Pluralism in a Democratic Society

edited by
Melvin M. Tumin
Walter Plotch

Published in cooperation
with the Anti-Defamation
League of B'nai B'rith

The Praeger Special Studies program—
utilizing the most modern and efficient book
production techniques and a selective
worldwide distribution network—makes
available to the academic, government, and
business communities significant, timely
research in U.S. and international economic, social, and political development.

Pluralism in a Democratic Society

PRAEGER SPECIAL STUDIES IN U.S. ECONOMIC, SOCIAL, AND POLITICAL ISSUES

Praeger Publishers   New York   Washington   London

Library of Congress Cataloging in Publication Data
Main entry under title:

Pluralism in a democratic society.

  (Praeger special studies in U.S. economic, social,
and political issues)
  Includes bibliographies.
  1. Ethnicity—Addresses, essays, lectures. 2. Pluralism
(Social sciences)—Addresses, essays, lectures. 3. Socialization—
Addresses, essays, lectures. 4. United States—Civilization—
1945-   —Addresses, essays, lectures. I. Tumin,
Melvin Marvin, 1919-   II. Plotch, Walter, 1932-
HM291. P58   301. 15'7   76-12877
ISBN 0-275-23310-3

PRAEGER PUBLISHERS
111 Fourth Avenue, New York, N.Y. 10003, U.S.A.

Published in the United States of America in 1977
by Praeger Publishers, Inc.

Printed in the United States of America

FOREWORD
Theodore Freedman

Although the population of the United States is comprised of a number of ethnic, cultural, and nationality groups, the legitimacy of a culturally plural society is still to be accepted by most Americans. Indeed, many Americans strive to conform to a popular norm and avoid identification with their own heritage, stifling the free contribution of that heritage to the quality of American life.

A conference, which was called Pluralism in a Democratic Society: An Interdisciplinary Inquiry into Its Meaning and Educational Uses, was held in April 1975 in New York. The purpose of the conference, which was convened by the Anti-Defamation League of B'nai B'rith and funded under a grant from the Ethnic Heritage Studies Program of the U.S. Office of Education, was to confirm that American life consists of a mosaic of different groups, each retaining its own richness and identity and each contributing to the strength and diversity of its traditions.

The aims of this conference were twofold: first, to arrive at a clear definition of cultural pluralism, and second, to search out the best ways to teach--and learn--about cultural pluralism in the classroom.

In much of the literature that has appeared on the subject since the mid-1960s, the interpretations and definitions of cultural pluralism are unclear. Assimilationist and sometimes acculturationist views, which are often confused and both labeled "melting pot," are rejected; yet what cultural pluralism does mean is not made clear, and instead the views propounded often sound very much like ethnic or racial chauvinism. For the educator who is seeking alternatives to assimilationist and separatist viewpoints, these simplistic, propagandistic interpretations are not very useful.

How, for example, can the U.S. history teacher who wishes to introduce ethnic studies into the classroom deal with each ethnic group in the United States without twisting history totally out of context? What key themes in cultural pluralism provide the structure with which to define and delimit the topic? Similarly, what forms of ethnic behavior can be discussed by social studies teachers without losing sight of uniqueness? In short, how is it possible to teach

---

Theodore Freedman is Director of the National Community Service and Program Divisions, Anti-Defamation League of B'nai B'rith.

about ethnic groups in U.S. history and give full dimension to the possibilities implicit in a truly plural multi-ethnic approach to these studies?

Other matters also require clarification and fresh definition. Although scholars tell us that the early childhood and elementary school years are the most important in the formulation of the identity, attitudes, and fundamental ideas of a person, the research in this area has not been systematically explored in order to determine the best educational strategies to draw young people into a culturally plural view of the world.

These challenging considerations led to the April 1975 conference. The papers that emerged from that conference form the body of this book. However, a conference is more than a collection of papers; it is also a collection of people. The participants in this conference brought an especially noteworthy sense of commitment and dedication to their task. The Anti-Defamation League of B'nai B'rith wishes to express its deepest appreciation to all of the participants, as well as to the Office of Education of the U.S. Department of Health, Education and Welfare, which provided support for this project.

ACKNOWLEDGMENTS

This book is the result of a joint effort involving not only the talents of those scholars whose work is represented here, but also the ideas of a number of educators who attended the conference at which these papers were given and many others who assisted in this process. For assistance in developing the conference, we wish to thank several members of the ADL staff: Betty Cantor, Eleanor Blumenberg, Oscar Cohen, Theodore Freedman, Harold Adler, and Stan Wexler. Others who were particularly helpful in identifying problem areas or suggesting possible contributors to this volume were Jerome Kagan, Professor of Psychology at Harvard University; Steven Graubard, the editor of Daedalus; David Sills of the Social Science Research Council; Gerald Lesser, Department of Education and Developmental Psychology, Harvard University; Donald Merachnik, Superintendent of Schools, Union County Regional High School District, New Jersey; and the following members of the Advisory Committee of the Ethnic Heritage Grant of the Anti-Defamation League: Rose Shapiro, Chairman of the Committee; Henry Lee Moon of NAACP; Frank Bianco, Director of the Columbian Coalition; Pedro Castillo, Professor of History at Yale University; Miss Marina Mercado, Instructor, School of Education, City University of New York; and Harry Rivlin, formerly Dean, School of Education, Fordham University.

John Carpenter of the University of Southern California, who was formerly head of the Ethnic Heritage Branch, U.S. Office of Education, played a major role in helping to conceptualize this project. He and a number of his colleagues at the Office of Education, including Carl Epstein, Elizabeth Farquhar, and Donald Bigelow, were unusually helpful.

Our hope is that the materials presented here will be of assistance to all those interested in cultural pluralism and in helping people of all ages to develop understanding and respect for cultural differences. We wish also to thank all of those who attended the conference or who assisted in any way for the time they freely gave to this project. Deficiencies in editorial areas or in selection are of course the fault of the editors.

CONTENTS

LIST OF TABLES AND FIGURES

INTRODUCTION
Melvin M. Tumin

The sociological model of a stable and orderly society calls for a population that is relatively homogeneous in its tastes, interests, and habits and shares a widespread consensus on basic values and goals. Such conditions can best be achieved, sociologists believe, when the population is relatively homogeneous in religious, racial, ethnic, and national origins. The more heterogeneous the people of a society are in these regards, the more likely it is that they will disagree on interests, standards, goals, and values and that conflict and disorder will ensue.

Seen in light of these expectations, the United States can only be judged to be a sociological anomaly. If one were to invent a country that would appear to have the least likelihood of enduring and that would probably be torn by violent strife in its brief existence, one might well invent the United States as it exists in 1975. Its people worship in over 220 different denominational institutions, not to mention the many who do not worship at all. There are at least five prominent categories of racial membership and more than 100 different national origins. The nationality groups, as commonly described, are themselves often names that cover numbers of quite distinct ethnic groups; to complicate matters further, these often cross national boundary lines. There are at least six, if not more, regional subcultures, often with large differences in dialect and life style. Moreover, the numerous and diverse Indian tribes should not be ignored; all of them had distinct cultures at one time and many still do or wish to revive their ancient cultures. Crosscutting these national, ethnic, racial, religious, regional, and tribal distinctions are the subcultures of the age groups, the socioeconomic classes, and the sexes.

One might very well marvel at the ability of this nation to contain such diversity within its boundaries for even a decade, much less to have survived for 200 years to become the oldest stable democracy in the world. How, we might well ask, has it been possible to manage such diversity within the framework of one society?

Among the most important reasons for this has been the gradualness of the introduction of diverse peoples into the national framework. More than two centuries have been witness to the successive introduction of immigrants from the major national groups of all the other continents. The task of incorporating these immigrants has thus been much easier than it would have been if the diversity had had to be dealt with in a shorter period.

Equally important has been the fact that the two most culturally strange groups, the Indians and the blacks, were dealt with in peremptory fashion, including expropriation of lands, forced concentrations in territorial enclaves, enslavement, deportation to undesirable territories, and wars of near extermination. These two major groups had the misfortune to differ in racial, as well as in all other regards, from the host population and suffered the consequences.

Implicit in this manner of dealing with the Indians and the blacks is the crucial historical fact that the social, economic, and political power to decide how to deal with "foreign" peoples has traditionally resided in the hands of a relatively small number of people, a so-called Anglo elite, who have been able to set and enforce the terms under which immigrants came to the country and what they had to do to make their way into the society.

Those terms have by no means been uniformly invidious. They have included such crucial features as the most open socioeconomic system found anywhere in the world; the indispensable instrument of that society of open possibilities, namely, the common educational system; and an extraordinarily expanding economy. The rule of this Anglo elite has also been characterized by an absence of the feudalistic and familistic barriers to social and economic prominence and power that are found virtually everywhere else, so that effort and achievement could come to count. The correlative emphasis has been upon the fundamental equality of rights of all people, regardless of origin; this equality has been tainted only by persistent racial prejudice and discrimination. Under the Anglo elite were achieved the protections, however bitterly won, of law and the Constitution; the freedom of religious worship; and the crucial separation of church and state.

The net result of these systems of opportunity and freedom has been the creation of a society in which, however disproportionate the representation of a certain Anglo type in circles of prominence and power, representatives of all nationalities and ethnic, racial, and religious groups have come to occupy important places in all the significant major institutions: government, business, education, the arts, religion, communication, and the military. Moreover, they have been able to expedite and enhance the career opportunities of their children with ever-lessening encumbrance from the traditional criteria of discrimination.

Of course, stress on the theme of opportunity rather than the theme of encumbrance depends, in part, on the groups to which the speaker belongs and, in part, on his or her tendency, metaphorically, to evaluate half a glass of water as half full or half empty. It is my own inclination to say that, although an enormous amount remains to be achieved by way of genuine equality of opportunity in this country, an enormous amount has in fact been achieved.

Equality of opportunity refers to what sociologists call life chances, that is, the chances of having the relevant talents and powers of an individual discovered, trained, recruited, and employed in the competition for making a living and for securing a place on the ladders of property, prestige, and power that characterize this society. Equality of opportunity does not refer to something that is quite distinct, though closely connected to life chances, namely life styles, or the distinctive ways in which individuals spend their lives, including their forms of worshipping, eating, dressing, speaking, associating, thinking about the world, recreating, educating their children, and working out family problems.

It is to the freedom to choose a life style that the question of cultural pluralism mainly refers. Many of the national, ethnic, racial, and tribal groups who have felt required to surrender their distinctive life styles in their quest for equal life chances now find themselves sufficiently assured of the chance to make a living and can turn their attention to the restoration of their former ethnic distinctiveness. Having become Americanized and thus in some degree homogenized in a common culture of the larger society, numerous groups now seek to reclaim their former ethnic heritage, to add their ethnic identity, even if in a hyphenated way, to their American identity.* Whether the ethnic group name is put before or after the all-embracing designation of "American" seems to matter little. The important fact is that numerous groups are insisting on bringing their formerly separate group identities and ways of life back into more active play in the daily conduct of their lives and of those of their children.

There is no serious contention that people who seek to assert their ethnic identities may not do so; what is questioned, however, is whether there is a public obligation to sponsor such a revivification of ethnicity, especially in the schools and in other community facilities, such as arts councils and the media.

The arguments on behalf of a restoration of ethnicity in one form or another are many and diverse. Many believe that this would provide a basis of group pride; give children a sense of membership and a secure self-image; construct a basis for small-group solidarity in an impersonal world; and enrich the common culture through ethnic diversification.

---

*By the same process, an increasing number of women, especially in professional circles, seek to reclaim their "identities" as individuals by insistence on the use of their family names along with their married names.

In the case of Indians and blacks, the pressure for restoration of ethnic identity also takes the very consequential form of a demand for indemnification for historical injustices through "affirmative action" and "compensatory justice," by which at least some of the losses suffered historically by these groups might be recompensed by special awards and privileges to their contemporary members, on the grounds that the latter have inherited the disadvantages that have historically been imposed on their groups. The demands of various Indian tribal units for compensation for their seized tribal lands are perhaps the largest of the whole array of compensatory claims being advanced.

It is against this background of a renascent ethnicity that the papers of this conference are to be considered. Sponsored by the U.S. Office of Education and the Anti-Defamation League of B'nai B'rith, the most active Jewish organization in the field of public education and community affairs, the conference was designed to explore the problems and possibilities of constructing units of school experience and curricula that might serve the basic requirement of cultural pluralism, which is to insure the fullest freedom of expression to distinctive life styles that is possible without interfering with the opportunity to secure equal life chances.

Such an inquiry necessarily addresses many troubling questions, most particularly in the matter of using a part of the common school experience of all children for education in ethnic diversity and cultural pluralism. What should be done in pursuit of this goal? What kinds of educational experiences would be most serviceable? How are these to be integrated into the common core of educational effort? What should children be taught about group differences? By whom? With what techniques? Can children find any profit or pleasure in handling the theme of differences and similarities? How early in the curriculum should such special education be introduced? How far into the curriculum should it run? How many separate ethnic history units should be introduced? Should we confine ourselves to the four or five most populous ethnic groups or include the many others? Are the problems of demeaned racial groups so much more severe than those of any others to justify spending most time and attention on the problems of interaction of particular groups, such as black-white or Anglo-Chicano problems? Is interreligious prejudice and discrimination still enough of a problem to justify serious attention?

Do we know enough to establish policy on such things as the effect of various curricular materials on the minds and hearts of children? Do we know enough about the cognitive, affective, and moral developmental sequences in children to plot our course wisely? What do we know about the impact of the mass media?

What dangers do we run of dividing the children against each other along restored and reinvigorated lines of ethnic, racial, religious, and tribal identities? Will the common fabric of a united society, which has taken so long to create, be torn apart by new divisiveness through resurgent ethnicity? Can the rights and freedoms of the most secure and prosperous groups be preserved while the society seeks to bring full first-class citizenship to the less fortunate groups?

How can we evaluate the success or failure of various school programs and of educational experiences outside of school, such as the daily hours spent with the mass media? How can we tell whether the resulting balance is for the better or worse? Are we agreed on the goals of ethnic education; and are these goals operationalized well enough to allow us to evaluate our trial programs effectively?

These were among the many questions that were addressed by the participants in this conference. It would be pointless, because impossible, to try to report briefly here what the participants said in reply. The special flavors and distinctive substantive contributions of their papers can only be appreciated if they are read in their entirety.

However, there was substantial agreement on the desirability of a flourishing and productive cultural pluralism, but pronounced disagreement about how such a condition might best be realized, if at all, particularly in regard to the curriculum innovations that might be introduced.

The main line of division among the conferees was between those, on the one hand, who out of concern for the preservation of social unity and the democratic process, doubted the wisdom of making significant additions to ethnic matters in the curriculum and those, on the other hand, who felt that the probable benefits of such revived ethnicity were great enough to justify developing such programs in the schools.

This cleavage seems relatively mild, but in fact it has some rather disturbing implications. For one thing it suggests that underneath the surface of nominal agreement on abstract values such as cultural pluralism, there are some very serious disagreements when the requirements for the realization of those values are stated in operational terms. Thus, there is nominal agreement about the value of equal access to education for all children, but there is serious disagreement about what to do to provide that equal access; this is especially true, for instance, when considering how to abide by the 1954 ruling that segregated schools are inherently unequal. Again, there is nominal agreement on the notion that every child needs a healthy self-image, but there is substantial disagreement about what should be done in pursuit of this goal, especially if the measures taken to improve the self-images of the children in one group may entail some negative consequences for children of other groups.

The disagreements that lie underneath the surfaces of nominal agreements need to be brought to light, not all at once, and not in their most extreme versions, yet brought to light over time and dealt with in ways that all parties can reluctantly agree are fair and just, however unsatisfactory the solutions may be as measured by the fullness of the program of any one party.

If we are to be able to reach such fair, albeit partial solutions and at the same time maintain a stable and productive society, one thing above all is imperative, and that is the preservation of the rules of democratic decision making. Only these rules can enable us to make important changes without destroying the core values of our society and the institutional arrangements that embody those values. Only these democratic rules and processes can safeguard the minorities while they struggle to realize more and more of what they consider to be their rightful entitlements. Only by the democratic process do minority viewpoints have a chance, over time, to become the convictions of a majority.

The history of our society is replete with alternations between periods when we have been prepared as a people to accept, if not enthusiastically sponsor, basic social changes and periods in which we have shown great reluctance to alter existing arrangements even trivially. These swings in mood and readiness for change are not simply a reflection of fickleness and volatility in our national character. Rather, they are better seen as alternations between justifiable optimism in the face of extraordinary realizations of national and individual possibilities, and subsequent periods of retreat and pessimism when our national well-being and our individual stakes in that well-being seem much less promising.

We have gone through a period of significant optimism and uplifted mood and are entering a period of considerable doubt and hesitation. The downturn in the economy is one major cause in the shift. Many of our people, particularly lower-middle-class white ethnics who had just begun to "make it" in American society, are now experiencing very stringent economic and social pressures. As a result they are ill-prepared to accept the persistent demands for rapid change advanced by other minority groups that have been traditionally behind them on the socioeconomic ladder.

Each of the competing groups sees itself as righteously entitled to a larger share of the goods and services of the society and of its honorific recognition, and each group sees itself as having struggled hard to achieve what it now possesses. If the demands for new rights by even more hard pressed peoples can be interpreted as threats to the hard-won shares of the newly rising members of this society, those demands are likely to be resisted at the most elemental levels and in the most elemental ways, and there is a high probability that they will evoke primitive sentiments of hostile ethnicity.

It would be unfair to the richness of thought shared at the conference to imply that the debate about the pros and cons of curricular programs on ethnicity was conducted mainly in terms of the probability of resistance by various groups who feel beleaguered by the current situation in our society. Those who advocated a significant increase in ethnic education did so on the grounds of the probable contribution to the children's self-image, group unity, and pride and to the enhancement of the reputation and image of demeaned groups in the eyes of others and the general enrichment of our cultural fabric. Those who opposed or were hesitant about any increase in ethnic content in the curriculum expressed their concern about adding new stereotypes to old, promoting further social divisiveness, placing obstacles in the path of socioeconomic mobility for members of highly visible ethnic groups, interfering in the process of adjustment through assimilation, or introducing artificially constructed or reconstructed ethnic identities of dubious value.

Most of these disagreements, it is plain, revolve around questions of fact that could be settled if the research evidence on these matters were more adequate. However, the evidence is very sparse and indecisive on most of these issues. No amount of deep belief, however sincere, in the positive or negative value of heightened ethnic visibility and identification will substitute for hard evidence about the consequences of such heightened ethnicity for the life chances of the individuals concerned.

Since we do not know with any confidence what may result, we are well advised to go slow in our curricular reforms, to be very experimental in making them, to hold modest expectations with regard to them, and above all to see to it that we develop effective means for objectively evaluating the numerous and diverse impacts of such curricular innovations. Otherwise we may, out of the goodness of our intentions, cause considerable harm and damage to those we most sincerely mean to benefit.

The reader will not find here any handy shopping list of curricular suggestions. Although the aim of the conference was to prepare the ground for such curriculum construction, it could not possibly engage in the actual task of building curricula in the short time available to it and with the basic issues of principle, philosophy, and fact still so very much in debate. The task of constructing a curriculum, even of one four-week unit for one semester for only one grade level, is, as everyone who has ever engaged in such a task knows, a complex and weighty procedure.

As we move toward constructing such a curriculum, we know we must observe certain imperatives. These include a delicate balancing of the value of individual freedom with that of social responsibility and of the value of the integrity of subgroup cultures with that of the requirements of national unity. We want cultural awareness and group identity, but we do not want political divisiveness. In the realm of the development of the child, we seek that optimal combination of affective, cognitive, and moral growth, the ingredients of which are as yet so vague and elusive.

Perhaps, however, we can say that we seek to have our students engage in educational transactions that will make them concerned and also effective in their efforts to realize their most valued potentials, both as individuals and as citizens of a democratic society.

Toward that end, we may think of a series of problem-themes that need to be solved in every aspect of our common social life. These are the themes of freedom and responsibility, of the one and the many, of equality and inequality, of conformity and deviation, of unity and diversity, and of stability and change.

These themes pervade all the experiences of organized human social life. They occur as problems in families, friendship pairs, schools, neighborhoods, local communities, cities, states, nations, and the international community. Every child must deal with these problems at some level of complexity appropriate to his situation. Since these are such ubiquitous problem-themes, they can serve admirably as the vertical spine or core of a school curriculum in social studies through all eight, twelve, or sixteen years.

These problem-themes have the further advantage of representing problems that all children experience immediately and intimately in their daily lives and to which they can therefore bring their own experiences to bear, as these issues are raised for consideration in their school settings. Because of their immediacy and relevance, a curriculum constructed around these themes has a chance of being lively and interesting for most children and can serve as a common core of education for all students at all grade levels.

Under the terms of the questions implied by these problem-themes, the most searching and wide-ranging inquiries can be conducted into the requirements of constructive cultural pluralism in democratic society. The exploration of these themes makes it mandatory for students to analyze the costs and the consequences of alternative social arrangements. Moreover, they can bring to bear the evidence from many cultures and they can examine for their relevance the experiences of our own national past. So, too, the materials formulated by social scientists of all disciplines--sociology, anthropology, economics, political science, social geography, and psychology--can be introduced at every juncture to inform students of what is possible and probable and at what gain and loss to whom, enabling the students to make more informed decisions about what is desirable.

As we move toward the construction, implementation, and dissemination of such a curriculum, we are strengthened by the realization, which conferences such as this both underscore and enrich, that a stable, productive, and fair democratic society is one of the most extraordinary social inventions in the whole history of mankind. The preservation and strengthening of such a society is, therefore, as worthy and important a social enterprise as one might envision. To contribute to that enterprise within the schools, which are our main public instrument for the fashioning of concerned and effective citizens, is thus, in turn, as worthy and important an educational venture as we might undertake.

We are therefore particularly appreciative of the efforts of the Office of Education and the Anti-Defamation League in sponsoring and organizing this conference and of the contributions of the many conferees who participated in the discussions of the papers that follow. We regret only that the many illuminating and enriching observations that were made during the discussions of the theme papers have not been able to be included here. However, the papers themselves are so very diverse in their approaches to the problem of cultural pluralism that the reader may be assured that a full array of agreement and disagreement on basic issues is presented here.

I take it to be a rather handsome testimonial to the confidence of everyone concerned in the importance of democratic process, that the presentation of sharply conflicting views on basic issues is seen as an important contribution to the future well-being of the society. It is through the operation of such ideological pluralism in open debate that we may yet achieve the fullness of our hopes for a rich, culturally pluralist, democratic society.

PART

I

A SEARCH FOR
DEFINITION

1

CULTURAL PLURALISM:
THE SOCIAL ASPECT
Nathan Glazer

"Cultural pluralism" seems to have won out, at least tempo-
rarily, as the preferred model for responding to the reality of a
multi-racial and multi-ethnic society. Now that it has won, however, we do not appear to be very sure of what it means. It denotes
a broad middle ground, stretching between "assimilation" and "acculturation" at one end, and "separatism" at the other end--or at
least this is one way of stating the two extremes between which cultural pluralism falls.

In each sphere of life it may mean something entirely different,
however. We are not sure of its political implications, of its social
and economic implications, or even of its implications in the sphere
that most concerns us here, which is education. This is true in spite
of an endless array of proposals, programs, and even laws and judicial decisions that is available to guide or confuse us. As we know,
cultural pluralism is now not only an academic model for education
in a multi-ethnic society, but also a matter for federal, state, and
municipal legislation and for determination by the ever-more-intrusive
courts, spurred by public legal advocates who seem convinced that
the most complex problems will submit to judiciary determinations.
Three presentations, such as we have in this conference, are scarcely
enough to explore cultural pluralism. A fuller study would need an
examination of the federal and state laws, of the ideas that guide
federal and state officials, and of the ways these ideas are being
implemented. It would be necessary to examine the specific ways
these ideas are expressed in some of the thousands of school districts and perhaps tens of thousands of schools in which something
of the order of cultural pluralism now exists. A fuller study would
also cover other aspects, such as the manner in which textbook
publishers are responding to the new concern. The nature of the

U.S. federal system makes no simple description possible of any development, in view of the variety that may (and does) exist in our tens of thousands of semi-independent units. One thing is possible, however, and that is a clarification of our thinking about cultural pluralism, particularly in light of the conception we have of a desirable social order for our very distinctive nation, made up of many national strands.

THE ASSIMILATIONISM OF 1900-40

Certainly we have to begin with the terms that define the parameters of cultural pluralism. At one end, as I have suggested, there is "assimilation" and "acculturation," to which we may add as a third, "Americanization." These terms defined at one level the aim of almost all those involved in the discussion of the multinational aspect of the U.S. population from 1900 to 1940. There were two writers, now well known among the students of cultural pluralism, who spoke out against the prevailing trend, who were Randolph Bourne and Horace M. Kallen, but the prevailing voices were in favor of assimilation, acculturation, and Americanization. This attitude is now presented to us as a form of domestic imperialism or colonialism. We are told by most contemporaries that instead of colonizing foreign peoples in their homelands the United States imported them and then subjected them to colonial conditions. These conditions involved an arrogant dismissal of any possible virtues of their native cultures and an insistence that they recast themselves as Americans. At the same time, argues the prevailing critique of the assimilationism of the early part of the century, the Americans had no intention of accepting the members of the new groups as equals, even if stripped of their original cultures by these policies of assimilation. They were to be left nothing of their own to stand with against Anglo-American culture, but they were not to be allowed entry into American society on fully equal terms.

This is certainly a severe criticism of policies of Americanization, but there is enough to support it. On the one hand the new immigrants were attacked for their foreignness; their inability to speak English; their presumed high crime rates (never proven); their crowding in slums, which was an inevitable consequence, after all, of their poverty; their continued attachment to their homelands, particularly if these homelands were, like Germany, enemies of the United States in war; their susceptibility to the city political machines; their uncertain knowledge of democracy; and their tendency to adopt socialist, anarchist, and communist doctrines. These arguments against them were used to exclude immigrants almost completely, from the early 1920s on. Once here, they were to be "Americanized." In the meantime Jews and Catholics and, even more, blacks, orientals, and Mexican-Americans suffered from various forms of prejudice and discrimination, and it was not at all clear that their "Americanization" would lead to the reduction of such prejudice and discrimination. The only hope held out was that a full assimilation, that is, a total disappearance, would indeed end the prejudice and discrimination directed against them, since at that point they would exist, not as individuals with some given inheritance, but as individuals who could not be identified as being different from other Americans. "Acculturation" was a stage on the way to "assimilation."

This criticism of policies of assimilation is familiar enough, but the problem with it is that assimilation was not the objective only of the reactionary, conservative, and ethnocentric forces in American life, but also the objective of liberal forces. It was not the objective only of the old American element, but also that of the new immigrants, for the most part, insofar as it was given voice by their representatives. In social science studies of the United States, we have long been familiar with the fact that it was possible to be populist and progressive and also to oppose immigration on the grounds of the presumed unassimilability of the new immigrants. This was the point of view of John R. Commons, Edward Allsworth Ross, Henry Pratt Fairchild, and others.

However, there was a stronger current in American sociology that was not so strongly populist and more basically liberal, which was identified with Robert E. Park, whose career included a long stretch as secretary and close associate of Booker T. Washington and who founded a school of sociology at the University of Chicago that reflected sympathy with, concern for, and curiosity about the various races and streams of immigration that were making up the American population. This was a severely empirical school and was ethnographic in its emphasis. However, insofar as it had a direction, that is, a proposal for the American multi-ethnic society, that direction was also assimilationist. The paradigm of race and ethnic relations that Park suggested ran from contact to conflict to accommodation to assimilation.

We sociologists, in our search for "theory," have made more of this simple scheme than it warrants, but as a matter of fact it did reflect the values, perhaps insufficiently thought through, of Park and his leading students. Louis Wirth, who was the chief successor to Park, made clear in The Ghetto that his preference was for assimilation: the Jew continued to exist only because of prejudice and discrimination; all the reactions of the Jew to this antagonism were humanly limiting; and assimilation, which to be

sure required lowering the barriers to assimilation, was the desirable end result of the interaction of Jews and non-Jews in contemporary society.

The major works of E. Franklin Frazier on the black family
went in the same direction. Insofar as the black family was stable
and puritanical it was good--that was unquestioned. There was no
hint, or scarcely any, that any distinctive cultural feature should
survive as specifically Negro or black, or that there should be any
effort to seek for such features.

This was not cultural arrogance or imperialism; instead, it
was the point of view of the best informed, most liberal, and most
sympathetic analysts of the ethnic and racial scene. Assimilation
was a consequence to be desired of the reduction of prejudice and
discrimination, while acculturation, that is, becoming more like
the majority, would contribute to the reduction of discrimination and
prejudice. This was the dominant liberal view until at least the
1950s.

It was also the view, insofar as there was anything that could
be called a view, of the representatives of racial and ethnic groups.
The NAACP and the Urban League were clearly "assimilationist."
Although it was clear that blacks could never because of race be in-
distinguishable from whites, it was desirable that they become culturally, socially, economically, and politically assimilated, that
they be simply Americans with dark skins. All public agencies, including the government and the schools, and all private agencies
that affected individual circumstances, including banks, businesses,
housing producers, and renters, were to be "color blind." In the
1950s the only legitimate form of differentiation proposed for American life was religious. The distinction of Catholic, Protestant, and
Jew (and Jew in religion) was acceptable, but racial differences of
any significance were to disappear through fair treatment, while
ethnic differences were to remain, if at all, only in religious form.
It was Will Herberg who held that the religious differences had also
disappeared, in a common "American" religion. They existed, to
his mind, only to maintain surviving ethnic differences.

Admittedly, in each group there were the maintainers and up-
holders of the ethnic conscience and consciousness, including
schools, ethnically colored churches, philanthropic and civic organizations, networks of insurance societies, and social groups,
but except by those whose direct interest was in maintaining them
and the jobs they offered, these were regarded as survivals, fated
to fall away as acculturation and assimilation progressed.

Acculturation and assimilation, if not the cruder "Americanization," were not simply positions of the old-fashioned Americans
and of those who were antagonistic to new immigrants and distinctive

racial elements in American life, but were also the positions taken by those who were most sympathetic to these groups and who understood them best, and even of the representatives of these groups.

Why was there such blindness to the possibility that these groups or elements within them would not want to acculturate and assimilate but would want to preserve their corporate characters and distinctiveness even if prejudice and discrimination disappeared? One reason seems to explain it: the focus of concern was with the immediate position of these groups and the problem that they did meet prejudice and discrimination and that their economic and social position was low. How could the transition to a better position be managed? First by becoming more like other Americans, and then by persuading other Americans to abandon this prejudice and discrimination on the grounds that the ethnic groups and different races were really just like them anyway. The main aim of propaganda for tolerance in the 1930s and 1940s, a propaganda the need for which was heightened by the rise of Hitler and the greater salience of anti-Semitism and racist propaganda and feeling, was that really the groups that were objects of hostility were just like other Americans: there was nothing different about them.

This strategy seemed to be reasonable, but as time went on it was to create a confusion between the point of view within liberalism that argues, They are just like everyone else, so they should not be objects of prejudice and discrimination, and the one that asserts, They are different and have a right to be different, and this difference does not justify any antagonism.

THE WEAK CULTURAL PLURALISM OF THE 1940s

There were thus, and there still are, in the area of ethnic and racial issues two liberalisms in conflict, one that looks to acculturation and assimilation and one that looks to the freedom to maintain differences. Some of the first efforts to introduce what we may call cultural pluralism into the curriculum served the first type of liberalism and not the second. The intercultural perspective of the 1940s arose in opposition to Hitler's racism. This was the liberalism that taught that people did come from different backgrounds; its hallmark in the schools was the multi-ethnic festival in which children of different backgrounds wore costumes to school that even their parents had abandoned or never wore. The purpose of intercultural education was to teach tolerance, not for the maintenance of cultures, but for individuals of different backgrounds who were now presumed to be the same and who could not help coming from different backgrounds. The purpose of this tolerance was not to

maintain differences but to create the kind of situation, through
tolerance, in which differences could disappear.

This was clearly a very weak form of cultural pluralism. We
are now familiar with much stronger forms, and these stronger
forms are now the focus of our concern. The weak cultural pluralism reflected a period of accommodation on the part of ethnic and
minority groups. Of course, they would say, our intention is to
acculturate and Americanize and perhaps assimilate; but meanwhile
our need is for toleration, and this can be assisted by an understanding of something of our background and culture.

STRONG CULTURAL PLURALISM

Strong cultural pluralism comes out of quite another perspective, in which the ethnic groups and minorities, with the assistance
of liberal allies, are on the offensive. Strong cultural pluralism
derives from a different perspective of U.S. history, one in which
the dominant note is exploitation and in which the extremes of this
exploitation are actually described as cultural or physical genocide,
such as slavery and colonialism.

Certainly the notion that the aim of cultural pluralism is
simply greater toleration for differences while all take the common
road to Americanization is now not very popular. It is this strong
cultural pluralism that we must subject to some analysis in the light
of the actual history of ethnic and minority groups, of their needs
today, and of the social future we envision for our multi-ethnic
society.

The new cultural pluralism is not based on the desire for a
transient period of tolerance to ease the way to full acculturation and
assimilation. Instead it is based on the assumption or expectation
that separate groups in the United States will continue to exist, that
they have value, and that there are both pragmatic and moral reasons why the government should provide some assistance to their
maintenance. Each of these phrases raises some questions that
require analysis if we are to develop some coherent basis for programs of cultural pluralism in the United States.

THE ATTITUDES TOWARD CULTURAL
PLURALISM OF 1965-75

In roughly chronological order I wish to describe the patterns
of cultural pluralism and the rationales for cultural pluralism that
have been current since 1965.

In 1965 there was as yet almost no acknowledgment of a public responsibility to provide any assistance to groups that would assist them in maintaining their cultures or corporate characters. Indeed, in 1964 legislation was passed that seemed at the time to mark the full triumph of the color-blind and thus, in a sense, the assimilationist position. The language of the Civil Rights Act asserted that no place of public accommodation could limit its patronage "on the ground of race, color, religion, or national origin"; that no public facility could deny the right to equal protection of the laws "on account of . . . race, color, religion, or national origin"; that the Attorney General would intervene if there were a complaint that any public school or college were denying admission "by reason of race, color, religion, or national origin"; that no employer could practice discrimination "because of . . . race, color, religion, . . . or national origin"; and most sweepingly, that "no person in the United States shall, on the ground of race, color, or national origin, be excluded from participation in, be denied the benefits of, or be subjected to discrimination under any program or activity receiving Federal financial assistance." At about the same time, all racial and national origin references were expunged from the immigration laws. Justice Harlan's dissent in Plessy v. Ferguson, that "our constitution is color-blind" had now apparently been written, sweepingly and with no possible restriction, into law.

Although this development meant that government, and a good deal of private activity with a public character, could not in any way make distinctions that would harm anyone because of ethnicity, by implication it would appear that the same institutions were also enjoined from making distinctions that would aid anyone because of ethnicity.

This did not mean that cultural pluralism was dead, however, since the entire private realm available for the maintenance of distinctive cultures still existed. Private religion existed for the maintenance of religious distinction and, if desired, of ethnic distinction. The entire realm of education existed, under Constitutional protection, for the maintenance of ethnic cultures. The Constitutional protection of speech, publication, and assembly protected the thinking, writing, orating, and disseminating of any image or argument or information that enhanced the survival of any ethnic group and culture. It was as if the United States had been struggling since its birth to define some coherent relationship between the universalistic sentiments of the Declaration of Independence and the Constitution, which seemed to establish or call for a nation based on principles rather than on race or ethnicity--on rational exposition rather than on primitive sentiment--and the reality of a nation in which one major ethnic stock dominated in various degrees and others faced

discrimination and prejudice and even, in various degrees, denial of
the rights guaranteed to all. The relationship between law and reality
could become coherent only if the original principles were abandoned
and one stock was raised to dominance by law, or if they prevailed
and no stock was given any recognition by law. The Civil Rights Act
of 1964 and the Immigration Act of 1965 determined that the initial
principle should prevail over any lingering attachment to the English
or Anglo-Saxon or Protestant or English-speaking original founders
of the republic. However, the same principles also guaranteed a
wide range of freedom for the voluntary maintenance of whatever
ethnic distinctiveness anyone wanted to maintain. The limit of protection, it appeared, was tax exemption for religious, educational,
and philanthropic organizations. The rest was up to each individual
and each group.

Under these circumstances, the range of alternatives that had
been selected by each group was extensive. Undoubtedly the fullest
network of independent organization of any ethnic group was that of
the Jews. This elaborate network was encouraged, first, by the
fact that in the case of the Jews ethnicity and religion largely coin-
cided and the institutions of religion and ethnicity were established
to serve the same group, sometimes in cooperation, sometimes in
antagonism, and sometimes in such a way that one institution, such
as the local synagogue or temple, seemed to serve the interests of
both in equal measure; and second, because the special situation of
Israel, a unique homeland in a uniquely dangerous situation, encouraged the strongest measure of ethnic attachment.

Religion was mixed in with the maintenance of ethnic attachment in the case of most other groups, too. Religious institutions
were the main form in which some knowledge of the ethnic groups
and their cultures and characters were handed on, and some effort
was made to maintain this attachment, though in many groups political, philanthropic, and religiously neutral educational institutions
contributed to the task. Aside from any institutional network, and
perhaps more important than it, were the informal networks of
family connection, neighborhood, and friendship.

This was, to my mind, the emerging and distinctive ethnic
pattern of America in the mid-1960s; indeed, it could be argued a
consensus about the proper arrangement of a multiethnic society in
the United States had been emerging over some time: the consensus
called for public neutrality and private freedom. Admittedly, the
movement in this direction had been marred by many aberrations,
including public denigration of and discrimination against some
groups (blacks, Mexican-Americans, American Indians, and orientals). Public encouragement and support had been given to others
by the Bible-reading and Christmas celebrations in the schools and

the assumption in textbooks that ours was a history made only by Anglo-Americans. However, the direction of opinion, law, and judicial decisions was toward public neutrality and toward the elimination of restrictions on private efforts to maintain distinctiveness.

Other elements might be added to this emerging pattern. Public neutrality did not necessarily mean that there was no official consciousness of diversity, but much of this consciousness was in effect ceremonial, expressed in the opening of conventions and sessions of Congress by ministers representing all religions and groups; in public recognition of groups through recognition of certain days dear to one or another as holidays and through the pronouncement of history weeks for each group; and in the recognition of festivals and the like. More significantly, there was a realm of informal recognition of group reality by the public authorities; perhaps the chief example of this was the balanced ticket that prevailed in so many elective bodies. In New York and San Francisco, for example, school boards were balanced by religion, and when new groups not defined by religion came to the fore, particularly the blacks, they were balanced racially. In the arrangements of political bosses, groups received recognition when one of their number was nominated for public office.

The private realm was also not completely removed from public intervention. There were three important areas of private decision making in which the public authorities, with the increasing support of public opinion, intervened in order to overcome discrimination that significantly hampered persons in certain groups; these three areas were employment, housing, and education. Action by certain states and by the courts supposedly ended these kinds of discrimination with the Civil Rights Act of 1964 and the act banning discrimination in housing in 1968.

Separatism

Cultural pluralism did not remain the responsibility of the private sphere of action for long. A confused period opened with the black power and black pride movement of the mid-1960s and has continued since then. If in the earlier period the challenge to cultural pluralism was from the end of the spectrum that posited acculturation, assimilation, and Americanization as the most desirable outcome for a multi-ethnic America, in the past ten years the challenge, or at least the disputed ground, has been between cultural pluralism and the other end of the spectrum, the end we may label "separatism."

All the words we deal with have multiple meanings, of course, and separatism is no exception. The most extreme definition of

separatism is that of a political separation of certain groups from
the American society. This separation might literally take the form
of separate territorial areas under the control of these groups. Only
certain black nationalists and Mexican-American nationalists ever
made this claim seriously, and they were few in numbers. For
American Indians there were already separate territories identified
as the domains of certain tribes, and the issue that has arisen in
recent years is what political powers come along with this territorial
area. The separatists demand the fullest control possible, the
status of separate nations.

There was a certain lack of realism in the demand by black
nationalists and Mexican-Americans. In the 1930s the Communist
party had called for a black nation in the South, basically in the
black majority areas, which were then still extensive; indeed, there
were then two black majority states, South Carolina and Mississippi.
However, the demographic basis for a separate black state disin-
tegrated as blacks moved to the North in large numbers. The ghettos of the North became so extensive that some of the extreme
separatists fantasized a separate nation based in the black areas in
the cities.

Colonial Status

We need not spend much time on the possibilities of political
separatism, which were extremely slight; however, there was one
thread in the argument for separatism that was rather more important than the demand for political separation. This argument
was broadly accepted, even though political separation was not. It
was based on a definition of the situation of blacks, Mexican-
Americans, and Puerto Ricans as colonial peoples. This definition
found broad acceptance among social scientists. The colonial
imagery began with the blacks and spread rapidly to other groups.

To define the status of a nationality as colonial has very different implications from the assertion that it is being subjected to
discrimination and prejudice. In the latter case the course to be
followed is clear: ban the discrimination and overcome the prejudice.
The implication is that a group is being prevented from becoming
part of a larger group through prejudice and discrimination and thus
that the process of assimilation will be aided by eliminating prejudice
and discrimination. If a group is defined as "colonized," however,
a different course of action is envisaged to overcome the deficiency.
In the modern world colonies are expected to be freed, not for the
purpose of permitting the colonized groups to become like the
peoples of the mother countries but for the purpose of permitting

them to find their own distinctive courses of political, economic, and cultural development.

ETHNIC STUDIES PROGRAMS

Clearly if the proper image for the relationship of ethnic groups to American society is that of colonies, we have a powerful political justification for cultural pluralism in a strong form. For instance it would imply control of institutions or parts of institutions that deal with subjects of interest to the group in question. It would also foster a demand that special forms of education strengthening individual attachment and allegiance to the group be instituted.

This was, I believe, the first and major justification for the rapid spread of black studies programs, Mexican-American studies programs, Puerto Rican studies programs, Oriental-American studies programs, and Native American studies programs. The wave as spread, in reduced form, to Italian, Jewish, Polish, and other groups. This was only one motivation for the spread of distinctive ethnic studies programs, but it was a powerful one. It will be argued that this is an extreme and tendentious view of the explosion of ethnic studies programs, since there were clearly two other strong justifications. One justification was scholarly: the contribution of these groups to American life had indeed been ignored or suppressed, and a fair handling of the information required that the lives and cultures and problems of these groups be introduced into the curricula of colleges and indeed of high schools, basically to redress the truth. A second argument was pragmatic: this was necessary to make possible the effective education of the groups in question.

In order to illustrate the degree to which ideology, truth, and practical necessity have contributed to the establishment of ethnic studies programs, we must describe a few of their characteristics. First, it was taken for granted, and in fact it was generally a key demand, that these programs be taught by members of the groups that were being studied. Blacks should teach black studies, Oriental-Americans should teach oriental studies, and so on. Leaving aside the fact that this contradicted one of the key elements of the consensus of the Civil Rights Act of 1964, it should be pointed out how remarkable a demand this was. In American universities there had been, of course, studies of the great cultures of the world aside from Western culture. China, Japan, Latin America, and Africa had been subjects of research and teaching by historians, anthropologists, sociologists, political scientists, literary scholars, art historians, and the like. The new demand was that these studies were now to be taught by members of the groups studied, on the theory that only they could understand them. A George Foote Moore would no longer be permitted to teach about Judaism or a Melville Herskovits to teach about Afro-Americans: membership and allegiance were now set forth as a prerequisite.

Second, it was demanded that the major focus must not be on the study of great cultural areas but on the problems and contributions of the immigrant groups that had come to the United States from these areas. This was a legitimate scholarly demand. It is always possible that a neglected subject can be added to the curriculum, but there are mechanisms within higher education for determining when a new subject should be given independent existence, and instruction in it expanded. However, as a matter of fact, the determination for, let us say, a program of black studies was rarely settled on scholarly grounds: instead these programs were instituted on political grounds.

Third, there was an element in the new demand that indicated its motivation, which was that the new programs were to be intended for the members of the groups taught. In many cases, others interested in learning about a group and its culture felt uncomfortable when they appeared to take the new courses: they were told, by signs or directly, that they were not welcome. This was a truly surprising development in U.S. higher education. All kinds of extracurricular activities have existed for a distinctive ethnic or racial group, but it was unheard of for a racial or ethnic test to be set for a given academic course.

Fourth, these programs, it was assumed and intended, were to advocate instead of analyzing, exploring, considering. What they were designed to advocate was commitment to the group as well as a distinctive view of its history and problems. Thus, for example, it was generally the colonial view of its history in the United States that was presented; assimilation and acculturation were attacked as surrender to the colonial power; and commitment to the more militant elements of the group was encouraged. This description may be considered somewhat heightened, but I believe it describes the earlier years of the history of the new strong cultural pluralism, even though there have been some modifications. It is still true that these are the only areas of the colleges and universities and, insofar as they exist, in the high schools, in which racial and ethnic tests for employment are taken for granted and are not as yet challenged by the Equal Employment Opportunity Commission; the Office of Civil Rights of the Department of Health, Education and Welfare; the Civil Rights Commission; the Department of Justice; or any of the state agencies the duty of which is to prevent discrimination on account of race, religion, or national origin. Insofar as persons not of the groups are involved in this form of education, they too are generally advocates rather than scholars or teachers because this has become the predominant tone of these programs.

Thus we had the rise of programs taught by members of groups, devoted to the problems of the members of the groups in this country, taught to members of the groups, and advocating a distinctive point of view about their past, problems, and futures, all under public auspices.

There were terribly important legitimate educational reasons for bringing the study of these groups into the curriculum. Along with the older groups, they are part of the United States. They have contributed importantly to the history of the country, and they have been part of its history, culture, economy, and society. They had also been neglected in the curriculum.

As a student of ethnic issues for 30 years now, I am fully aware of the important place of ethnic studies in American life, and I could probably be gotten to agree that they have not been given their full due. Nevertheless, it is hard to think of any area of American life that, from the point of view of those studying it, has received full and sufficient recognition by granting agencies, university and college administrations, textbook writers, students, or fellow scholars. I myself do not think the study of the racial groups in American life has been much neglected. A better case can be made for the neglect of the history of some white ethnic groups. The best case can be made for the neglect of the integration of our knowledge of these areas into the general curriculum. There was a scholarly case, and there still is a scholarly case; but there is no good argument why only members of these groups must teach about the groups or why only members of the groups need to learn about them.

Finally, let us consider the pragmatic argument. This, too, has a good deal of legitimacy. It asserted that the members of different racial and ethnic groups either could not learn well or learned to be ashamed of their heritage when it played no role in the awesome institution of the public school and the college. There are of course limits to this pragmatic argument, even if we grant, as I do, that there is a solid basis to it   There is still the common knowledge of humanity to be transmitted--skills in reading and calculation and the knowledge of science and history. The pragmatic argument comes up against the pragmatic need to set some limit to the kind of teaching and learning the purpose of which is to give people a good opinion of themselves and to convince them they are accepted, in order to allow for the kind that is simply valuable and necessary for them and for all people. The pragmatic argument has been carried to extremes, as when special schools were set up in Berkeley, under

the auspices of the public school system, for Mexican-Americans
and for blacks. Perhaps they could be justified as experiments, and
they were basically experimental, but I can scarcely accept the
argument that learning for some groups can only go on in separate
enclaves for the groups themselves. On some college campuses
something perilously close to this was instituted at the height of this
movement.

INTEGRATION

I have defined a weak cultural pluralism, which was basically
a kind of tolerance on the way to an expected acculturation and assimilation, and a strong culutral pluralism, which was based primarily
on an ideological view of the position of racial and ethnic groups in
American life, one that emphasizes their colonial status and the
repression of their cultures by Anglo-Americans. These may be
seen as two extremes in cultural pluralism. We can define something that stands between these two extremes, and here "integration,"
another ambiguous term, will be helpful. Integration implies, on
the one hand, an organic relationship: just as a personality may be
integrated, so may a society. On the other hand it implies that
there is still a clear articulation of the parts, that is, some degree
of identifiability of each part. I wish to divorce the word from its
most current usage, as in an integrated school or an integrated
organization, but even there the meanings I want to emphasize are
apparent, as indicated by the fact that we differentiate desegregated,
which means numerically distributed, from integrated, which is
assumed to imply some organic connection between the races.
    The form of cultural pluralism that to my mind would be in
the interests of both individual groups and the entire nation is one in
which the emphasis on distinctive histories and cultures is integrated
into a larger sense of American history and the American experience.
    To show how this may be done, I shall emphasize the situation
in the elementary and secondary schools rather than in the colleges
and universities. In the latter, all points of view should properly be
in conflict, as long as they are presented by teachers committed
basically to the search for truth, in a situation in which students are
not presented with a single exclusive view. The colleges and universities, because they are committed to a search for truth, para-
doxically may tolerate a greater degree of extremism and error.
We assume, even though the facts often do not support this assumption, that we deal with mature, if young, people and that if extreme
positions are presented--we are speaking of positions supported by
evidence, presented according to the canons of science rather than

propaganda--the students will be able to determine what position they want to take.

The situation in lower schools I believe is really quite different. In these schools we are engaged in the introduction of basic skills. Although there may be arguments about how to teach reading or writing or calculating skills or foreign languages or the large structure of historical events, there can be no argument about what the end product of such a process must be, even when we deal with the most ambiguous of these elements, such as history. It is important that students should know, for example, that the New World became known as a result of the voyages of Southern and Western European navigators in the late fifteenth and sixteenth centuries and that Spaniards and Englishmen were the first significant European settlers of North America, rather than that they should believe, for example, that the New World was really first settled by the ten tribes of Israel, or by black people from Africa, or by travelers from outer space.

We are also engaged in a process of socialization. We want to teach the students to work on their own and in groups, to respect the common rules of any social order, to regard achievement through their own efforts as possible and rewarding, to understand that blaming others for their own failings is self-defeating and frustrating, and to comprehend all the other things that make for a good and satisfying social order.

Finally, we are still engaged in the process of making a nation, a distinctive nation that is based on the primacy of no single ethnic group, but still one with a defined history, character, and ideals. In other words, in the schools we are still engaged, and must continue to be, in the making of Americans, since this is still a country of mass immigration with large populations still imperfectly integrated into a common nation, both for reasons of past prejudice and discrimination and current parochialism.

These objectives, the teaching of skills, socialization, and the making of Americans, are crucial to the elementary and secondary education process, and they must be held in mind when we talk about truth in education. There are many levels of truth, and we must judge what we teach by what we want to attain. We could emphasize in our teaching that a dominant ethnic group, the Anglo-Americans, enslaved, suppressed, and carried out genocide, physical or cultural, against all other groups. We could emphasize that these other groups attained equality through organization, force, and violence. We could emphasize that it is a betrayal of manhood and authenticity to surrender to Anglo-American cultural values and that the values of each group are good for it and must forever be maintained. We could concentrate on every gap in education, income,

or political influence between the groups and ascribe that gap fully
to prejudice and discrimination. I could continue the litany. Some
evidence can be found for each of these views, though all distort some
other kind of evidence.

We do exercise selection in our teaching of history and current
problems; but our selection and choice in history, economics, and
sociology must be guided not only by truth, a difficult enterprise in
itself because scholars disagree, but also by our conception of a
desirable society, of the relationship between what we select to
teach and the ability of people to achieve such a society and live together in it. In other words, our view of the future, the future we
want, must in some sense determine our teaching about the past and
present.

Thus, after World War II there was a great concern in Europe
with the way history should be taught, because it was believed that
the kind of teaching done might encourage nationalism and antagonism
toward other nations, or the opposite. I would make the same argument about cultural pluralism in American schools: we must decide
whether we will teach separatism or antagonism to the formerly
dominant ethnic elements or whether we will emphasize for each
group the contribution of that group to the United States, the maintenance of its culture in as full a form as possible, and perhaps
criticism of members of each group who prefer acculturation and
assimilation; or the opposing assimilationist views. It is my impression that there are those who would want to teach loyalty to a
single nation that has virtues, but that they are so intimidated and
demoralized by the events of 1965-75 and the way these have been
interpreted in the dominant media and in many scholarly circles,
that the problem is not that minority groups will be crushed by
American culture but that, quite the opposite, they will be taught an
unrealistic and unrewarding emphasis on the independence and
separate virtue of each group, and the necessity for it to defend itself from the basically corrupt Anglo-American-dominated society.

THE RELATIVE WEIGHT GIVEN TO ETHNIC STUDIES
FOR BLACKS AND THE SPANISH-SPEAKING

The argument is sometimes made that at least for some groups
a stronger culturally pluralist emphasis is both politically justified
and socially necessary. Many in the black and Spanish-speaking
groups feel that their need for an education that recognizes special
needs and a special cultural distinctiveness, and that raises their
group consciousness, is much greater than that of the white ethnic
groups, and that their right to it is more solidly established. They

point out that statistically and otherwise they are truly deprived, especially in income and jobs. The blacks point out that the extermination of their cultural traits was almost total, while the white immigrants could, if they wished, maintain their cultures in churches, afternoon schools, and parochial schools. The Spanish-speaking point out that they have a distinctive language situation. Both blacks and the Spanish-speaking point to a distinctive political situation: the blacks were brought as slaves, and the Spanish-speaking, that is, the Mexicans and Puerto Ricans, were conquered. The American Indians were also conquered. The white ethnic groups, however, came as free immigrants. Thus the blacks, the Spanish-speaking groups, the American Indians, and perhaps some other groups can make stronger claims on U.S. institutions for public support of their distinctive cultures than can European groups, since the former were forcibly deprived of cultures, while the latter voluntarily chose to assimilate.

I think there is a good deal of weight in the argument that the distinctive cultural differences of blacks, the Spanish-speaking, and American Indians have a larger moral claim on American society than do European ethnic groups. However, we should not exaggerate the weight of this argument. After all, many blacks are also "free immigrants" from the West Indies and elsewhere. Most Mexican-Americans are free immigrants or the descendants of free immigrants, and the Puerto Ricans choose voluntarily whether will enter the English-speaking environment. If the argument is that the black and Spanish-speaking immigrants were forced to migrate for economic reasons, why, so did the immigrant ancestors of the present-day European ethnic groups.

The fact is, we cannot separate ethnic and racial groups into two classes: those that have suffered, economically and culturally, in American society and therefore deserve redress; and those that have not. Perhaps at the extremes we might make such a distinction, but the history of each group is so unique that a broad separation does not make sense. Consider the Asian Americans, the Chinese and Japanese, who have been among the most successful in introducing special programs devoted to their heritage in the colleges. They did not come as slaves, and they were not conquered, but they did suffer racial prejudice and in the case of the Japanese-Americans, confiscation of their property and incarceration. Nevertheless, they do well in school and well economically. Therefore the question arises: Does deprivation give special rights to ethnic programs?

Another powerful argument gives special weight to the claims of black and Spanish-speaking groups as against those of white immigrant groups. This is the pragmatic argument that as a matter of fact the blacks do poorly in school, and so do the members of the major Spanish-speaking groups and that for that reason alone some special attention to ethnic studies programs is required. The first claim is made on the basis of a past deprivation, and the second on the basis of a present deprivation; but since this is a pragmatic argument, there are pragmatic questions. Do ethnic studies actually raise the scholastic achievements of the students? There are many reasons why an ethnic studies emphasis might improve the achievement of blacks or of the Spanish-speaking, but the arguments are quite different and we do not know how much weight to give them. One argument is that the present dominant curriculum is alien to members of certain groups; there is no way for the black or Mexican-American or Puerto Rican child to relate to a middle-class curriculum based on Dick and Mary. In other words, the argument is that relatedness is necessary, and that this must be a relatedness the objective of which is to bring the black or Spanish-speaking child to competence in what we may call the general curriculum, which is sometimes and improperly called the "white" or "middle class" curriculum--I say improperly because the ability to read and calculate is a general human need, not based on class or color. Whether this ethnically related curriculum is more effective, I do not know. It may be. We should find out.

There is a second and quite different pragmatic argument for ethnic studies, which is not so much that they directly serve to make the curriculum more attractive and meaningful but that they give a greater sense of self-respect to the child of a minority group and in so doing make the child a more competent and self-assured learner. Discovering that blacks and Mexican-Americans and Puerto Ricans have played a major role in the United States, according to this argument, the child will display greater self-confidence in his or her studies.

The first pragmatic argument asserts that the child will do better in his or her studies if their content relates directly to the child's actual, concrete life. The second argument says the child will do better if his or her group or members of that group are visibly reflected in the curriculum, because that will raise the child's pride and self-confidence, the sense that he or she is part of the educational enterprise rather than an outsider in it. Yet a third pragmatic argument is that ethnic studies will of course bring more blacks and Spanish-surnamed teachers into the school and that this will increase the number of role models and will again lead the child to achieve more.

All this may well be true; yet it is also true that Chinese, Japanese, Armenians, Greeks, Jews, and some other groups learned well when nothing about their ways of life or about their groups was in the curriculum, and when none of the people of these groups served as teachers or administrators in the schools. However, there are many ways of learning, and perhaps the direct contact through the curriculum with their actual ways of life, with the histories of their ethnic groups, and with individuals from their groups is needed by the children of some groups or by some children in all groups. Once again we see, as I said earlier, that we cannot assume that ethnic groups are as alike as peas in a pod. Not only are they concretely different, but their differences may result in very different educational needs; for this reason some groups may need ethnic studies while other groups do not.

When we contrast Chinese, Japanese, Armenian, and Jewish students with black, Mexican-American, and Puerto Rican students we are contrasting groups that have seemed to achieve academically even in the total absence of any public recognition of their cultures and group lives with the groups that have achieved least of all, which might be benefited by a recognition of their cultures and group lives. However, we have left out a host of groups in the middle: Polish, other East European, Irish, and German, the achievements of which have been neither remarkable for speedy progress in the face of adverse circumstances nor for its backwardness. Would the children of these groups be helped academically if recognition were to be given to their group characters and their cultural backgrounds? This is not at all clear. In some cases the descendants of these groups have only a distant and vague sense of their group characters. In any case, their demands for the recognition of their group characters are not based on either a deprived political condition (conquest or slavery) or on particular backwardness in academic or economic achievement. Instead they are based on the demand that all cultures be recognized, that all group heritages be of equal significance, and that all be given roles in education and in the curriculum.

CONCLUSION

The claims of truth, of the pragmatic educational necessities of certain groups, and of what I would call the nation as a whole may thus give different answers about the place of cultural pluralism in American life and in the school curriculum. I have suggested the word "integration" as the key by which we can evaluate the place of cultural pluralism. We reject in this term the absolute demands of assimilationists on the one hand and of cultural separatists on the other. I don't believe that either of these rejected positions is dominant; the issue is the definition of the middle ground. There we have many problems. Even a small amount of cultural pluralism

begins by raising troubling questions. Should ethnic studies be only
for the children of the group having that heritage, or should ethnic
studies be for all? Should ethnic studies be required for members of
the groups to which they pertain, or should they be offered as elec-
tives? Should ethnic studies be a separate enclave in the curriculum,
or should they be diffused through and affect the entire curriculum?
Should ethnic studies be taught only by persons who belong to the
groups they teach about, or is the teaching of ethnic studies available
to all, from any background? Should ethnic studies be seen as ad-
vocacy--"belong to the group, have pride in it, study its language"
--or should they point out the varied courses that individuals in the
United States have taken to their heritages?

These are all enormously difficult questions, and the talisman
of "integration" does not give all the answers; nevertheless, it suggests, for example, that we should not limit enrollment in ethnic
studies to those of a given heritage, though it is understandable that
those of a given heritage will be more interested. The model here
should be the teaching of foreign languages in the high schools. They
are all considered of value and are made available because they are
of value; yet it is understandable that one will find Italian taught more
commonly where there are many students of Italian background, and
many will study the language for that reason. In other words, the
achievements of a group should be taught insofar as they play a part
in American history. Understandably, blacks have a much larger
share in American history, and thus should take a larger place in
the curriculum, than Polish Americans. However, in areas where
there are many Polish Americans, additional attention should be
given to their contribution.

The teaching of ethnic studies must not be the teaching of resentment and antagonism. Here our argument is the same as that
which leads us to reject a chauvinistic emphasis in history in general.

Teaching must be open to all on the basis of their real qualifications. Real qualification will very often mean that members of
the group in question are much better qualified than anyone else,
since they have more background and motivation.

Ethnic studies should be integrated into those parts of the
curriculum where they have a place: into history, first of all; but
also into economics, sociology, social science, and literature. In
each case distortion must be avoided, both for the sake of truth in
education and for the sake of the country. I think a black literature
of resentment and anger has played a larger role in teaching in recent years than can be justified by any large view of American and
English literature.

My view of cultural pluralism in the schools and in the society
is that we should not support the creation of sharp differences, with

the children of an ethnic background, neatly labeled and numbered, automatically taking special courses in that background. That is not the reality of U.S. society, for here all groups are to some variable extent acculturated and assimilated. Not all black children should be taught as if black English were their language, nor all Chinese as if they were deficient in English. We should think of teaching about a subgroup in American society as a focus of interest and subject of relevance; primarily it will turn out to be most useful for members of that group, but not exclusively for them. A focus of interest and a subject of relevance is not a means of mobilization. Indeed, education in general should not be a means of mobilization of any sort.

This general picture of cultural pluralism in the schools is based on my view of ethnic groups in their relationship to the general society: ideally, this place is also not defined by sharp differences. The society should be generally open to those who have no interest in a background defined by their descent and have no desire to maintain it or make claims for it; but it should also be open to those who do take an interest in their background and wish to maintain it and instill it in their children. The public agencies should take a position toward ethnic inheritance that I would describe as benign neutrality. We are not interested in a situation such as that of the Soviet Union, in which every person must carry his nationality on his identity card and may not change it even if he has no interest in it. Subnations and subgroups have no legal identity in this country, and should have none. They are protected against discrimination and prejudice, and they are given the liberty, as all individuals and groups are, to maintain whatever part of an ethnic heritage or a distinct identity they wish, as long as that does not transgress on the rights of others. I don't think, however, that it is the place of public agencies to go beyond a benign neutrality toward ethnicity, either to suppress it or to strengthen it.

We want a truthful account of our past and our present, and this involves considerably more attention to race and ethnicity than it has received in the curriculum. We want effective teaching in common skills and knowledge, and this pragmatically may involve paying attention to the fact that many children do not know English or that they need role models or need material that relates to their interests. This is a pragmatic concern, however, and I do not think most of the American people, including most of the people who are defined or see themselves as members of distinctive subgroups, want the government to maintain an interest in their survival as a distinctive group. This would raise the problem of how the government should deal with the claims of many subgroups, which are poorly defined, and with the varying relations among those who may be considered their members. There are mechanisms for going beyond what the public and the common agencies of government and education can or should do to maintain distinct groups; these mechanisms are the independent churches, schools, and organizations. The definition and survival of a fuller and more robust subculture for those groups who find a need for it should be the function of these institutions and not that of the government and the public school.

    We should still engage in the work of the creation of a single, distinct, and unique nation, and this requires that our main attention be centered on the common culture. Cultural pluralism describes a supplement to the emerging common interests and common ideals that bind all groups in the society; it does not, and should not, describe the whole.

2

CULTURAL PLURALISM
FOR INDIVIDUALS:
A SOCIAL VISION
Michael Novak

There is a danger in writing about ethnicity solely in the context of culture and consciousness, since ethnicity, and not only in
America, has direct and indirect relationships with the distribution
of power, wealth, status, and occupations. An ethnic analysis of the
executive suites of major corporations in such cities as Chicago and
Detroit, or an ethnic analysis of universities, of the major media,
of the highest offices of government, of foundations, and of other institutions, reveals that if there is a "melting pot" in American society, it does not exist at the top. The proper focus of ethnic awareness is on issues of power, wealth, and influence: Who are the
decision makers? Also, since power in America now depends largely on communications, who are the opinion makers? A new ethnic
awareness portends changes in the social, political, and economic
order. The "rise" of the unmeltable ethnics suggests new energies,
new purposes, and a new advancement.

Still, the subject assigned for our consideration, although it is
heavy with political and economic consequences, is of a rather different order, which is that of self-perception and world-perception.
Our concern here is what goes on in the soul. "Politics," Charles
Péguy used to say, "begins in mysticism. And mysticism always
ends in politics." The same is true of ethnicity and of other issues
the primary locus of which is consciousness.

BACKGROUND

Intense discussions among social scientists, historians, and
political scientists over the last few years, both in conferences and
in print, have made the lack of theoretical consensus about the con-

cept and significance of ethnicity abundantly clear. We lack elementary distinctions. We lack an accurate and serviceable vocabulary. For over a generation most social scientists in America have considered ethnicity a fading and dysfunctional variable; the emphasis of their research has fallen upon terms such as race, class, and caste, to the exclusion of ethnicity. Since the early 1970s a burst of work has attempted to bring the discussion of ethnicity to comparable sophistication, but the state of this discussion is nevertheless still primitive.

Since I am not by training a social scientist, my own most useful contribution to the discussion must lie in the effort to put into words some experiences with ethnicity, a creative philosophical task, rather than in an attempt to develop concepts satisfactory to social scientists. The philosopher, at this level of activity, presents a body of data, as sensitive and exact as he can render it, and a set of preliminary definitions that beg to be tested. Perhaps philosophical inquiry, by drawing certain distinctions, can draw the attention of social scientists to promising materials. An assiduous reading of the literature of social science in this area has not satisfied me that my own experience and those of many others (I am tempted to say millions of others) has been adequately accounted for.

Naturally I take my earlier written work for granted; there is no use in repeating it. (See the References section at the end of this chapter.) My present aim is to shed further light on the subtle ways and byways of difference in the ethnic traits of one individual from those of another. These subtle areas of consciousness are of considerable intellectual, moral, and educational significance, and the usual set of explanations seems inadequate for expressing what actually happens to many of us in the United States.

I would like to make sense out of my own experience, but efforts in this direction far exceed merely autobiographical reference. Orlando Patterson accounts for the differences between growing up black in the West Indies as opposed to growing up black in the United States; Philip Roth wrestles publicly with the tensions of growing up Jewish in a non-Jewish world; Michael J. Arlen writes in the New Yorker (February 3, 10, and 17, 1975) of his voyage to discover what it means to have roots in Armenia; Richard Gambino explores the Italian experience in America, as he has lived it; Andrew Greeley writes of "the taming of the American Irish"; Ottavio Paz in Labyrinth of Solitude writes powerfully of the anomie of Mexican American youths in a southwestern city; Vine de Loria writes of growing up as an American Indian; Willie Morris describes what it is like to discover Mississippi in New York; and so forth.

The present generation of intellectuals has been brought up to function within a national network formed by television, by the national news magazines, and by the highly mobile culture of the universities and the national corporations. Such intellectuals have had to begin to explore, often without institutional or cultural support, the sources of their own originality, identity, and creativity. There may be a difference here among the generations. Thomas Wolfe and Sinclair Lewis fled the southern and midwest cultures from which they sprang, and F. Scott Fitzgerald entered the high WASP world at Princeton and never looked back. It used to seem obligatory to leave home, to become enlightened, and to join sides with the "larger" world.

By contrast, many today have discovered that you can, and must, go home again, because somewhere there, behind secret doors, hidden behind the branches, lost in mists--somewhere lies the treasure that nourishes their work. The national university system and the national communications network, both created since World War II, may be most responsible for this emergence of ethnic and regional consciousness, since it is in part by meeting "others" and in part by learning the ways of self-consciousness and the tools of self-analysis that one is prompted to notice one's own "difference" and to be puzzled by it. One is obliged, by a certain intellectual honesty and by a certain intellectual exigency, to see things precisely in their proper intellectual horizon and to call things precisely by their proper names. The higher education of the masses was bound to cause an explosion in American self-consciousness, insofar as the masses were not all Anglo-Americans whose lives were already well articulated in the dominant cultural symbols.

For myself, I mark the appointment, after a certain struggle, of Lionel Trilling to a chair in American literature at Columbia University as a major cultural turning point. If a Jew could be an arbiter of English language and literature, a master of American culture, and if at the same time he could bring to bear on traditional literary materials the psychoanalytic methods and social criticism that had been imported into America preeminently by Jewish culture, then sooner or later the cultural horizon of Anglo-American traditions was bound to be expanded by still other imports, still other methods, and still other tastes. After 1950 the war between Jewish writer-critic and Anglo-American writer-critic replaced the older literary war between paleface and Indian; since 1965 the battles have widened, as historians like Oscar Handlin and sociologists like Daniel Bell have quietly enlarged the pillars and bases of Anglo-American consciousness. The publication of Beyond the Melting Pot, by Nathan Glazer and Daniel Moynihan (1963), also suggested the long-range need of a more realistic interpretation of the U.S. urban reality.

The great expansion of higher education after World War II brought hundreds of thousands of blacks into the universities;

compared to this quiet and steady social transformation, the "black revolution" of the 1960s was an evanescent media event. The structural change was both economic and inward. The newly educated blacks could hardly help noting the anomalies of their lot: their own family culture and group history were hardly mentioned in the humanities and not adequately treated in the social sciences. Because great feelings of guilt attended Anglo-American relations with blacks, and also because of a certain condescension, the blacks were easily conceded a right to be "different" and even "separatist"; it was "legitimate" for them to think of themselves as a group. Although black consciousness was following in the tracks already opened up by Jewish consciousness, the legitimation it won from the Anglo-American arbiters of culture, the academics, editors, and publicists, not only extended logically to every other minority, but also raised new problems. In the generation of Trilling, Handlin, and Bell, many Jewish scholars had struggled to gain a universality of range and personal transcendence that exceeded their desire to think of themselves as Jewish; they belonged to America as a whole, to the "mainstream," to the "common culture." The debate that raged around William Styron's Nat Turner showed that the new black consciousness was, by and large, choosing a more particularist route. Some asserted that only a black could properly understand the black experience; that only a black could effectively teach blacks, and so on. The problems of intellectual pluralism that are implicit in these differing approaches are not easy even to state correctly, let alone to resolve.

The situation in 1975 is somewhat different from that of the late 1960s. The great taboo has been broken. Every day new works appear as evidence that each human being does emanate from a particular social world and that there is intellectual gain in self-consciousness about one's own beginnings. Michael J. Arlen's beautiful three-part essay in the New Yorker is not an exercise in chauvinism, boasting of the glories of being Armenian, but is rather a kind of elegy, haunting and sad, exploring the mystery of why for two generations being Armenian had been an object of secrecy, unconsciousness, and hidden shame in his family. To be Armenian and American is not a sign of failed universality or flawed self-transcendence; it is, as Michael Arlen exemplifies it, an admirable expression of what it is to be of flesh and blood, inspirited by a large soul: he is who he is, unpretending, perceptive, at home in a pluralistic world, rooted, unhomogenized, living consciously in a history different perhaps from yours or mine, and yet living also in a history that you and I share.

No one of us speaks for all humanity; yet each of us, if we are so committed, does try to speak to and within a human history increasingly shared in common, even though shared by each of us from a different chair in the total symphony.

I should like, indeed, to propose that the metaphor underlying our search for a theory adequate to our diverse personal experience is best taken from the world of music. Our society is not best understood as a melting pot, a salad, a stew, a mosaic--such metaphors are far too static, ugly, and mechanical for the life of the spirit. In the world of music, the chief sense is the ear, the most personal of all the senses, the most attuned to inner ways, the most complex and subtle in its range, the best suited to the perception of many levels of meaning simultaneously, drawing upon quite distinct instruments and following interweaving motifs. In music, underlying melodies may rise and fall, emerge and recede; and many diverse sounds may mingle or suddenly be heard alone or in crystal-clear counterpoint. The whole effect may include the contributions of all-- present a "common culture"--without thereby requiring that flutes be drums or sonatas symphonies. Dissonance has its uses; and variation; and sudden harmony.

Enough of metaphor: we need some fairly precise words, to disentangle the many levels of experience involved in pluralistic living.

DEFINITIONS

I say "fairly precise" advisedly. It is a mark of wisdom, Aristotle instructs us, to expect of each inquiry only that degree of clarity appropriate to it. Most of our most important social and political concepts do not lend themselves to univocal definition, being neither clear, nor pat, nor universally applicable, nor tame. In my own field, which is religious studies, no one has given a definition of religion that would be adequate to describe every historical manifestation of the phenomena we are driven to term religious. The same is true, I am instructed, of concepts in social science such as class, and even caste, as well as of democracy, liberalism, and equality. The most basic concepts are the hardest to define. We should not expect that a definition of ethnicity, or of its components, will be any more neat than these others; what we should hope, however, is that the definitions offered are at least heuristic, that is, that they will channel our attention in fruitful ways, will not preclude the raising of important further questions, and will not avert our eyes from those discrepant experiences that still elude the embrace of our definitions. In this area, definitions are more like searchlights than like maxims carved in stone. The test of a good definition is not whether it covers all cases--smothers them, ties all their edges down--but whether it brings to light, or at least allows to emerge, everything relevant and significant.

I sometimes imagine that there is a finite number of characteristics that various authors have listed as constituting an ethnic group. Let us suppose, for the sake of simplicity, that the number is twenty. Are Texans an ethnic group? Are the Syrian-Lebanese in America one ethnic group (Arabs); or are they two (Syrians and Lebanese, at least since Syria and Lebanon became independent nations in the twentieth century) or four (Syrian-Moslem, Syrian-Christian, Lebanese-Moslem, and Lebanese-Christian)? Is each Indian tribe of North America an ethnic group? Are contemporary intellectuals an ethnic group? Are the Jews, Poles, Italians, Slovaks, Irish, West Indians, and American blacks ethnic groups in the same sense? No two of these groups, let us admit, have identical sets of characteristics constituting them as ethnic groups. From my finite list of constitutive characteristics, each group has perhaps ten or twelve. Perhaps having a greater number of such characteristics may mark a group as an ethnic group in the strictest sense, while having a smaller number may mark it as an ethnic group in a looser, but informative, sense. A theory of ethnicity arrived at in this way would provide, as it were, a map, a scale, a field, in which fruitful analogies might be constructed. Such a theory might also be imagined as containing a historical dimension, enabling us to chart the coming into being and the dying out of certain forms of group consciousness. For instance, most immigrants from Central Europe had "Hungarian" on their passports, but thought of themselves in much more local terms than that, and were only to be sorted out, and to sort themselves out, in such shifting categories as "bohunks," then "Bohemians," then "Slovaks," and then, perhaps, "Czechoslovaks."

The French have begun to use the word ethné to signify an ethnic group. It would be beyond my range to list all the elements constitutive of an ethné, as required for the theory mentioned above; nevertheless, some of the following propositions may make a contribution in that direction. The field I have in view is the people of the United States, and not all the people of the planet as a whole.

1. Ethnic belonging is a phenomenon of consciousness; it is not merely genetic. It is ascribed by others or self-ascribed. When the young Michael Arlen replied sincerely to a schoolmaster that his nationality was English, the schoolmaster retorted, "You couldn't be English." There are genetic factors involved in ethnic belonging, since it involves the transmission of certain genes from a relatively limited gene pool, and over a long period of time environmental factors, including diet, may deeply affect the character of an ethné; but in the United States, at least, much is to be gained by concentrating on the effects of ethnicity upon consciousness. How does ethnicity work in consciousness? On how many levels?

2. Ethnicity affects consciousness below the threshold of self-consciousness or self-analysis. Behavior or perceptions that seem natural, normal, and universal to the person participating in them may be "different" or "distinctive" in the eyes of others. Even those who try to erase from their behavior, emotions, and perceptions the characteristics they identify with their past may nevertheless unconsciously signal to others that they are different. When Senator Muskie cried in New Hampshire in 1972, some thought his learned Yankee composure had cracked. It does not follow that those whose consciousness has been shaped by ethnic belonging "know themselves" thoroughly enough to discern how, to what degree, and in which ways it has been changed, or that everyone wants to know these things. It also does not follow that those who do know them necessarily wish to reinforce or inhibit them. Efforts at more exact self-knowledge may reveal the impact of ethnicity upon our own consciousness; for it has had such an impact, even if we have never adverted to it. Explore and see.

3. Ethnicity is, in a loose, preliminary definition, participation in a shared social horizon and in its way of structuring self and the world, in its affects, and in its history. Such participation is usually transmitted un-self-consciously by our parents in their behavior and attitudes and by the structure of family relations and the relationship of the family to larger worlds. It tends to be transmitted tacitly and without conceptual or even verbal articulation, although in some cases elaborate rituals, social codes, activities, symbols, games, tales, and stories may objectify the tacit transmission. The learning of a language and the study of a specific literature and history may further objectify the tacit transmission. Implied here is a possible, and in America statistically frequent, breakdown between the objectified world and the tacit transmission. Most public symbols, language, and activities may run counter to the tacit transmission. Inner experience may lack cultural objectification, and the tongue to reveal itself. A Croatian-American may have learned feelings and ways of perceiving from the family but may never encounter symbols that express such inner feelings in the schools, in the media, or in public life.

4. The shared social history that constitutes ethnicity is not identical to religion, although in some cultures religion is a primary component thereof. To a Lebanese, being Christian or Moslem may be of greater salience than being Lebanese; yet being Lebanese Moslem rather than Egyptian Moslem is also significant. Being Jewish is not identical with being a participant in Judaism as a religion or even with believing in God; yet the tie between Judaism and Jewishness is culturally decisive. The Slovak Catholic, the Slovak Orthodox, and the Slovak Lutheran do, and yet do not, share the same

social history; the issue is complex because Lutheran cultural leaders did so much to develop the distinctive Slovak language and cultural identity, while the Orthodox have maintained symbols that look eastward. The connections among religion, nationality, and culture are experienced differently, and the distinctions among them are drawn differently, in different cultures.

5. The shared social history that constitutes ethnicity is not identical with national heritage or national origin. Many nations are composed of more than one ethnic group. A Scotsman in London may be a citizen of Great Britain and yet identify himself ethnically in clear opposition to English or Welsh citizens.

6. A shared social history endures over time because, and inasmuch as, it offers illumination and support in changing circumstances, changing environments, and changing times. Ethnic consciousness waxes and wanes; ethnic groups seem to appear, to disappear, to "melt," and to be stirred back to life according to various conditions. On the other hand, one must distinguish between a "shared social history," insofar as it is conscious and insofar as it is unconscious. Forgotten historical events can be brought back to memory, with a galvanizing effect. A mythical history can slso be invented. To some extent, every exercise in historical reconstruction reflects a present sense of reality and present criteria of relevance; history is always being rewritten as an exercise in present self-understanding. One can learn new, or forgotten, elements from the past that throw light upon the present. The historical reconstruction of an ethnic history, even of the sort Michael Arlen undertook, is done because it has utility, in Arlen's case because a writer's identity is the most precious resource he or she has.

7. A shared social history, if it is not to be merely episodic or part of a larger whole, must in some way be related both to the whole of human history and to cosmic time. Territorial or regional experience over a relatively short period of time, in Appalachia, in Texas, or in the American South, for instance, approaches, or recedes from, "a shared social history" in the strict sense, insofar as it aspires to convey an entire world view. If the regional experience presents itself as a subplot of a larger story, the story of the United States, for example, or the story of English-speaking peoples, they are rather like those group variations that every <u>ethné</u> includes within it. Such variations, however, are full of interest and psychological power and are often characterized by specific economic and social structures, making their influence at least very much like that of a "shared social history" in the fuller sense. Thus the inner geography of many persons in the South, or in Appalachia, with respect to the dominant and taste-making culture of the Northeastern upper class, includes elements of self-doubt, cultural insecurity,

and self-hatred that are remarkably analogous to those discerned by
Michael Arlen in his father. The cultural dominance of the North-
east in the U.S. educational structure imposes a somewhat false
self-image on the vast majority of Americans: U.S. history is too
much written from Boston westward and southward and from the upper
class downward. The chief television production supported by the
National Endowment for the Humanities for the Bicentennial concerns
the life of Abigail Adams.

8. A shared social history may give rise to an "ethnic culture,"
an "ethnic identification," and an "appropriated ethnic heritage." An
ethnic culture is observable when attitudes, styles of personality, and
behaviors are ethnically distinctive, as when Polish-Americans prove
more likely to vote on election day than any other ethnic group in
America. An ethnic identification arises when one places oneself on
an ethnic chart: "I am West Indian." An ethnic heritage may be unconscious and implicit, but it is appropriated as one's own when one
explicitly and consciously explores one's social history, its symbols,
and its historical objectifications. Under present conditions, the
second and third of these moments frequently come first, making us
conscious, for the first time, of the third. Thus Michael Arlen was
identified, and then identified himself, as a person of Armenian
descent. Then he began to appropriate a particular social history,
that of his family and his people, by reading, study, and travel. Then
he began to draw connections between some of his own tastes, interests, values, and activities and those of the culture he had, even unconsciously, been sharing. He was a kinsman, and he began to become conscious of his kinship with his father, his grandfather, and
others, along lines that in the first part of his life he had studiously
guarded from acknowledging.

A young Serbian student in Winona, Minnesota, recently told
me how for years he had been protected by his mother, and passive-
ly by his father, from learning of his father's "foreign" family; contact with them was regarded as a downward pull. The student's
handsome profile, black mustache, and wavy hair reminded me un-
cannily of a painting of a hussar I had just seen in a Serbian restau-
rant in Vienna. (On these distinctions, see Andrew Greeley, 1974.)

9. A shared social history does not imply tribalism, group
think, or collective action. Even when living at a distance from one
another, without neighborhood ties, and virtually apart from all but
occasional group contacts, individuals may participate in a shared
social history. Often individuals live in diaspora and yet maintain a
remarkable sense of group connectedness that is consonant with daily
existence at great distance from other members of their group.
Thus the Syrian-Lebanese in America, although for the most part
scattered in individual families across the whole United States,

retain a remarkable sense of shared social history. To speak of
group solidarity in their case is to speak only analogously; for while
there are many evidences of national cooperation and association and
of organized initiatives, the dominant pattern of their living seems
to be as individual families in the midst of others different from themselves. In contemporary life, many carry their ethnic connections
internally, without living in an ethnic group.

10. There is no contradiction between living as a responsible
and autonomous individual and appropriating one's own shared social
history, that is, between the celebration of individuality and the
celebration of ethnicity. There would be such a contradiction only
if the human being were not a social animal, but atomic and singular
and alone. Thus Orlando Patterson (1975) in attacking "the fallacy
of cultural pluralism" is not denying his own shared social history
as a black from the West Indies nor that of David Riesman, whom he
cites, as a scholar of uncommonly large sympathies and yet much in
debt to his Jewish heritage.

11. The phrase "cultural pluralism" conjures up at least five
social models, each of which should be distinguished from the others
(Greeley 1974). First is the model of Anglo-American conformity.
The plurality of cultures entering into America should adapt to the
cultural history of the Anglo-American part of the population.

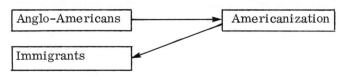

Second is the model of the melting pot. The Anglo-American
part of the population is modified, at least in part, by the other immigrant cultures and the result is a new common culture. In practice this view usually gives way to Anglo-American conformity.

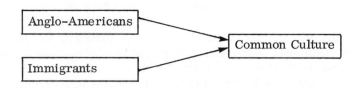

Third is the model of simple cultural pluralism. The non-
Anglo, immigrant parts of the population are affected by the dominant Anglo-American population and so do not remain as they were,
and yet they remain somewhat separate from the Anglo-American
population. This model may represent the pluralism of Switzerland,

Holland, Ulster, Sri Lanka, and some African countries. However,
it does not explain the situation of Michael Arlen and many others.

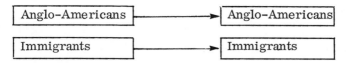

Fourth is the model of acculturation but not assimilation. The
immigrant cultures pick up some traits from the dominant Anglo-
American culture, and the dominant culture picks up some traits
from the various non-Anglo cultures, so that an area of "common
culture" is created. On the other hand, the non-Anglo cultures retain some of their other traits. Anglo-American culture retains
some of its own special psychic territory. Members of groups discover a fairly ample distance, especially between themselves and
members of other groups, but only in the private sphere, such as
in marriage, friendships, occupations, habits, and vacations.

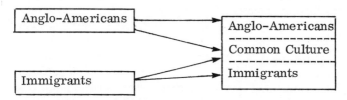

Fifth is the model of ethnogenesis. Some at least of the non-
Anglo groups had shared traits and resources with Anglo-American
culture even before their meeting in America. Depending on the experience of various groups in America at the diverse times and
places of their arrival and depending on their subsequent experiences,
reinforcements, and negative shocks, individuals may proceed along
various trajectories. In some ways they may pick up traits from
Anglo-American culture or from other American cultures and may
try to set aside some traits they have brought with them. The re-
sultant mix of traits may still remain quite distinctive; indeed, in
some respects they or their children may be more different from
their fellow Anglo-Americans after three generations than their
ancestors were from Anglo-Americans three generations earlier.
For example, they may more keenly distrust certain "American"
ideas that were celebrated three generations ago. The shared social
history in which they now participate may include Anglo-American
traits, symbols, and history while also going quite considerably beyond them. Thus a Lithuanian-American in the third generation
may share a quite different social history from that of Orlando

Patterson, Willie Morris, Philip Roth, Mohammed Ali, James Reston, Jr., or Robert Kennedy, Jr. An individual might, moreover, test his or her own attitudes, opinions, convictions, and behavior and discern remarkable differences between them and those of other ethnic traditions, assuming the same residence, income, class, and other variables. Of course, acculturation is like a glass of water: some say it is half full, while others say it is half empty.

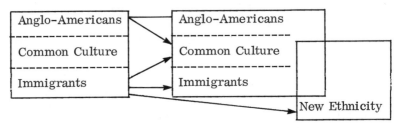

12. Research is needed on free use by the individual of his or her own ethnic inheritance, especially its resources for nourishing sensibility, imagination, moral perception, and intellectual style. Most discussions of ethnicity seem to have the tribal group in mind and to look for the characteristics of group solidarity, group behavior, and group perception. One distinctive feature of a pluralistic society like that of the United States is that the individual, living and acting and thinking as an individual, may continue to nourish ethnically differentiated symbolic materials. At this point it is logical to ask in how many ways this is done and whether the ways must be conscious.

13. Ethnic inheritance affects the rate, direction, symbols, and style of moral development. The extent to which the moral agent imagines himself or herself as a solitary, autonomous individual or, by contrast, as an autonomous member of a family or other communal network, varies ethnically. The extent to which morality is imagined as obedience to moral principles; loyalty to one's bonded fellows; or fidelity to an ideal type of conduct or code of honor, varies ethnically. The valuation of obedience, dissent, loyalty, and priority vary ethnically. The starting places of moral development are especially diverse: at the heights (or the depths) of moral development, moral geniuses may have more in common.

14. Ethnic inheritance affects the symbolic field within which religious perceptions occur. It may determine whether the symbol "God" is linked to morality or to nature, to historical optimism or historical fatalism, to distance or proximity; or to personal crises or impersonal detachment. It may be observed that architecture, religious rituals, and rites of marriage, birth, and death evoke

symbolically diverse materials in ethnically diverse traditions.
Even quite secular symbol systems, whether those of groups such as
Ethical Culture or those of individuals, tend to reflect ethnically di-
verse symbolic fields.

15. Literary symbols diverge ethnically. To read Portnoy's
Complaint (Roth, 1969) alongside Couples is to move in two ethnically
diverse symbolic worlds. The sexual vagaries of the hero of American Mischief diverge according to the ethnic backgrounds of his mis-
tresses. Codes of honor, the role of the individual, family expectations, and other materials differ quite remarkably in the literary
works that derive from different ethnic traditions. Giants in the
Earth, by O. E. Rolvaag; America! America!, by Elia Kazan; Out
of This Furnace, by Thomas Bell (Belejak); The Fortunate Pilgrim,
by Mario Puzo; The Virginian, by Owen Wister; and other novels re-
create significantly diverse symbolic worlds. It is one of the functions of literature to render particular worlds accessible to a universal audience; but the interplay between the particular and the universal is complex and fascinating.

16. The perception of political symbols varies ethnically.
Frequently used political words, such as "conscience," "change,"
"quotas," "welfare," "compassion," "loyalty," "patronage," "neighborhood," "family," "humane," "peace," and others, have associations that affect those who hear them on more than one level simultaneously and in ethnically significant patterns. The political actions of a person can link that person with certain allies even when
the political symbols surrounding such actions affect him or her differently from the way they affect those allies. Some persons voted
for George McGovern who reacted quite negatively to his moral self-
presentation; others wished he had been even more vigorously moral.
A distinction should be made between perception and behavior, along
the lines of which ethnic inheritance varies significantly. Some traditions have symbolic and behavioral resources that others lack. To
certain symbols and behavior some individuals have logical responses
that are different from their emotional responses. An individual cannot be determined by an ethnic inheritance to perceive or to behave
in one way only, but the resources for perception and behavior of that
individual may be significantly affected by a social history different
from that of others.

If the preceding propositions are generally acceptable, then
certain deficiencies in U.S. educational institutions and networks of
communication come to light. We are not very well prepared, even
by many years of education, to discern nuances of difference in our
ways of thinking. Our statistical reporting, for instance, reveals
the narrowness of our preoccupations; it is fixated on racial and

sexual differentiation to the neglect of ethnic differentiation. In February 1975 unemployment among blacks was 13.4 percent, while the national average was 8.2 percent. A harder look shows that unemployment among all blue-collar workers was 11 percent, which was much closer to the black average. Considering the situation in Detroit and in the minefields, what was the unemployment rate among Slavs? This figure, however it might turn out, would throw black unemployment into a more significant light. Similarly, proportionally more blacks go to college than Slavs or Italians. Why do the statisticians only compare blacks to whites, as if "white" were a homogeneous category?

ETHNIC DEPRIVATION

What most concerns me here, however, are the resources that an appropriation of ethnicity provides to the individual, even in isolation from his or her ethnic group. My strategy for presenting them is to set forth a utopian view of the way we ought to manage cultural pluralism. The fifth of Greeley's models seems to me the least inadequate for interpreting our present circumstance. It also supplies the conceptual skeleton for a more adequate use of educational and other resources.

Imagine a typical third-generation Polish person who is now a professional in academic, political, or corporate life. Let us call him John Kubek. Kubek is a graduate of Cornell with a doctorate in political science. He grew up in Buffalo but has never had any affiliation with an ethnic fraternal association or with any other kind of ethnic association. Most of the students in the parochial school he attended were Polish, but many of the students and most of the teachers were Irish, along with a few Italians, blacks, and others. The parish he attended as a child was Polish, but Polish-language sermons had already almost disappeared, although confessions in Polish were still available for old timers.

Polish was not spoken in his home except when the parents wished the children not to know what they were saying. For instance his mother seemed to warn his father in Polish when he was being too hard on the children. His father was proud to be a foreman in the mill. Not many Polacks, he repeated, had made it to the rank of foreman because the Irish kept pushing their own. Neither in the parochial school nor in the public high school, where with some qualms his ambitious parents had sent him, did Kubek learn anything significant about Polish literature or history. He learned a little about St. Patrick's day in the parochial elementary school, as well as how to dance the Irish jig (for the pastor's silver jubilee) and about the Easter Rebellion. "Orange" was a taunt he could use against the Irish; once on St. Patrick's day he wore an orange sweater to school and a minor fist fight resulted, after which the eighth-grade nun admonished him verbally about his "bad judgment" but emotionally about his gross insensitivity.

To Kubek the university seemed to be a great liberation. He thought that many of his professors were quite complacently anti-Catholic and, indeed, moralistic and impractical in their social ideas, exactly as his father had predicted. However, a freer sexual ethic, an attitude of openness to shocking ideas, and a genial atmosphere of virtual laissez faire attracted him. He did indeed feel liberated and enlightened by virtue of his university experience. He felt he had a strength in political practicality and toughness that his instructors lacked, especially with respect to urban politics and urban history. He tended to idealize early labor union history less than they did and would not feign shock that labor union leaders earn more than full professors. He was early won to a form of radical politics in the early 1960s, and he enjoyed shocking some of his professors by contradicting their expectations that he would be conservative, although he had been implicitly expected to because he had been Polish and Catholic. Liberalism seemed to him a fairly elitist and complacent view of the world, a little too Jewish and high Protestant in its intellectual and social base. It represented an establishment toward which he had quite ambivalent feelings. It presented itself as weak and in opposition, when in fact it seemed to him strong, even dominant, and virtually unopposed, at least intellectually. On the other hand, many of his colleagues in radicalism seemed to carry Jewish and high Protestant tendencies to even further extremes and to be too fond, for his taste, of witness, martyrdom, and failure. He had an instinctive sympathy for underdogs but disdained losers.

He was pleased that his relationships with blacks seemed to be on tougher and more elemental grounds than those of his academic colleagues; he neither felt guilt nor permitted himself to be emotionally bullied. He liked to disagree openly with blacks, to call their bluffs, and to tear away the moral rhetoric ("oppression," "reparations," and even "racist society") from their real claims. "We outnumber you nine to one," he would say. "If we wanted to be racists, to oppress, and to commit genocide, why shouldn't we? If you want jobs, say so. Don't expect me to go down the sawdust trail, preacher man." Blacks would wink and elbow him.

When he heard of the "new ethnicity," Kubek ridiculed it. Hell, he wasn't Polish. He had assimilated. He couldn't speak Polish and didn't want to. His children showed hardly a sign of Polishness, whatever that might be. The old neighborhoods in Buffalo were going or gone. Of course the "ethnics"--he hated the

word, didn't like being any place where labels might be stuck on him--
were "melting." The evidence was overwhelming.

On the other hand, every evidence that "melting" was not taking
place irritated him. He was sick of smiling weakly at Polish jokes;
among colleagues who wouldn't tell black jokes or Jewish jokes. He
did believe that the statistical evidence was fairly systematically distorted, by colleagues who spoke of political attitudes, voting behavior,
and rhetorical symbols among blue-collar workers generally, and
among ethnic populations in particular, in ways that the figures did
not warrant. He thought of this as part of his own tough-mindedness
in such matters, given his social rooting in such communities.

He did not feel as though he was a political ally of white ethnic
working-class populations: he made jokes about Boss Daley and his
machine as bitingly as the next man (Mike Royko was a favorite of
his, actually); but he didn't particularly like the "feel" of many of
the "creeps" he was in alliance with, either. (Mike Royko's column
on "Jet-stream [Jesse] Jackson" gave him a special exhilaration,
like an evanescent ray of honesty in a fog.) He worked for, but
loathed, McGovern. He wished someone else besides Nixon were the
Republican candidate so he could prove to himself that he was independent and didn't always vote Democratic. Is John Kubek an "ethnic"
or not?

More to the point, would a different public conception of cultural pluralism and a different educational system have been of assistance to him, enhancing his creativity and increasing the probability
of his making a distinctive and significant intellectual contribution to
this society? In two respects John Kubek's potential has been aborted:
he has been deprived of self-knowledge and he lacks a serviceable intellectual language.

Both these deficiencies have practical consequences. With more
thorough self-knowledge he might lose less time and energy on un-
necessary inner conflict, and his own self-image and the image others
have of him might fall into sharper focus. It is not paradoxical that
John Kubek is in some ways more radical and more progressive than
his colleagues and in other ways more progressive in a different way,
a way they at first perceived to be "conservative." On abortion, for
example, he early raised issues about the rights of the fetus that they
then ridiculed but later, about the time of the February 1975 cover
of Newsweek, also began to worry about. His own early reaction had
been stimulated by the translation of "24 weeks" into "six months,"
at a time when his wife Betsy was six-months pregnant.

With a more serviceable intellectual language, Kubek would be
able to say some of the things he obscurely feels about family life and
family culture, about what distinguishes a "good" neighborhood from
an alienated neighborhood and the like, in terms that others could

readily understand. The language of U.S. politics sometimes seems incredibly impoverished. "Left" and "right" are terms borrowed from nineteenth-century France; "liberal" and "conservative" from nineteenth-century England; and "progressive" and "populist" from the rural United States. For the politics of the immigrant white urban working class there is no uniquely appropriate language. The perception of its values is somehow askew, and even its self-perception is askew. Perhaps if such a language were generally accessible, the present political situation of the nation might be quite differently understood and the nature and structure of American society might be differently imagined. One of every four Americans is Catholic. Perhaps a theory that began with Catholicism might shed light upon the whole.

To put the matter briefly, the present system of acculturation and assimilation has two drawbacks: it alienates many citizens from a genuine self-knowledge, and it inhibits the growth of genuine intellectual creativity. In effect, the processes of acculturation and assimilation strengthen the mechanisms of conformity, both outward and inward. They do not liberate the unique and differentiated resources of the individual; instead they reward capitulation.

PRESERVING ETHNIC ADVANTAGES

Thus the third- or fourth-generation descendant of "white-ethnic" immigrants with professional aspirations has three choices, the first of which is a rather high degree of Anglo-American conformity, not only in outward behavior but also in comfortable inwardness. It is important to be "at home" among those who set the cultural style in professional circles.

The second choice is some degree of involvement, which is usually small or nonexistent unless fairly direct economic trade-offs result in explicitly ethnic neighborhoods or organizations. Leadership in any subgroup ought not to be disdained, since between state totalitarianism and isolated individuals, well-organized and semivoluntary subgroups make essential social contributions to a healthy society. Nevertheless, the larger society tends to regard active participation in ethnic subgroups with a certain uneasiness or condescension. Therefore this choice, unless special compensations are involved, is usually discouraged by the prevailing social climate. Ordinarily, education means education "away from" the ethnic group; the ethnic group is one of the darknesses with which "enlightenment" is set in contrast.

The third choice is a personal, usually unaided search for one's family and cultural roots that is possible only after a certain economic and social success has been established. Here one may find identification with a cultural stream that is differentiated both from the host culture and from the immigrant organizational structure.

With respect to each of these choices, an intelligent cultural pluralism might provide certain assistances that are not now available. In the best of all possible Americas, here is what I believe such assistance would look like.

First, in the home young children would be provided with folk tales, images, and rituals that would objectify the actual emotional and intellectual rhythms that govern family relations. When family relations move on levels that have no objectification, or an objectification that does not actually fit, serious emotional distortion arises. Anger, resentment, misunderstandings, and dreadful silences multiply, intertwine, and feed on each other, not only those that occur in the complexity of all human relationships, but also special cultural distortions that heighten them.

Young Slavs in the Pittsburgh area, for example, frequently manifest an unusual docility, modesty, passivity in school; there is about them some sense of already having been defeated. They are prey, too, to flashes of anger, to deep hostility, and to an ambivalent self-hatred and feeling of inferiority. Some of the passages in Dostoevsky about the self-grovelling and the exhilarating extremes in the Russian character capture, in their Russian version, the swings of emotion of these young Slavs.

Dostoevsky's tales do not represent the peasant culture from which most immigrants come. Most immigrants have in their homes no access to books or stories that exemplify their own spontaneous tendencies to anger, to ecstasy, to fear, to envy, and the rest. The process of acculturation provides them solely with "American" ways of disposing of these emotions. However, Anglo-Americans do not have to contain in these channels the same structure of passion and feeling. Jewish culture, by contrast, provides in story and image a wide variety of self-understanding. Jews have possibilities of being "American" but also, where useful, of not being limited by American ways.

Second, the curricula of the public and parochial elementary schools offer virtually no illumination to the Italian, Greek, Slavic, and other children concerning the different family patterns and emotional contexts out of which they come. Dick and Jane in the elementary readers are plainly white Anglo-Saxon Protestant in attitude, behavior, and image. The objects in the home and their attitudes with respect to them are not those of all U.S. families, even in the third and fourth generations. Perhaps all children experience the schools as a somewhat unreal environment; but in values and style the schools are still more distant from Southern and Eastern European traditions. The problem has been more acute since the mid-1950s because the cultural dissonance is internal rather than external. The world of plastics and mass production floods all homes more or less homogeneously, but the emotional currents in the home still tend to follow patterns thousands of years old. Anger is a legitimate and frequently exhibited emotion in some traditions, but is regarded as a lapse in self-control in others. Ambition is nourished in some, but much chided in others. Children are lavishly praised in some traditions, and systematically "humbled" in others. School curricula that do not help students objectify their own inner tendencies contribute to the general dissonance, to a merely extrinsic conformity, and to enormous psychic wastage.

Third, the curricula of universities systematically exclude the cultures of a very large minority, perhaps a majority, of their students. In studying U.S. history, for example, it is important that all students learn something of the formative experiences of the nation: of the Puritan divines, of the great Virginians, and of Abraham Lincoln, Theodore Roosevelt, Woodrow Wilson, Franklin Delano Roosevelt, and so on. On the other hand, historical studies that regard as unimportant the great formative influences of the industrial and urban turmoil of the last 100 years, thereby neglecting the history of the great immigration, leave out of account one of the most powerful of all American realities. A systematic distortion is introduced by the fact that so many historians and teachers do not resonate to immigrant history as their own. Few translators have been available, from the beginning and even today, to provide the children of the immigrants with an accessible literature. Except in the case of the Jews, the structures of immigrant societies did not include due proportions of teachers and intellectual workers; nor were those who came with the immigrants valued for their intellectual skills. Enormous cultural and emotional costs are still being paid for this structural flaw.

Fourth, few descendants of the immigrants have appeared on state boards of regents, on the boards of trustees of the state universities, or in other comparable educational positions, and of those who have, far fewer have grasped the extent of the inner distortion being suffered under the existing policies of Americanization. Often those from ethnic groups who are so honored are proud of the honor, and in their minds the honor confirms the justice of the processes of Americanization; its costs are not so apparent to them.

Fifth, even if individual parents try to compensate for the egregious failures of the schools, the local public libraries are extremely deficient in resources. Books on England, France, and Germany abound. English culture is indeed wed to Norman and to

Saxon culture, and the wedding continues; but concerning Southern and Eastern Europe the holdings are slim indeed. The publishers' lists suggest the same pattern.

In a word, the tasks before us are immense. The basic intellectual work, that of translation and creation, has often not been done; nor can those who want to do it find the supporting resources. Work in curriculum design has not been done, and the texts, workbooks, and teacher training that would undergird it do not exist. Finally, many parents are not aware that much of the cultural dissonance they and their children face is not essential or irremovable; they often feel left out, cheated, and resentful without diagnosing this aspect of their frustration. Many of them do not see the importance of cultural, intellectual, and artistic forms in bringing inner life into harmony with outer life. Their anti-intellectualism costs them more than they know; and it does not occur to them that this anti-intellectualism might be occasioned by the failure of intellectuals to come to their support.

What ought to be done? So much needs to be done on every level that it is difficult to see where to begin. Perhaps our greatest requirement is a sound justification for doing anything at all. In the following pages I will list the negative and positive reasons for a long-range strategy in multicultural self-understanding in all our cultural institutions.

The Negative Reasons for a Long-Range Strategy

1. Suppressed anger. Even a casual watcher of television in the mid-1970s can hardly help noticing the undercurrent of anger in most successful prime-time shows, in Don Rickles, Archie Bunker, Maude, the Jeffersons, Rodney Dangerfield, the Smothers Brothers, and many others. A persistent claim is "lack of respect." One ingredient of this undifferentiated anger is, I believe, the fundamentally bad faith in which Anglo-American conformity involves the major part of our population. The gap between public and private self-presentation is emotionally very costly. The policies of assimilation and acculturation, while admirable in many respects, demand an enormous amount of repression. Each generation is obliged to shape its emotional patterns to a public standard that is native to very few. Even Anglo-Americans are forced away from old and respected habits. For instance, a person's word is no longer a bond, as it once would have been.

2. Distorted self-knowledge. Without culturally sophisticated self-understanding, the models and standards individuals apply to themselves may not be in keeping with their resources. They may

pretend, or try to be, what they are not, being ignorant of ample historical repertoires that are more nearly attuned to their own possibilities. An assumption should here be made explicit: I do not believe that any human being is entirely malleable, a blank sheet, an Eliza Doolittle. Whatever restructuring of the psyche is done after a certain age carries with it certain costs. Human beings are extraordinarily free, and it is a mistake to underestimate their freedom, but they are not pure spirits, and total conversions are exceedingly rare. In most of us the limits of assimilation, of acculturation, or even of consciousness raising are quite impressive.

3. Inadequate social policy. If it is assumed that all whites are homogeneous in culture, perception, values, and needs, and if social policy is merely formulated around issues of race, great resentments will certainly be stirred in those who feel called upon to be patient while feeling acutely misunderstood.

4. Wasted resources for international understanding. An event can hardly happen any place upon this planet without galvanizing some cultural group in the United States. A revolution in Cyprus, a tornado in the Dominican Republic, danger in Thailand, a political struggle in Puerto Rico, repression in South Africa, a war in the Middle East, an uprising in Prague or Budapest--each of these events travels as though on a planetary nervous system to nerve endings in some U.S. citizens. Nevertheless, far from encouraging our citizens to become expert in their native languages and cultures so as to make the United States the most sensitive and intelligent of all nations in multicultural understanding, we have, as it were, plucked out our eyes and stuffed our ears. The same cultural arrogance that leads to the undervaluing of "foreigners" who immigrate to the United States often marks our conduct abroad, even when it springs from good will and good intentions.

5. The constriction of the creative arts. In a healthy culture the streams of interior life and ordinary circumstances among all the people feed the streams of high literature, music, and the arts. How unprepossessing are the homes of Beethoven, Mozart, Shakespeare, and Goethe! Classic works spring from and codify perceptions that great and small, each in due measure, appreciate. In the United States a marked class and ethnic bias seems to render such high culture as we attain, which is far too little, too often unrooted and inaccessible. (The secret to the success of Jewish writers and artists is that they have been brilliantly particular and universal.) These are difficult issues, but a few suggestions may at least open the matter up. One of the greatest traumatic experiences of history was the separation of millions of individuals from their families and roots in the most massive migration of human history; yet our playwrights, novelists, and cinematographers have virtually neglected

the anguish and ambivalence involved, though they are still in living
memory and continuing experience.

Again, public television affects a class bias so remarkable
that it cries out for popular revolt; its programs are aimed almost
solely to the tastes and interests of the top 10 percent of the population in income, education, and professional standing. It is not "public" television but elitist television; not quality television, either,
but most often merely snobbish. It goes often to Great Britain, but
seldom to any other part of the world, such as Japan, Eastern Europe,
Italy, Germany, France, or Scandinavia, for its dramas and imagina-
tive materials.

In many parts of Europe, opera and high music and certain
kinds of drama reach a public that is not confined solely to the upper
classes. Here, too, if the arts spoke more directly to our diverse
citizens, who are rooted more in their own lives, fresh sources of
creativity and public response might be opened up. Andy Warhol is
a Czech from Pittsburgh, whose irreverence and sarcasm are rather
more like those of Good Soldier Schweik than like those of Jonathan
Swift; I wish the cultural climate did not inhibit his turning to Wilkins-
burg, Homestead, and East Miffin Township for artistic materials.
The soup cans might at least be Heinz's.

The Positive Reasons for a Long-Range Strategy

1. More accurate and liberating self-understanding. A multicultural self-understanding would increase the freedom of individuals
to be themselves and would allow for recognition of the difference between mere conformity and a genuine act of inner appropriation.

2. Sharper discernment in interpersonal perception. A distinction would be observed between individual characteristics and
cultural styles. Diagnosis would be possible of the correct meaning
of interpersonal cues, gestures, behavior, and speech.

3. Less stereotyping and a more accurate sense of nuance in
interpreting group behavior. Anti-Catholic innuendos abound. The
behaviors and symbols of many groups are misinterpreted by others.
Anti-Semitism and racism assume protean forms, and even sophisticated people exhibit bigotries they are hardly aware of. It is impossible to develop a mental hygiene that preserves us from all possible
errors of perception; but it is not impossible to develop a competence
in multicultural insight that enables us to set off down the long road
of mutual appreciation.

4. A wiser and more multiculturally differentiated social policy. There are, of course, limits to social policy; but there is also
a form of practical wisdom the aim of which is cultural ecology;

that is, there is at least as much respect for the survival of specific
traditions and cultures as for the needs of rivers, forests, moun-
tains, and air. Human beings do not learn virtue in general; rather,
they learn particular ways of behaving. They do not learn inquiry in
general, but rather specific patterns of curiosity and intellectual
boldness. Family tradition is the most basic constitutive element
in moral and intellectual development. Where it is lacking, enormous compensations are required; with it the rest comes naturally.
Family tradition is the most concrete form of ethnic transmission.
A social policy that injures family tradition destroys itself.

5. A school curriculum, in K-12 and in college as well, that
begins with the social subconscious of individuals; encourages them
to explore their own social, and not merely solipsistic, resources;
and teaches them to respond accurately to the cultural and individual
differences others also present. Such a curriculum would not only
"cover ground" but would also "touch ground." In my own village
perhaps 60 percent of the population is Italian American. I deeply
wish the school offered courses in the Italian language and culture,
in which our children could also be enrolled. There are only a few
Slavic families here, so courses in Slovak, which I would also like
to take, are not practical.

It would be of some help in our village if each of our several
communities knew more about itself and its neighbors; as it is, the
children study Japan, Mexico, anything not too close to home. Here,
as in most localities, the number of ethnic traditions is not infinite
but rather small. Five or six would cover 95 percent of us. Even
our suburbs are remarkably, if subtly, ethnic-specific. Older
people who retain a native language should be encouraged to perfect
their skills, to bring them up to date, and to give them a wider cultural range; many immigrants speak nonmodern, peasant dialects
only. My brothers and I were encouraged to "forget" Slovak but
were given credit for learning Spanish, French, or Latin. Unreal!

6. An international multicultural competence that is encouraged throughout our population at every level. The United States
ought to be the nation in the world that is the most responsive to cultural currents at every point on the planet. Our citizens ought to be
rewarded for keeping in contact with their cultures of origin.

CONCLUSION

America belongs to the entire planet. For three generations
Americans have tried to unify their population, even at rather severe
emotional cost. Much good came of this effort. I, for one, am glad
to have learned so many of the values and practices that are the genius

of Anglo-American culture which is unexampled in any other culture
to which my family might have emigrated three generations ago.
Now, under the almost worldwide threat of homogenization and modernization, perhaps it is time to reverse ourselves in the long zig-
zag of history. Diversity, approached in an inward and creative
fashion, could become our highest genius. We might live out in advance the sort of multicultural unity the planet as a whole so desperately seeks. Ethnicity is not to be conceived, in our conditions, as
a merely primordial, fateful, and tribal bond; on the contrary, it can
be freely chosen, developed as part of a multicultural competence,
and rooted in the socially aware individual rather than in the unthink-
ing group. A self-conscious and freely chosen ethnicity is not the
same as a merely inherited, inexperienced, and relatively closed
ethnicity. We are in a position to make something new of ourselves
as individuals and something new of our nation as a multiculturally
aware society. There is really not much hope, except through the
instrumentality of the totalitarian state, of homogenizing every individual on this planet. Indeed, the strengthening of the social bonds
that mediate between the solitary individual and the state is one of
our greatest defenses against the totalitarian state and against the
dreadful "Coca-Colanization" of the world. The new ethnicity is an
authentic cry of the human spirit in search of human freedom under
modern conditions.

Perhaps, under the auspices of the Anti-Defamation League,
it would be appropriate to say that the model of ethnicity and pluralism I have described here coheres thoroughly with the best practice
of many American Jews, with those who are neither "ethnic" nor
"non-Jewish," but who are cosmopolitan, humanistic, autonomous,
and at the same time richly and gratefully rooted.

APPENDIX

Minority Report: The Representation of Poles, Italians,
Latins and Blacks in the Executive Suites of
Chicago's Largest Corporations*

The question "How many are there?" has become one of the
most provocative and unsettling questions being raised on all levels
of American society. It reflects the national preoccupation with
evaluating the success or failure of various ethnic groups in gaining
their share in the American system for distributing income and power.
Thus, in just a matter of a few years questions regarding a person's
race or ethnic background, once felt to have no public relevance and
even considered illegitimate, now not only are being asked but even
require answers by law. Companies with government contracts are
now required to file reports indicating their utilization rate of blacks,
Latins, American Indians, Eskimos, and women. In January, 1973,
the U.S. Department of Labor, Office of Federal Contract Compliance,
issued new guidelines to cover discrimination against persons because
of religion or ethnic origin. These guidelines said:

> Members of various religious and ethnic groups,
> primarily but not exclusively of Eastern, Middle,
> and Southern European ancestry, such as Jews,
> Catholics, Italians, Greeks, and Slavic groups
> continue to be excluded from executive middle
> management, and other job levels because of dis-
> crimination based upon their religion and/or na-
> tional origin. These guidelines are intended to
> remedy such unfair treatment.†

---

*This report was prepared by the Institute of Urban Life, 820
North Michigan Avenue, Chicago, Illinois 60611, for the National
Center for Urban Ethnic Affairs, 4408 Eighth Street NE, Washington, D.C. 20017. Copyright held by Institute of Urban Life.
†60-50.1 of Chapter 60, Title 41, Code of Federal Regulations.

Russell Barta, the author of this report, is professor of social
science at Mundelein College of Chicago. He had the assistance of
Helen A. Smith of the Graduate Program in Urban Studies at Loyola
University.

What the guidelines in effect recognize is that, despite the
powerful American rhetoric which emphasizes individual achievement, power and affluence in reality still flow along group lines, and
that an individual's religious or ethnic affiliation may in fact still be
an obstacle to his advancement.

The purpose of this study was to investigate the extent to which
members of the Polish, Italian, Latin, and black communities have
penetrated the centers of power and influence in Chicago-based corporations. This was done by determining how many Poles, Italians,
Latins, and blacks either serve on the board of directors or occupy
the highest executive positions in Chicago's largest corporations.

In focusing on Poles, Italians, Latins, and blacks, this study
selected a combination of minority groups which at this point in time
is historically significant. The 1960s saw the rise of group consciousness among blacks and Latins, and their relentless pursuit of
parity with other groups in the United States. This process released
the latent consciousness of other groups, such as Poles and Italians,
who are becoming increasingly aware that like blacks and Latins,
they may not be sharing equally in the affluence of American society.

Thus, although this study originated at the request of leaders
of the Polish American Congress, Illinois Division, and the Joint
Civic Committee of Italian-Americans in Chicago, they were more
than willing to see the study expanded to include blacks and Latins.
In the Chicago metropolitan area, where nearly 34 percent of the
seven million population is either Polish, Italian, Latin, or black,
such a perception of mutual concerns could have a positive influence
on the future of group relations and thus on the very shape and tone
of life in the city and suburbs.

The corporations reviewed in this study were identified by combining the Chicago Daily News and Chicago Tribune lists of the Chicago area's largest corporations in 1972. Among the thousands of
corporations based in the Chicago area, 106 were identified as the
largest industrial firms, retailers, utilities, transportation companies, banks, and savings and loan institutions. More than half of
them (66 percent) were included in Fortune magazine's 1972 list of
the largest 500 industrial corporations or Fortune's lists of the
largest non-industrial firms in the United States. These 106 corporations, therefore, comprise the top layers of the economic and financial power structure of Chicago--and of the nation. It was the top
management of these corporate giants and their boards of directors
who were scrutinized in order to determine the representation of
Poles, Italians, Latins, and blacks.

Information about directors and officers was taken directly
from the 1972 annual report of each corporation. The number of
directors of all 106 corporations totaled 1,341; the number of officers,

1,355. For the purposes of this study, honorary board members were not included, nor were officers of less than vice-presidential rank such as assistant vice-presidents, assistant secretaries, or assistant treasurers. Where a firm was controlled by a holding company, only the directors and officers of the holding company were counted. An officer who also was a member of the board of directors of the same firm was counted twice, once as director, again as officer.

Findings and Conclusions

Thirty-six, or less than three percent, of the 1,341 directors were Polish,* Italian, Latin, or black. These four groups make up approximately 34 percent of the metropolitan area's population. When translated into individual percentages, the findings indicate that 0.3 percent of all directors were Polish, 1.9 percent Italian,[†] 0.1 percent Latin, and 0.4 percent black. Out of all officers, 0.7 percent were Polish, 2.9 percent Italian, 0.1 percent Latin, and 0.1 percent black. (See Table 2.1.)

How does one make a judgment about such information? How can it be used to evaluate the extent to which Poles, Italians, Latins, and blacks have entered the executive suites of Chicago's major corporations? Are Poles, Italians, Latins, and blacks equitably represented there?

To answer such questions the executive suite data were compared to the population of each of the four groups in the Chicago metropolitan area. This comparison provides a rough but fair guide for determining whether each group has achieved parity or whether it is underrepresented.[‡]

If one compares (Table 2.1) the percentages of officers and directors whose backgrounds are Polish, Italian, Latin, or black to the percentage distribution of these four groups in the population, it

---

*In referring to Poles, Italians, Latins, or blacks, the author means Americans who are of Polish, Italian, Latin (Spanish-speaking background), or black ancestry.

[†]One person of Italian background serves on nine different boards. If he were to be counted only once, the percentage of directors who are Italian would be reduced from 1.9 percent to 1.3 percent.

[‡]What should serve as an equitable norm, and how to apply it, is, of course, open to discussion. One can anticipate increasing public discussion of the matter as more groups pursue group gains.

becomes clear that all four groups were grossly underrepresented on the boards of directors and in the executive positions of Chicago's major corporations. Thus, although Poles make up 6.9 percent of the metropolitan population, only 0.3 percent of the directors are Polish. Italians make up 4.8 percent of the population, but only 1.9 percent of the directors are Italian. Blacks comprise 17.6 percent of the population yet only 0.4 percent of the directors are black. Latins are 4.4 percent of the population yet only 0.1 percent of the directors are Latin. The same general pattern holds if one compares the percentages of officers who are Polish, Italian, Latin, or black to the percentage distribution of these four groups in the population.

TABLE 2.1

Representation of Select Ethnic Groups in the Chicago Metropolitan
Area Population, on Boards of Directors, and Among
Officers of 106 Largest Area Corporations

	Area Population (percent)	Directors		Officers	
		Number	Percent	Number	Percent
Poles	6.9	4	0.3	10	0.7
Italians	4.8	26	1.9	39	2.9
Latins	4.4	1	0.1	2	0.1
Blacks	17.6	5	0.4	1	0.1
All other	66.3	1,305	97.3	1,303	96.2
Total	100.0	1,341	100.0	1,355	100.0

Notes: The "area population" refers to the Chicago metropolitan area: the six counties of Cook, Kane, Will, DuPage, Lake, and McHenry, whose population in 1970 was 6,979,000.

The percentages of area population were prepared by Michael E. Schiltz, Director of Loyola University's Graduate Program in Urban Studies. For Poles, Italians, and Latins, the estimates include first, second, and third generations, based on U.S. Bureau of Census data.

The black population is based on 1970 data from the U.S. Census Bureau.

As a matter of fact, Poles, Latins, and blacks were virtually absent from the upper echelons of Chicago's largest corporations. 102 out of the 106 corporations had no directors who were Polish; 97 had no officers who were Polish. Only one corporation had a black officer and only two had Latin officers. While the Italians were more numerous in the executive suite than the other three groups, 84 corporations out of 106 still had no directors who were Italian and 75 had no officers who were Italian. Finally, 55 out of the 106 corporations had no Poles, Italians, Latins, or blacks, either as directors or as officers. (See Table 2.2.)

TABLE 2.2

Number of Corporations, of 106 Examined, with No Directors or Officers Who Were Poles, Italians, Latins, or Blacks*

	Number of Corporations Without Director	Number of Corporations Without Officer
Poles	102	97
Italians	84	75
Latins	105	104
Blacks	101	105

*55 of the 106 corporations had no Poles, Italians, Latins, or blacks either as directors or as officers.

Other significant patterns emerge from the data. Poles and Italians do better in their representation in executive positions than they do as board members. The opposite is true of blacks, whose major source of representation comes from appointments to boards of directors rather than from holding top executive positions. No Poles were located among the public utilities and banks reviewed in this study, either as directors or as officers. As for Italians, 16 were associated with banks or savings and loan institutions. However, there were no Italians in the executive suites of the utilities.*

---

*An Italian, however, does serve as an officer of the two subsidiaries of one of the utilities.

On the other hand, three out of the five corporations with black directors were public utilities. The number of Latins was not large enough to yield any significant pattern.

Hopefully, this study of four ethnic groups in the corporate structure of metropolitan Chicago will be extended to include their representation in major civic groups such as public boards and commissions, influential private agencies and associations, foundations, and social clubs. Similar studies of other ethnic groups such as Czechs, Greeks, Lithuanians, etc. should be conducted in the Chicago area. Given the lack of adequate research on American ethnic groups, similar surveys should be undertaken in other large cities.

As such studies accumulate, the result may be a national profile for each of America's ethnic groups showing precisely the extent to which each of them share in the power and affluence of the nation. In the process the nation will learn to what extent the American corporation is a "truly public institution bound to the same criteria of selection that today affect government service--freedom from bias, and the requirement at the same time to represent and reflect all parts of the American population."*

A Note on Method

Trying to determine ethnic origin is a hazardous enterprise. In order to make this study as accurate as possible, knowledgeable leaders from the Polish, Italian, and Latin communities were asked to identify ethnic names by studying the lists of directors and officers in each annual report. In cases of doubtful ethnic origin the individual's office was contacted directly. Each corporation having no apparent representation from any of the four ethnic communities was informally contacted to double check the preliminary findings. In regard to blacks, all available studies were utilized and persons familiar with the black community were consulted. Also helpful were several lawyers and business leaders who were generally knowledgeable about many of the corporations studied. If there are any errors in the final tally for each group, the margin of error would not be sufficiently great to invalidate the findings of this study.

A manual describing in full the method used is being prepared by the author and will be distributed through the National Center for Urban Ethnic Affairs in Washington and the Institute of Urban Life in Chicago.

----

*Nathan Glazer and Daniel P. Moynihan, Beyond the Melting Pot, 1963, p. 208.

The 106 Chicago-based Corporations

Abbott Laboratories
Admiral
Allied Mills
Allied Van Lines
American Bakeries
American Hospital Supply
American National
Amsted Industries
Baxter Laboratories
Beatrice Foods
Bell Federal
Bell & Howell
Borg-Warner
Brunswick
Bunker Ramo
Carson Pirie Scott
CECO
CENCO
Central National Bank
CFS Continental
Chemetron
Citizens Bank Park Ridge
Chicago Bridge and Iron
Chicago-Milwaukee
Chicago and North Western
Chicago, Rock Island and
    Pacific
Combined Insurance
Commonwealth Edison
Consolidated Foods
Continental Illinois Corporation
CNA Financial
De Soto
Donnelley (R.R.) & Sons
Drovers National Bank
Exchange National Bank
First Chicago
First Federal
FMC
General American
    Transportation
Goldblatt Brothers
Gould

Harris Bankcorp
Hart, Schaffner & Marx
Heller (Walter E.) International
Hilton Hotels
Home Federal
Household Finance
Illinois Bell Telephone
Illinois Central Industries
Illinois Tool Works
Interlake
Inland Steel
International Harvester
International Minerals & Chemical
Jewel
Kemperco
Kraftco
Lakeview Trust
LaSalle National Bank
Libby, McNeill and Libby
Marcor
Maremont
Marleman
Marshall Field
Masonite
McDonald's
McGraw-Edison
Morton-Norwich Products
Motorola
Nalco Chemical
National Boulevard Bank
National Can
National Tea
Northern Illinois Gas
Northern Indiana Public Service
Nortrust
Northwest Industries
Northwestern National Bank
Outboard Marine
People's Gas
Pioneer Trust
Pullman
Quaker Oats
St. Paul Federal

Santa Fe Industries
Searle (G. D.)
Sears Bank & Trust
Sears, Roebuck
Signode
Spector Industries
Square D
Standard Oil (Indiana)
Sunbeam
Swift
Talman Federal

Trans Union
UAL
U.S. Gypsum
UNICOA
Universal Oil Products
Walgreen
Ward Foods
Washington National
Wieboldt Stores
Wrigley (William) Jr.
Zenith Radio

REFERENCES

Barta, Russell. 1973. "Minority Report: The Representation of Poles, Italians, Latins and Blacks in the Executive Suites of Chicago's Largest Corporations." Report. Chicago: Institute of Urban Life, December.

Greeley, Andrew. 1974. Ethnicity in the United States. New York: John Wiley.

Novak, Michael. 1972a. "New Ethnic Politics vs. Old Ethnic Politics." In Pieces of a Dream, ed. Michael Wenk. New York: Center for Migration Studies.

_____. 1972b. The Rise of the Unmeltable Ethnics. New York: Macmillan. Also new introduction in paperback edition, 1973.

_____. 1974a. "How American Are You if Your Grandmother Came from Serbia in 1888?" In The Rediscovery of Ethnicity, ed. Sallie Teselle. New York: Harper Torchbooks. A longer version of the middle part of 1972a.

_____. 1974b. "The New Ethnicity." The Center Magazine, June.

_____. 1974c. "One Species, Many Cultures." The American Scholar, Winter.

_____. 1974d. "The Social World of Individuals." The Hastings Center Review, Autumn.

_____. 1974e. "To Be American Is to Come from Somewhere."
In Liberty and Justice for All. Washington, D.C.: National
Catholic Conference.

_____. 1975. "The People and the News." In Moments of Truth,
ed. Marvin Barrett. New York: Apollo Editions.

Patterson, Orlando. 1975. "Ethnicity and the Pluralist Fallacy."
Change, March.

U.S., Department of Labor, Office of Federal Contract Compliance.
1973. Code of Federal Regulations, Chapter 60, Article 50.1.

3

**POLITICAL LIFE
AND PLURALISM**
David E. Apter

THE ASSIMILATIONIST FALLACY

Let us consider our subject in its broadest possible context, on a world scale, and in history. To do that and avoid getting completely lost in complexity, our discussion should be centered on a particular aspect of the topic, what might be called the war between assimilationism and primordialism. This war, which we had pretty much assumed would by now have been decided in favor of assimilation, goes on unabated. It is not a nice war, and for those of us in the field of development studies, the victory of assimilationism is associated in our minds with good things: with tolerance, an acceptance of diversity, and above all democracy. The primordial enemy represents the reverse. Primordialism is intolerant, atavistic, and not well disposed toward democracy. When primordial revivals occur, whether in our own country or abroad, we find them difficult to cope with. Particularly in an immigrant society such as ours, we are sensitive to the need for assimilation, for the building up of a common set of values, and we are above all aware of the fragility of the network of self-imposed constraints, which, when open, is sufficiently instructive to allow people to understand each other and function in terms of each other. "Primordial hotspots" threaten the fabric of such self-imposed constraints.

The threats themselves are made in the name of democracy and accompanied by great piety and self-righteousness. The challenge to assimilationism is posed on some of its own terms. Primordialists take diversity and transform it into a weapon.

Accordingly, it might be helpful to review assimilationism as an evolutionary idea and take a second look at its significance in our thinking. I shall then turn to primordialism, treating it as a situation,

58

a case, in order to illustrate its complexities. The next step will
be to consider how the alternative forms of assimilationism, liberal
and socialist, have evolved and to review the history of the idea. I
will discuss the liberal and pluralist solution of regarding primordialism mainly as pathological. Finally, I will consider some of the
differences between pathology and belief and the pluralist implications of political primordialism.

Since the procedure that will be followed in this chapter is a
little unusual, it may be worthwhile to describe why it has been
chosen. The different sections represent different ways of thinking
about the subject. The introduction considers assimilationism in a
developmental contest. The case examined illustrates what Clifford
Geertz has called the "thick" texture of primordialism in a developing country. In this examination of the assimilationist ideal, following the case, it will be helpful to consider some alternative views of
the relation between assimilationism and progress. Then it will be
possible to show how pluralist solutions make most sense where they
treat primordialism as pathological and remedial. To grant it a
greater credibility than that jeopardizes pluralism itself as a possible political solution. Underlying the entire discussion is my conviction that the thinking that has been done on the subject has been
inadequate and that the problems posed by primordialism remain
more serious than had been believed.

Before beginning this discussion I want to make my own position
clear. I am a professor of social and political development. The
chair I occupy is a testimonial to the belief shared by the university
and the donor who provided the funds, that development and particularly its political and social consequences will result in benefits
for mankind. To consider these matters I spend a good deal of time
studying and working on various parts of the world, in Africa, in
Latin America, in Europe, and occasionally in Asia. For better or
worse I am an assimilationist, a universalist, and a pluralist. I
represent a kind of thinking that I am about to challenge in this essay.
I believe in the benefits of an enlightened culture and development.
It should be clear that in expressing the views that follow, I am
arguing with myself.

The argument itself is simple. We are all, or at least most
of us, believers in the assimilationist fallacy. Briefly stated, this
is that history, most particularly modern history, represents an
evolution from a primitive and limited condition to a more universal,
open, democratic, pluralistic, and popular one. The new order
drives out previous and more primitive affiliations, primordial
attachments, and less rational solidarities. These primordial attachments are linguistic, tribal, ethnic, and religious. Not only do
we think that blood, race, and tongue are not good criteria for

affiliation, but that when passionately believed they become monopolistic, racist, prejudiced, and indeed redolent of fascism. The real primordial stuff is dangerous to mankind and is irrational. In contrast the enlightenment is the triumph of human civility over such attachments, which we hope will disappear. Modern science and development, together, provide an ever more complete and democratic alternative. Deprived of their primordial stigmata, the surviving diversity of tongues and cultures will speak with one voice in the more universalistic, pluralistic, and relativistic framework.

I want to argue that the assimilationist fallacy is not so much wrong as insufficient. Clearly such historical forces are at work. There is a widening of universalistic and pluralistic beliefs. However, primordialism is at work too. It pops up where we least expect it, in Scotland, Wales, and Quebec, and among the Basques, Catalans, and Bretons. Old primordialisms can fade away and yet revive. The reasons why are puzzling to pluralists and liberals, who have not expected it or have considered it to be of passing significance.

Clearly primordialism has something. If we accept the idea that it will not disappear but is capable of continuous revival, taking new forms, expressions, and meanings, not simply among the less educated, but also among the most highly educated, then we do not quite know how to deal with it. The survival and prosperity of primordialism challenges most of our views about the way the world evolves, how people learn, what they emulate. It renders problematic a good many of our fondest hopes that the world of nations will consist of people whose like-mindedness on important matters of common interest, environmental problems, population, and development will serve as a basis for solid political cooperation. If now we conclude that the world as it is, is the world as it is likely to be, that the personae and the names of places and specific events will change but that religious, linguistic, racial, and other conflicts are likely to remain and indeed grow as development occurs, then evolution takes on more frightening aspects. We can no longer see the end in the beginning. Our articles of faith begin to disappear.

Most of us, no matter how sophisticated, secretly believe that, despite clear and present dangers, the growing force of education and knowledge, a desire for detente among the great powers, and a general growing up in the world constitute net gains, a continuous improvement in our affairs. We believe that no matter how slow or halting the process, it is the force of an immanent rationality, the enlightenment itself, working its way into the world. A world in which such a progressive evolution can no longer be taken for granted is hard for us to accept; yet it is this kind of possibility that I want to debate, with you and with myself.

It will be necessary to state the pluralist view and expose the assimilationist fallacy within it. We will examine a developmental case, Nigeria, in which a democratic pluralist political solution was applied to problems of ethnic, racial, and religious diversity and failed. I will examine the origins and evolution of assimilationism itself and show how fundamental it is to both the liberal and socialist varieties of modern thought. I will then consider the argument that prejudice and discrimination are the main reasons for the survival of primordialist conditions, which can be rectified by greater equality and political opportunity. Finally, I will suggest an alternative explanation for the significance of primordialism, treating it as a direct consequence of the thinness and inadequacy of assimilationism and most particularly of the culture of the enlightenment. I do not urge as a solution that our contemporary enlightenment culture should contain more depth, texture, and metaphorical or other power because to do so is a purely rhetorical exercise, but I do hold that it will develop such depth as the enlightenment myth, which is the correlate of the assimilationist fallacy, confronts primordial challenges. Win or lose, such conflict is bound to be ugly. Science, the search for knowledge, and the achievements of technology will be punctuated by the revival, permutation, and transformation of all the old fashioned solidarities.

A solution will not be easy to find. The Jews, perhaps, have a culture that combines the two, enlightenment and primordialism; no doubt this is one of the reasons people on the whole do not like them. Certainly this aspect troubled Marx, as it did Stalin, as we shall show. Modern democrats believe that the two principles can be combined in democracy. The United States shows that it can. Nevertheless, there are few success stories, and even in the United States it involves so many problems that the satisfaction to be found in it is increasingly cold comfort.

The enlightenment myth on which the assimilationist fallacy rests is that modern history is moving in a single direction away from provincial and local attachments and toward a greater common consciousness of the world. In the nineteenth century this was regarded as natural or evolutionary. In the same way that lower forms of life evolved into higher, more complex ones that were closely linked together, so has social life. Additionally, it was widely believed that this evolution would provide a better human life.

Enlightenment remains very much at the core of most of our ideas about political life. With it, more and more people are enabled to come to terms with their existence. As they become less vulnerable to forces outside their control, the growth of knowledge goes hand in hand with more active participation in public political life. The opportunities of modernity represent the voluntary choices of people themselves. With enlightenment goes democracy and a belief in the ultimate equality of man, grounded in a common understanding.

Within this general tradition of an evolving and universal democratic enlightenment are two main strands. One is that the world is becoming more or less the same all over again, and the other is that as a culture is enriched and diversified, each group develops its own genius, expressed in its history, in its language, and in all its preferred metaphors, meanings, and myths.

The two can go hand in hand. Political democracy, enlightenment, and equality represent a kind of intellectual evolution. Cultural pluralism also evolves as a result of diversity. It becomes clear that no culture can be evaluated in terms of another because each form, no matter how eccentric, has its own contribution to make. Under the broad rubric of political democracy, universal enlightenment and cultural pluralism are international. Everyone assimilates certain common values and attitudes in an evolutionary or developmental way, while respecting the diversity and pluralism of the groups composing the society.

Such a view is rooted in our conception of history. From Greece and Rome to the present day, a more unified world culture has enveloped more and more parts of the globe. At the same time nations, that is, groups of people with common traditions and bonds of solidarity, tribes, races, and nationalities, have become more physically jumbled up. People move about constantly. Leads and lags develop. This motion requires more applied, deliberate, and purposeful thinking.

In the so-called third world of developing countries in Asia, Africa, and Latin America, economic growth and political development are objects of policy. Science and technology increase. Exclusive and parochial affiliations decline. Of course, we do not expect the "premodern" social organizations and beliefs to disappear all at once; but nevertheless, the primordial attachments of race, religion, language, and blood ties erode, and history repeats itself. Feudalism in Western Europe consisted of "struggles for power among more or less autonomous jurisdictions, whose members shared immunities and obligations--based on an established social hierarchy and on a fealty relation with the secular ruler whose authority has been consecrated by a universal church" (Bendix 1964, p. 39). In the same way, old loyalties and jurisdictions have been consolidated by new political leaders and nationalist movements. Just as a period of absolutist rule followed feudalism when kings imposed their powers through appointed officials in a fashion binding upon the hitherto separate and autonomous jurisdictions, so also with military rulers of new states. As absolutism gives way to representative government, so the traditions of the great English, American, and French revolutions are kept alive. Indeed, with technical assistance such transformations can now occur without the revolutions themselves.

All this would appear to be so self-evident as to provide un-shakeable grounds for the view that the unifying forces at work in the world will eventually triumph. The words we use to describe such processes, the teleology of terms such as modernization, develop-ment, and industrialization, are not out of date. For countries that lag behind, the problem is how to speed up change and with it a de-sirable political unity so that through the joint efforts of all sectors of a population, the talents of that population can be harnessed to the common tasks.

At the core of these views lies a profound belief in rational-ism, a belief that positive reasons can be found for all physical and social phenomena. If this is so, then planning and the application of science enable us to predict and apply theory to the problems of the human condition. Moreover, such rationalistic principles are universal: whether its students are black or white, English or Amer-ican, Chinese or Jewish, liberal or communist, science is the same. This view, as old as Francis Bacon, is incorporated in the main current of positivist, empiricist, and materialist thought. In human terms it means that structural changes in social life can be planned and directed, publicly or privately, to bring about self-sustained growth, urbanization, and social mobilization. Secular education is required. Grievances and antagonisms may remain, especially in the less modernized sectors, and this is perhaps unfortunate; such problems can be handled remedially.

Few have criticized this view. An Indian scholar suggests that "scholars studying the modernization process basically generalize on the basis of their study of capitalist societies, be they highly in-dustrialized neo-capitalist societies of the west or that section of underdeveloped societies which has taken the capitalist path of devel-opment after independence" (Desai 1971, p. 459).

Robert Packenham (1973, pp. 62-63) has described the pre-vailing "developmental" view.

> The message of the "Charles River group"--which
> directly influenced Kennedy and with which he agreed
> --was that aid should be designed to enable the under-
> developed countries to "take off" into self-sustaining
> economic growth. They believed that "take off" was
> feasible in most countries; when it was reached, the
> need for aid would end. To achieve "take-off" and
> to "reduce the explosiveness of the modernization

process" required not only economic inputs but also
social change--land reform, tax reform, more voluntary organizations, greater political participation.
The result of all this, they believed, would be a host
of good things politically: more democracy, less
Communism, greater national independence, and
greater political stability--ultimately a "world
community" of stable, independent, democratic and
peaceful states (Packenham 1973, pp. 62-63).

That, at any rate, was the ideal.

What went wrong? Today Arab nationalism; Kurdish separatism; Welsh, Scottish, and Basque revivalism; Sunnite Arab antagonism against the Shiites; Macedonian consciousness; Greek ortho-
doxy in Bosnia; and Catholicism in Croatia--the list is endless--are
more intense than ever. Whatever happened to history as the evolution of a world of stable, independent, democratic, and peaceful
states?

There is more primordialism than ever before. By the mid-
1970s, ten years later, it appears that assimilationism was wrong,
not only for the politicians, but also for the men on the spot, the
community development officers intent on local development in India
or Kenya, the American Agency for International Development (AID)
officials for whom Point Four was the voice of the prophet and who
devoutly believed that a few good men on the spot could universalize
benefits, given a little technical assistance, a little luck and skill,
some windfall funding, and bright local initiative.

How many men on the spot?

In 1968 alone, there were over 100,000 experts and
volunteers working in the developing countries,
financed under official programs, and over 80,000
students and trainees were studying in the indus-
trialized countries. To these must be added the
consultants, engineers, and analysts engaged in
preparing and implementing capital projects as
well as those experts and trainees supported by
private organizations; these are nearly equal in
numbers to officially financed personnel.

This two-way flow of people has powerfully
stimulated change, introduced new management
skills, raised educational standards, and helped
to create much infrastructure and expanded in-
dustry (Commission on International Development,
1970, p. 51).

Such networks, large though they were, represented only the tip of the iceberg. Underneath were the concrete activities aimed at transforming village life, bringing the Green Revolution, and attracting the multinational corporations and jet-set administrative power.

Disappointments were to be expected. Populations grew too quickly. Dynamic leaders were assassinated or overthrown. However, none of these events could shake the belief in the universalizing spread of modernity that would eventually bring nations together. Strengthening fragile political institutions and supporting local participation and democracy was much more difficult than anticipated; but that was precisely what "partnership" meant: if rich countries were to help poor countries to help themselves, patience and support would be required, the helping rather than the hiding hand.

Today all this is reversed. In Europe, where national conflicts were for a time submerged in the European community, in regional associations, in common markets, and in the fulfillment of the enlightenment ideal of a united Europe, there is an increase in parochial tensions; in French nationalism; and within France, in Breton nationalism.

Indeed, so rapidly is this happening that perhaps the only thing to do is to put a good face on it and try to turn such parochialism into a harmless cultural pluralism. This is hard to do, but certainly most governments are trying. They sponsor digs into the archeological past. They seek more authentic national traditions. They reject the "Americanization" of the world and try to purify their languages. Indeed, the more a revived primordialism and nationalism occurs, the more the coin of assimilationism loses its luster. There is a longing to preserve the national genius and the national language, or as in French Canada, to use this as a basis for secession or autonomy.

Does this represent a reversal of the tendency toward universalization or a rejection of assimilationism or the cultures of modernity and the enlightenment? Not necessarily. The two tendencies, toward and against primordialism, can go on at the same time. Indeed, the more development and growth take place, the more some primordial groupings have to gain by their parochialism. Similarly, it would be wrong to treat the primordial as if it were "irrational." As the prospect of North Sea oil brightens, there is great shrewdness to Scottish nationalism (see Begg and Stewart 1971, pp. 135-52).

In Africa, where nationalism, having replaced colonialism, is more threatened by separatist ethnic rivalries, no one quite knows whether assimilationism is increasing faster than primordialism or whether the two feed off each other. Since primordialism does not mean low culture, the assimilated technocrat who has been educated abroad can be as committed a Biafran nationalist as any farmer in the bush.

It is the assimilationist who rewrites the children's school books. Under colonialism a first English reader showed pictures with captions like the following: "The banana is a tropical fruit which does not grow in our country," while children in Mali learned that their ancestors were the Gauls.

It would seem that the universality of assimilated knowledge could blend easily with particular historical experience, an identity. Where then is the problem? It begins when experience becomes monopolistic, when race or religion becomes inflated as a remedial form of social therapy. The next step is that the assimilated join forces with the primordial. At this point we are told that only an African can teach African history; that only a black can understand the black experience; that only a Palestinian can speak for Palestinians. Manipulated identity and monopolistic experience quickly become political and challenge the pluralist ideal. The principle that human beings are pretty much alike, deserve the same treatment, and can with some understanding share in each others' experiences, declines under the hammer blows of a compensatory primordialism.

The odd thing about it is that what causes this is in part the desire to make men equal, to provide support, morale, depth, and a willingness to participate. Primordialism is not simply a lazy alternative to mind, a manipulated therapy; it is partly a result of the thinness and the dangers of the enlightenment culture and partly a way of mobilizing people for action.

The real alternative to primordialism would require so complete a utilization of individual genius and potentiality, so revolutionary a realization of each person's "species being," that people would need to be gods to achieve it. What we have overlooked in our desire for democratic solutions and developmental assistance is the need people have to revive myths as metaphors to enclose the spaces of their own lives. To look out at the world as a flat universal plane is a bore. Heights and depths are needed, and distance and promontory, texture, and light and shadow. All these are provided by primordialism. The symbolism of kin or ancestor and their connection to naturalistic cycles of birth and death is intertwined with national entities, races, tribes, and nations. Their embodiments in language, history, and tradition all display their own internal structure and logic. Perhaps primordialism is the poor man's poetry; or perhaps it is primitive aestheticism. Whatever its roots, it has passion and power. It returned a dispersed Israel to its homeland after thousands of years of wandering. Each "primordial" person carries a whole history.

A SITUATION: THE PARABLE OF THE MINISTER
AND THE TRUCK DRIVER

Such concerns are of course fearfully abstract. To show how
they come together in the context of a specific situation, I will describe an incident which I witnessed in Nigeria. The case of Nigeria
is useful in helping us understand how assimilationism and primordialism are often intertwined. In this case, liberal and democratic
pluralism came into conflict with primordial revivalism. The time
is early in the 1960s, the development decade. I was attending a
conference in Nigeria that had been designed to help set that country
on the right track. Experts from all parts of the developed world,
foundation executives, administrators, and local observers met at
the University of Ibadan. The organizations they represented were
busy carving out office space for more permanent missions. The
"Ford Flats" were already occupied. A number of former colonial
administrators had disappeared from the scene after independence,
to reappear as experts after taking "refresher" courses, while those
who were not able to make the grade had retired or become school
teachers, or moved to South Africa.

The Peace Corps was already in evidence, as were AID officials with their plastic brief cases and wide Kansas City smiles, big
men whose handshakes were stenciled on the aid packages arriving
from America and on the doors of official automobiles. Nigeria was
all set to go. The new federal constitution had been argued out in
tedious sessions by often hostile politicians and usually glum or
apologetic Colonial Office officials. Nigeria was to become a show-
piece of development in the Western tradition. Good will was evident
on all sides, and money followed those stenciled hands. A recently
published Carnegie Commission Report on Higher Education had
called for the rapid expansion of the university system, from one to
five, and had argued that the new universities, of high quality, should
be scattered in the various regions of the country. Michigan State
was called in to do a land-grant job in the eastern region, where the
Ibos were getting restless. The Muslim north, though a little afraid
that too much knowledge would be a dangerous thing, especially for
women, was becoming fearful of being left behind. The northerners
were considering a university and were consulting "experts" about
the special needs of a Muslim area. How were they to do a good job
for the locals, while not fostering a hotbed of pan-Arabism, Islamic
revivalism, or radical secularism?

It was in that capacity, wondering what I might contribute that
might be of any conceivable help, that I left the conference and
found myself bundled, at dawn's early light, into a Pontiac station
wagon belonging to the Minister of Education of the northern region,

whose guest I was. Traveling together, our object was to make
Kaduna, the northern capital, by tea time. It was a long journey,
and sufficient time had to be allowed for the minister, who previously
had been Minister of Works, to stop and pray at periodical intervals.

We sped along the glorious countryside. It was a hodge-podge
of peoples and things. Nigeria, like India, can never really be known
by an outsider. Everyone has the illusion of a little knowledge, but
most have only a kind of informed gossip. The handouts printed by
the Nigerian information service had marvelous photographs of Emirs
and Sultans on horseback, clad in medieval armor, looking grand
and Moorish. We were heading for their part of the country. Nigeria, which is composed of many ethnic, linguistic, and religious
groups, had become independent not too long before. The three most
politically powerful groups were the Hausa-Fulani in the north,
where we were headed; the Yoruba in the west, which we had just
left; and the Ibo in the east. The political leaders representing these
regions, the Sardauna of Sokoto, Chief Awolowo, and Dr. Azikiwe
had, after protracted negotiations, agreed to a federal constitution
organized on the principle of a three-legged stool; that is, if anyone
failed to cooperate, the thing fell down.

It was widely believed that this would not happen. The leaders
were reasonable, educated men. Azikiwe, the President, was a
graduate of Lincoln University. All had an interest in practicing the
democracy in Nigeria that for years the British had preached.

Under the federal arrangement, higher education was federal,
as were the army, the treasury, and foreign affairs. A parliamentary
system at the center allowed for regional legislatures composed of
many different subethnic and linguistic groups. The president was
an Ibo; the prime minister a Hausa-Fulani; and the leader of the opposition a Yoruba.

This was the prevailing arrangement as we drove north at a
quite unbelievable rate of speed. The minister was extremely articulate about the problems of his country. He described his own fore-
bodings about the future. There was opposition to his ideas for the
improvement of education for women from the more conservative
Mallams. He pointed out the need for technical institutes, which had
lagged behind those in the south, the lack of which put the north at
the mercy of southern civil servants, clerks, and officials, who in
time would undermine the authority of the northerners in their own
region. He was afraid his region would be finessed out of its share
of federal grants-in-aid by the smart sourthern civil servants who
dominated the federal service. For that reason he retained as his
permanent secretary an Englishman whom he could trust.

Periodically we stopped the car so that the minister could pray.
The minister washed his hands carefully while his driver unrolled a

mat, and then he would face toward Mecca and kneel and pray, touching his forehead on the ground repeatedly. Then, prayers said, he would jump up, the mat would be rolled, and the Pontiac would literally fly along the ridges in the road. After we crossed the Niger River the countryside was drastically different, becoming flat and dry and much poorer. As we sped through small villages, the ministerial standard flying, small children waved. It was all rather festive.

We had just begun to talk about whether or not exchanges could be established between U.S. universities and the university in northern Nigeria when the car skidded abruptly to a halt. The minister's small round embroidered hat fell into the front seat as we all pitched violently forward. We had passed a large sign that said Diversion. In front another sign said Halt. Our driver, without stopping, had passed very close to a dump truck spreading gravel on the road. A short, tough, cocky-looking truck driver wearing a broad-brimmed British army campaign hat at a jaunty angle stuck his head out of the cab and shouted, "Stop, stop, stop. Can't you read, stop." He was beside himself with anger and pointed to our car tracks, which had ploughed into fresh tarmac as well as graded gravel.

The minister retrieved his hat and got out of the car. Then he walked very slowly toward the truck, the driver still shouting. The minister said nothing but motioned him to get down from the cab. "No, no, no," said the driver. "You are not my master. No one is my master. We have self-government now."

Then one by one the day laborers, all northerners, who were working on the road picked up shovels, picks, crowbars, and hoes and moved toward the driver, forming a slowly shrinking circle. The driver glanced around, jumped down from the cab, looking very small next to the minister and disreputable in his torn shorts and army shirt. He took off his hat and threw it on the ground and then stamped on it himself. "All right," he said, "You may be my master. You be my master. You step on me." He stamped on his hat again.

The minister, in a rage, lectured him on respect for the ministerial car, the ministerial standard, the minister himself as representative of the northern government. Returning to the car we sped off, leaving a cloud of dust and great gaping ruts behind.

It took a few moments for the minister to compose himself. "You saw him," he said. "That lorry driver was an Ibo." The words came spilling out. The Ibos were like snakes, small, close to the ground, poisonous. They were everywhere. They took all the good jobs. They were filling up his country. They filled the schools with their children. I asked what he thought the solution was. They should "go back where they came from." They were too clannish, secretive, and untrustworthy. "If I had my way," he said,

"I would throw them all out of the country." I asked him which country and was told, in confidence, about negotiations underway between representatives of the Sardauna of Sokoto and the neighboring (formerly French) country of Niger, which had the same Hausa-Fulani population. They were at this very moment considering the declaration of an independent Niger state, separate from Nigeria.

Not too much later the three-legged federal stool collapsed. First the northerners and easterners ganged up on the west to divide up the western region. Then an Ibo general moved against the federal government and in the ensuing coup both the Sardauna of Sokoto and the prime minister of Nigeria were killed. Reprisals followed. The minister got his wish. An estimated 30,000 Ibos were massacred, the survivors fleeing to the eastern region, which declared itself the independent state of Biafra. The civil war was on in earnest. The result is history. A clear case of primordialism, you will say; such deep conflicts cannot be papered over by a pluralistic federalism. Cleavage following primordial lines intensifies with development. Assimilationism at the top only disguises primordialism at the bottom.

But who is the assimilationist? The minister was highly educated. Islam is a receiving religion. It is far more assimilating than Christianity. In this instance assimilationism and primordialism were so intertwined that it is not possible to distinguish which was which. They are mutually explosive. A territorial jurisdiction makes them mutually exclusive by generating polarities of conflict, resulting in political cleavage for which there seems to be no pluralist solution.

How is this episode to be evaluated? For one thing, it shows how mixed up and intertwined assimilationism and primordialism can be. Would it have helped to have had a different political framework? Probably not. Was the conflict inevitable? Who can know? The intricacies of the events and the actual feelings, attitudes, and inside stories will never be known. The same people who hated at one moment could be quite civil and pleasant at another. Primordialists could be assimilationists and back again, depending on the situation.

"Depending on the situation"--that is the problem. None of us knows enough about "the situation" or how many "situations" each situation contains. Nigeria made something of a shambles of the original predictions for it and of the optimism of the developmental theorists; not that Nigeria will not make a go of it; it will, but not for the reasons given.

A year ago (1974) I spoke to the head of the present Nigerian government, the man who won the civil war, General Gowon. A quiet, gracious northern Christian, he described his plans for

returning Nigeria to civilian rule. He told how well the defeated
Biafrans had been reincorporated into Nigeria. Instead of the three-
legged stool there were now 12 regions, giving minority representation and local self-government. The scars of war were rapidly dis-
appearing. Oil production had expanded dramatically, and the
national income was up. The rancor is almost gone, he said. He
seemed like the epitome of a senior British officer, come to life in
African dress, all that was needed was the sound of a bugle and the
short jacket of the regimental mess.

He is a product of the well-established network of schools that
Nigeria had well before independence. There was a good civil
service, headed by a distinguished and experienced civil servant.
The original hope was that a federal solution to a multi-lingual and
multi-ethnic state would point the way for other federations wherever
such diverse populations were to be found. That each ethnic group
would press hard for its own side was after all to be expected. That
was what party politics is all about. The ferocity of the civil war,
when it came, surprised the outsiders. Everyone was wise in hind-
sight. Among expatriates there was the unspoken premise that
underneath the exquisite courtesy of the Nigerians, except for Ibos
who are rather more brusque, lurked primordialism, tribalism, and
a host of other pathological conditions. It was all so African.

But was it? When Sukarno was overthrown in Indonesia it is
estimated that half a million "communists" were killed in Java. How
different is that from the Lod, or from the Munich massacres, or
from Northern Ireland?

The point is that primordialism never stands alone. It is not
a thing in itself. In Nigeria it meant a lot of things, including a
north more poor and more populous and yet able to dominate by
sheer size of population a richer and more economically aggressive
south. There was class struggle, the northern day laborers versus
the Ibo clerks and drivers, the new middle class. In the actual
moment of the case, the particular confrontation was of a self-
consciously tall Alhadji (a Muslim who had made the pilgrimage to
Mecca), standing in front of a runt of an Ibo foreigner who had
shouted at and demeaned the minister in his own country. The Ibo
was most likely a Catholic. He was ugly. His clothes were tattered.
He had screamed at the minister and defied his authority. He had
violated the ordered world of the minister, which was bounded by the
ritual and the ceremony of kings. With its antique and conquering
tradition, Northern Islam had the simplicity and knowledge of the
book, the Koran, in honor of which the minister prayed several
times a day. In that situation all the devoutness and simplicity of
Islam was affronted, a simplicity of hierarchy and deference between
men and women, nobles and serfs, yeomen and slaves, and between

ministers and Ibos too, if only the Ibo had had any sense. The day
laborers who had made weapons out of their picks and shovels were
serfs responding to a feudal obligation, an arrangement that had
prospered under the British administration and was far from destroyed. An enlightened Islam had allowed the Emirs, Sultans, and
chiefs to work in conjunction with foreign civil servants. They were
people of the book. The founder of the empire, Uthman Dan Fodio,
had been a great scholar as well as a king. Declaring a jihad, or
holy war, in the middle of the nineteenth century, he had built the
great Hausa-Fulani empire on a foundation of Islamic purification.

From the northerners' point of view, the Ibos were not only
interlopers, but they were unclean, a pariah population. They were
individualistic and had no chiefs. It required only a few of them,
banding together, to form a mobile, aggressive, flexible, and competitive enclave of outsiders visible to all. Rapidly they spread
through the countryside, like the plague. First a few in one village,
then in another, working for the Public Works Department or the
Ministry of Education. Soon they were a regular epidemic. They
made fools of the accepting and trusting northerners. Give an inch
and they took a mile. At every turn in the road, every office, every
bank, there they were. And what was their reply to this? Insolence
and arrogance; not gratitude for the opportunities so freely bestowed.
They considered themselves the great benefactors of a backward
north and not the parasites that they were, and they gracelessly
pointed out that if it were not for them the north would be even
further behind.

It is not necessary to dwell on the story. Equivalents for it
can be found in the situations created in every mutually penetrative
cultural exchange. The "situation" describes a whole universe, a
body the violation of which cries out for reprisal. One could no doubt
hear the same objections about Turks in Germany, Ukrainians in
Calgary, and Ewes in Ghana. It is familiar enough, and so is the
prejudice that goes with it; but what it reveals is not that discrimination or prejudice cause conflict but that there seems to be a need
for discrimination and prejudice, a need for boundaries, for situations, identities, conflict, and hostility. What is doubtful is that
mankind really can live entirely at peace or even wants peace instead
of some measure of constant antagonism.

The problem is the limitations inherent in our assimilationist,
relativistic, or pluralistic thinking, which accepts the view that
everyone in his right mind wants peace and universality. This may
be true, but the question is how much, in the midst of the desire for
peace, is there a need for conflict?

What we ought not to do is to consider the events in Nigeria as
the unfortunate consequence of a democracy prematurely given to a

backward people not far enough along on the way to development. It
is not that primordial affiliations had remained, too unassimilated
or partially assimilated, or insufficiently neutralized by the growth
of a modernizing culture. Rather, such conflicts go hand in hand
with assimilationism and with growth. It is only a step from the
competitive interests of ethnic minorities to the fundamental conflict
of primordial tribalism. Democracy does not need to change very
much for such a transition to be made.

What is shown by Nigeria, along with other cases, is not that
people want conflicts, but that in the composition and collision of
their worlds there is a predisposition for revivalism and conflict.
The flaw in the assimilationist argument is not that the political system was inadequate, or the development insufficient, or that there
was too much corruption or discrimination, which may all have been
true, but that the assimilationist alternative, the high culture of
modernity, has proved to be too shallow and too trivial to have replaced the primordial beliefs. That is as true in our own country
as any other. Indeed, primordialism is for the moment on the wane
in Nigeria, having expended itself for the time being in such a
ferocious war. It was no more pathological than it is anywhere else.
Its complex causes need to be recognized for what they are, both in
their "situation," when all primordialism is mobilized into the single
event, or in war, which mobilizes all the primordialisms along the
same lines of cleavage. Primordialism cannot be treated as a good
thing when it happens among Jews and a bad thing when it happens
among Arabs. The biggest problem is that it is not understood by
just the people who come to give advice; the experts; the palefaces;
the men with the Kansas City smiles; the representatives of modernity,
democracy, and the enlightenment. Is the real world elite attending
conferences on modernity and democracy, the candidate replacements
for the deep texture of primordialism?

The parable of the minister and the truck driver thus tells us
many things. It makes it clear that the condition was aggravated
but not caused by the three-legged stool of federalism. Perhaps the
present system of administrative units is better; but the improved
condition of Nigerian politics today is really a freedom from politics.
Nigeria is a country well and efficiently ruled under an exceptionally
able and intelligent army officer with presence, with a good eye for
subordinates, with a sharp nose for the future, and with a good ear
to the ground for saboteurs and plotters.

The civil war was not simply a matter of prejudice exacer-
bated by uneven development. If that had truly been what it was,
then we would always be in trouble. There is, willy-nilly, always
some sort of uneven development in the world, and to presume to
equality is to underestimate how many different ways human beings

can impose inequality of mind or matter on each other. The equality
argument, which is the political form of the assimilationist ideal,
is that when all are equal then conflict disappears. When Arab and
Jew are equally rich and equally sophisticated, and when both have
too much to lose from conflict, then they will make up as friends.
That is a fine argument, but what it would really mean is that when
Jews become Arabs, or Arabs Jews, or they all become Americans,
then there will be peace in the Middle East.

The following lessons can be learned from the case of Nigeria:

1. Do not believe in the assimilationist view of the world. It
is a product of a naive evolutionary idea that began with the Greeks
and has, in an uneven and episodic way, been muddling through our
consciousness as if the idea was the ideal and the ideal was real.
From the nineteenth-century rationalists through the nineteenth-
century evolutionists, this progressive evolutionism has defined and
embodied the hope of the world. As mythic and blind as any form of
utopianism, it only appears to be scientific; yet we accept it unthink-
ingly as the enlightened part of the enlightenment itself and associate
it with everyone from Marx to modern evolutionists like Talcott
Parsons.

2. Do not believe that there are wrong units, regions, territories, or jurisdictions, or that there are right ones, for that matter. Units are important of course; but there are no "natural" or
appropriate jurisdictions. They are like everything else, fictions
in people's minds that are drawn around some presumed reality.
That reality may be the representation of Scots in their Scottishness
or Ibos in their Ibo-ism; but that is precisely the problem. Jurisdictions that work for one purpose may be quite useless for another.

A pretty good parallel to the Nigerian federal arrangement
is the three-legged stool of world jurisdictions. Could anything be
more "primordial" than the relationship of the United States, the
"first world"; the USSR, the "second world"; and the developing
countries, the "third world"? If any two get together and gang up
on the third, the whole rickety structure falls apart and then where
are we? Indeed, compared to the fragile three-legged stool of
world jurisdictions, Nigeria under its federal system was a tower
of strength.

3. Do not believe in development. It is not true that as the
world becomes more developed both the culture of enlightenment
and the prospects of democracy are spread. Both are based on the
inadequate assumption that the unversalization of science and the
willingness to convert primordial feelings into interests and primordial affiliations into interest groups will go together. Quite the
contrary: for every primordial attachment that is converted to an

interest in the wheeling and dealing of democratic politics, new
primordialisms appear; and with every spread of enlightenment,
newly unenlightened primordialisms come along as well.

Primordialism is not a form of primitivism. It is not a simple
reactionary phenomenon, but it can take that form. It is not going
to disappear with education, development, or science, but these
erode it. It is not a reaction to the "meritocracy," but that stimu-
lates it. It is a thing in itself, continuously changing, capable of all
kinds of faces, good and bad. It can become quaint, or it can swell
to monstrous proportions, and the circumstances that bring these
things about are simply not well understood.

THE "THINNING" OF THE ENLIGHTENMENT CULTURE

One of my major arguments is that primordialism is a response to the thinning out of the enlightenment culture, the deteri-
oration of which is part of the process of democratization and plural-
ization. Reason and knowledge are no longer the property of the
enlightened few, the philosopher kings. The capacity to know the
truth or interpret it is extended to all. Popular sovereignty means
popular culture. Enlightenment is redefined as science and as a
shrewd and practical view of the world.

Assimilationism itself then vitiates the enlightenment culture.
As it does, it leaves what might be called a primordial space, a
space people try to fill when they believe they have lost something
fundamental and try to re-create it. Of course, they cannot really
do that. Mostly they combine a new commitment to primordial
affiliations with a very shrewd and practical manipulation of primordial ties, what we can call the "Egyptian Strategy." This enables the poor and weak to gain from the rich and powerful. The
Egyptian strategy turns primordialism into practical politics, a
compensatory primordialism.

This strategy and its results are discussed below, but before
doing so it is necessary to trace the decline in the depth and power
of assimilationism, because it is important to explode certain misunderstandings that have resulted from a too-easy acceptance of the
assimilationist fallacy.

Assimilationists find it hard to comprehend primordial attachments, especially when these are also held by the enlightened. It is
difficult to accept the view that the most militant Arabists are engineers, architects, writers, and senior civil servants. Moreover,
primordial remnants within an assimilationist enlightenment culture
can arouse deep (primordial) antagonism. The sight of Hassidic

Jews, with their long black coats and broad-brimmed hats and their beards drives modern Israeli assimilationists up the wall.

Membership in any primordial group is associated with mumbo-jumbo, with ritual purifications at conversion, with tests and initiations, and with elaborate rites and ceremonies using blood, water, wine, wafers, sacred rocks, and an occasional sacrifice. For assimilationists all these things are fine in their way, but belong in a museum. They are no more appropriate than camels on a superhighway.

Behind the antagonism is the belief that the technocrats, businessmen, scholars, and administrators represent a kind of triumph of civilization over the narrow exclusivism of the primordial. Indeed most assimilationists, liberal or socialist, regard the nation-state as a kind of halfway house between primordialism and assimilationism. It too has its ritual boundaries, its oaths of citizenship, flags, and insignia; not to speak of armies and coercive apparatus. For the socialist this must all be, in the long run, swept away. For the liberal the primordial aspects of nationalism will eventually be replaced by more practical considerations, requiring cooperation on common problems, environmental, developmental, legal and economic, and so on.

Not that these enlightenment beliefs should be suspect; the problem is that they obscure the need for a primordial attachment that grows alongside of pluralism, assimilationism, and the rest.

Consider what has happened. "Truth" was once the unique property of a prepossessing elite, a stand, on the basis of which claims to rule could be made. The philosopher kings, the Mandarins in China, and the Brahmins in India represented high culture. Their job was to refine it, to abstract it, and to give it greater and greater depth through commentaries, writings, and scriptures. In turn, much of this ancient form of high culture became the wisdom of primordialism, a scriptural depth and symbolic vibrancy, against which the enlightenment substitutes a much more workaday set of practices.

It was the Greeks who made the first distinction between wisdom as divination, mysticism, ascetic contemplation, and empirical knowledge. They distinguished between themselves and the barbarians, not only on the basis of language or custom, but also on the principle that the ideal of the rational and prudent man, a Pericles or an Aristotle, capable of abstract but discriminating judgment, was Greek. They also recognized the problems that this caused. When such knowledge became the property of all citizens, it was likely to be abused. Democracy forced Socrates to drink the hemlock. Nevertheless, the Greeks wisely concluded that the solution to that problem is more and better education and a more enlightened citizenry. We have accepted that argument, lock, stock, and barrel.

The Greeks had a great advantage. Their version of the enlightenment was never thin. It was festive and public, a continuous round of performances and theater, political and dramatic. Noblemen were educated by their tutors in arts, drama, music, philosophy, and politics. These, expressions of high culture, became spirit, honor, areté. Ability and superiority were idealized and venerated and passed down in idealized form through the humanistic revival into the essential Western culture in France, England, and Germany. So accumulated, it required only education and democracy to convert it into the universal human acquisition. (See Jaeger 1954, vol. 1.) Perhaps the best example was France, which transformed its classicism into a revolutionary doctrine only to have it expropriated by the bourgeoisie in the form of a salon culture, as any reader of Proust will remember. Such a hothouse flowering was not without its steel frame, the rigid, virtually mandarin educational system that, filtering out the best from the rest, put the most elegant enlightenment minds into higher education and out into the administration. What Weber (1951, p. 132) said about the Mandarins in China is not so far off the mark here: "It may seem strange to us that this sublimated 'salon' cultivation, tied to the classics, should enable men to administer large territories."

The French are a good case, because not only did they democratize the ideal, but they made an enlightened assimilationism into a colonial doctrine. In the 1930s it was accepted by both black and white that assimilation into French culture was not only desirable but should lead to an egalitarian legal status.

Indeed, such assimilation produced its own reaction and the accusation of racism by French West Indian poets and writers who believed that this seduction into French culture by assimilated Africans was destroying their identity, what Frantz Fanon (1956, p. 129) called being "encultured" and "decultured" at the same time.

This is very much to the point. The question is whether or not we have not begun to enculture and deculture ourselves altogether. How else can we account for that peculiar and aberrant form of assimilationism that, especially in America, elevates the counterculture figure, the pariah, into a heroic figure complete with macho dress, hair style, black talk, and so on, in the same way it did with the work shirts, work songs, and picket lines of the workers in the 1930s. Indeed, it is a fact that the attributes of pariah cultures become attractive precisely to the elite and the middle class, which are the most accepting of the enlightenment myth and all that goes with it.

This thinness of the enlightenment as a popular culture became a recognizable problem from the onset of the enlightenment itself. Those who first made the case that language is important because it expresses the unique unity of meanings of a people and contains a

special richness, or that religion expresses the unfolding properties
of the divine in a human being and that these, shrouded in myth and
fantasy, express a symbolic need to share certain common collective
meanings, were attacking a monopolistic and medieval alternative.
They opposed the "uniformity of popes" and the "true" church and of
Latin as the "true" language. Giovanni Battista Vico (1668-1744),
one of the first to oppose such medieval universalism, believed that
human consciousness manifested itself in the evolution from primitive to sophisticated forms. It would be necessary for each culture
to repeat the sequence until a new science formed, the true philosophy
of all men. With such common and enlightened ground, political
unity would follow and cultural diversity would disappear.

Johann Gottfried Herder (1744-1803), who has wrongly been
regarded as the forerunner of a mystical nationalism, regarded
modernizing impulses with more distaste. Vico's enlightenment
theory failed to reckon sufficiently with the dehumanizing and bu-
reaucratic impact of modernization. Herder believed in a world of
nations, based on the organic qualities of each people. Those who
best represented the particular popular culture should educate and
humanize, thus making possible an elective world political community based on cooperation. Language was the essence of nationhood,
and national and linguistic boundaries ought to coincide. Nations
would reach out to each other through their humanity. "Nations,
Herder thought, were in a sense comparable to individuals. Just as
the self-realization of the individual was an interactive process,
inconceivable in isolation, so also, Herder believed, did national
self-realization necessitate international cooperation" (Barnard
1965, p. 107).

Between them Vico and Herder represent both sides of the
issue. If cultural diversity was so important to the meaningful life
of people, what would prevent passionate conflict between peoples,
and how could a world of nations survive? Vico's solution was that
pluralism itself would be vitiated in a progressive and evolutionary
scientific enlightenment. Herder's was that the humanizing effects
of each culture upon its people would stimulate their desire for
negotiation.

Edmund Burke (1729-94) believed that religion, a respect for
ancient institutions, and constitutionalism could combine. There
was a need for uniqueness and for civility. Wisdom is on the side
of the past. Individualism is dangerous. Uniqueness inheres in
each state; but the state must be constitutional. Burke's solution,
like Herder's requires constitutional government.

Such cultural romanticism took a more well-defined shape in
the nineteenth century. Saint-Simon, Marx, Darwin, Spencer, and
a host of other evolutionists gave the entire enlightenment tradition

a different twist. Not the property of an elite or a universal es-
thetic and classical culture, nor of the unique genius of a people,
enlightenment was industrialization. Modernity was a class and a
thing in itself, capable of its own universalization. The enlightenment became not only developmental but predictive. One went from
primitive tribe to modern state, from anarchy to internationalism.
The economic system evolved from lower to higher forms. Absolutism evolved not only into democracy but eventually, as everyone
became equal, into a classless society. The state itself would wither
away. According to Marx, burgeoning capitalism, when thrust into
a world of nationalities, races, and religions, prompts insurrec-
tions and aborted uprisings such as the Paris Communes of 1848 and
1870. He saw all these as forming a developmental pattern of class
struggle and exploitation that put history into sequence and evolution.
Society evolved from feudal to bourgeois and then to socialist and
communist stages as the modes of production evolved. Only in one
case would this evolution be restricted, and that was in China and
India, where the indigenous pattern of life was despotic, fixed,
static, and based on the "oriental mode of production."

Like the liberals, Marx believed that cultural differentiation,
especially of the primordial kind, would resolve itself. He could
speak kindly about the barbarians, sorry that they were exploited by
capitalists; but nevertheless he called a spade a spade. Village life
in India was not sentimental communalism. Slavery, brigandage,
the suttee, child marriage, and superstition, all were products of
oriental despotism. Calitalism made them worse. The promised
land was the unalienated man of universal socialism. So much for
cultural diversity (see Avineri, 1971).

Marx's views about primordial attachments were particular
in regard to religion. He regarded religion as a "defect" (see Marx
1963, p. 9). To emancipate the Jews, for example, one does not
give them political rights, but emancipates the state from both
Christians and Jews and society from the state (Marx 1963, p. 9).
Then all such categories, Jew and Christian, Englishman and Indian,
black and white, would disappear together, leaving only man himself,
the pure thing, what Marx called his "species-being."

Marx agreed with Vico and had the additional advantage of
having a method of showing how cultural diversity, in the form of
broad social or cultural categories arising as a result of the various
modes of production, would also be resolved.

His views were picked up by that most Asiatic despot of them
all, Joseph Stalin. Stalin became Soviet Commissar for Nationalities
in 1919. "A nation," said Stalin (1942, p. 12), "is a historically
evolved, stable community of language, territory, economic life,
and psychological make-up manifested in a community of culture."

People might possess a common national character, but they "cannot be said to constitute a single nation if they are economically disunited, inhabit different territories, speak different languages, and so forth. Such, for instance, are the Russian, Galician, American, Georgian, and Caucasian Highland Jews, who do not, in our opinion constitute a single nation" (Stalin 1942, p. 13). The Jews were primordials, relics, composed of "petrified religious rites." The Bund, the organization of Marxist Jewry within the Bolshevik movement, he singled out for special attack. This group had the nerve to propose a federalism "in which this non-nation should be allowed to exist within the socialist nation, as the sole representative of the Jewish proletariat." Petty nationalism was the nice name for it. "The maintenance of everything Jewish, the preservation of all the national peculiarities of the Jews, even those that are patently noxious to the proletariat, the isolation of the Jews from everything non-Jewish, even the establishment of special hospitals--that is the level to which the Bund has sunk!" (Stalin 1942, p. 47.) Yet elsewhere Stalin also spoke of

> the blossoming of national cultures, national in
> form and socialist in content under a proletarian
> dictatorship in one country, with the object of their
> fusion into a single, common socialist (both in form
> and content) culture, with a single common language,
> when the proletariat is victorious throughout the
> world and socialism becomes an everyday matter--
> such is the dialectical nature of the Leninist pre-
> sentation of the question of national culture (Stalin
> 1942, p. 209).

Just as the Jewish Bundists believed that they could be both Jews and proletarians under Communism, so such attachments violated the essential universalism of the idea. One could not be a Jew and a Communist any more than one could be simultaneously a capitalist and a proletarian. Indeed, Stalin was right; if this were allowed to the Jews, it opened up the possibility that the unlinear drift of all mankind to a single universal classless society might be hoisted on the petard of any stubborn primordial affiliation. What could happen to the Jews then could happen to anyone: Stalin's Georgians; smart Armenians; the works. Let the Arabs behave like these Jews, or the Uzbeks, the Chinese, or the Turks, and the whole vision crumbles. So it does in many ways. Go to Buenos Aires, parts of which look like a London suburb. On one street is the appropriate lawn and tennis club. On another are the pubs. There are English-language "public" schools, whose pupils wear

the crest of St. George on their jacket pockets. Go to Chile, to see
towns literally transplanted from the Black Forest in Germany or
Alpine villages whose inhabitants, complete with Lederhosen and
cuckoo clocks, Bierstuben and close-cropped hair, need only an
occasional "Heil Hitler" to complete the picture.

PLURALISM AS A SOLUTION

The socialist solution is a world language and a single culture.
The liberal solution is a pluralist world of nations and cultures that,
no matter what their particularities, all share in a common enlightenment culture and accept its values. This pluralist solution seems
to have a practical wisdom about it. Even though it is populist and
sometimes unattractive, by the very nature of pluralism, primordial
values are seen as being converted into interest group competition.
Primordialism is simply an extreme form of compensatory demand.
Put in more familiar terms, the argument is that if blacks,
for example, need more, let them get together and organize, and
bargain and vote for a larger share of the pie. If they need black
consciousness and other primordial nonsense in order to do so, fine;
only that ought not to be taken too seriously. Changing the image
may require Black Panthers; but they will wind up giving breakfast
to babies. So much for primordial blackness.
It is not necessary for people to love each other. The history
of ethnic groups is not that of a waxing but that of a waning of primordial loyalties, and of a good bargain struck by their members
in the process. The Italian-Americans did not need to be loved by
the old Yankees; they just captured the governments of their towns.
The Irish had showed them how to do it. They turned hostility to
Catholicism into a discipline for elections. Sure enough, that is
exactly what blacks are doing in Newark, in Atlanta, in Cleveland,
and elsewhere.
Here, then, is the model for the world. Poor countries can
bargain with rich ones if they organize. Members of the Organization of Petroleum Exporting Countries (OPEC) can get oil revenues
if they hang together and blackmail the industrials. Who then is
dependent, and who independent? No one needs to love Americans
in order to make them pay off.
If the high culture of enlightenment is thin, a successful pay-
off brings in money that has its own thickness. This "American
solution" is abrasive, bumpy, and violent. Universal enlightenment
becomes universal self-interest and cynicism. However, it also
produces a new kind of individual, who is not the ideal "species-
being" contemplated by Marx. This kind of person is alienated,

smart, and fast moving, with a nose for highly organized and pack-
aged options. It is not the new socialist but the entrepreneur who
becomes the man (or woman) for all seasons. He or she functions
in mass politics and organizes the big political party. This is not
a prisoner of work or place, but a member of the active society, an
individual who uses empirical knowledge, common sense, and technical skill and who disposes of the product at will.

Such people are organizers as well as individualists. As politicians they are political entrepreneurs, brokers. They operate on
national levels and international levels. All they need is a framework, a set of rules that can be used or abused for a pay-off.

What is built can be called development or exchange; the end
result is the same, and that is modern informational and political
networks, connecting all parts of the community, that are integrated
more and more closely within each part. The larger frameworks
contain smaller ones, associations and groups that, interweaving
the community, produce more and more political and social options
for more and more people all the time. There is a constant process
of centralization for purposeful action and decentralization for feed-
ing out the results. Centralization gives individuals power. Decentralization promotes participation, and with it new people are
drawn into the process to learn the rules of the game. A familiarity
with international and national issues extends downward to the lowest levels, where decentralized small groups develop around the
sensitive and important focal points

> where people are in frequent contact: the place
> where people live--the home, school, neighbor-
> hood, town, and among intermediate groups the
> city, state, and region; the place where people
> work; the groups in which people meet to help set
> standards or make demands about work--profes-
> sional groups, trade unions, guilds, the gatherings
> of people who meet to exchange goods, services,
> and money--market groups of various kinds, in-
> cluding retail stores and consumer coops; ethnic
> and racial identification; the process of friendship.
> The last, of course, cuts across all the others; it
> is one of the vital functions of small groups that
> cannot be carried on by large ones (Dahl and
> Lindblom 1953, p. 267).

Pluralism, then, is a model for the world. The enlightenment
culture is transformed into a highly participatory and activist assimilationism. What people learn is, not to venerate ideas, but to

practice what they refuse to preach. Internationally the frameworks include the United Nations, regional associations, common markets, the World Bank, and mutual exchange. Nationally, as a result of the interchanges of commerce, the networks multiply daily. A Chinese engineer may use the same tools and criteria for design as does a Chilean German engineer in his Tyrolean hat.

What then is left of primordialism under pluralism? It is a perfectly understandable phenomenon; for an assimilationist plural- ist, primordial ties remain where the culture is underdeveloped and indeed are a measure of its underdevelopment, or they may survive where there is great discrimination.

The solution to underdevelopment is simply more development, aid, and technical assistance; but the solution to discrimination is more difficult. The assimilationist and pluralist solution is to study the causes of discrimination with a view to making people aware of its costs and enabling them to take remedial action.

For the assimilationist, then, primordialism is pathological. In a world of complex networks and political and social levels, dis- crimination forms an interlocking and mutually reinforcing con- spiracy of hostility and prejudice. When they are surrounded by networks of discrimination, migrants or immigrants have no choice but to stick together. If they can find gratification in their traditional cultures, they will rely on them; hence the survival of immigrant cultures in ghettos. If they have no such cultures, these groups will either disintegrate or create one. For the assimilationist, the solu- tion to primordialism is to remove hostility and discrimination. Once this has happened everyone will share in the common and popu- lar culture. Italian-Americans, Arabs, Jews, Bosnians, and Uzbeks--all will behave in the same way. Residual ethnic politics becomes an interest-group competition.

The pluralist solution, then, is to recognize that the causes of primordialism are discrimination and its correlate, which is fallout from the "meritocracy," in which open and competitive performance favors the advantaged. In a democratic society, competitive per- formance establishes its own hierarchy. The danger is that the majority will come to believe that those on the bottom belong on the bottom, which is a self-fulfilling prophecy. Pariah populations score significantly lower on tests in a variety of criteria, compared to others who have not felt intense discrimination. Take any indi- cators, including income, mobility, time in the community, family stability, child rearing practices, dependence on social welfare, and inability to make use of opportunity, and there is a direct cor- relation between low scores and prejudice. The low scorers in our society are the blacks, the Indians, and to a lesser extent the Mexican-Americans. These groups also comprise a large part of the

subculture of the damned (and there are few of those), who seek redress in public violence or in self-inflicted wounds such as drugs
or drinking. How can they compensate for a realistic limitation on
ambition by other than the twin motilities of crime and politics?
(See Shannon and Shannon 1973.) The minority poor, when pariahs,
not only are unable to find work, but they increasingly pass on their
incapacity. The idea that the minority poor will be upwardly mobile
in their third or fourth generation like the descendants of immigrants,
does not really work (see Richardson Report n.d., pp. 51-56).

Pluralists understand very well that such self-perpetuating
helplessness can be transformed into powerful primordial attachments, accompanied by violence and fear, such as a black power
movement or an Indian renaissance. With such primordialism goes
the search for significant symbols. Indeed, pluralists welcome
some of the changes that primordialism brings about. For example,
the rich texture of American black life today contrasts to an unbelievable extent with its poverty only a decade ago, exerting powerful influences upon the style of thinking and life of the entire society.

These are some of the liberal reasons why primordialism
survives. Lack of opportunities, few role models, and the prolonged
effects of discrimination can inhibit the growth of self-confidence.
The result is few marginals who can use what opportunities exist.
What does it mean to be black and poor and to be told to behave like
anyone else, when in high level professional occupations in 1966 the
proportion of blacks among accountants and auditors was .6 percent;
among chemists, 2.1 percent; among engineers, .5 percent; among
lawyers and judges, .9 percent; and among physicians and surgeons,
2 percent. These figures may have improved somewhat, but the
discrepancy is still dramatic. The advice to a young black must be
"go primordial my son" (David 1966, p. 57).

Such problems are even more profound among poor countries.
In the third world primordialism has increased, because cultural
groupings, like any other, magnify their claims when they feel dis-
criminated against. Push this far enough and it becomes separatism,
as in Nigeria. Primordial attachment is a function of prejudice plus
class or regional exploitation. In the Congo after independence,
rebellion sprang up everywhere, and although its predominant form
was ethnic, this was mixed with competition for new posts, antagonism against entrepreneurial elites, and a generalized political un-
rest caused by "relative deprivation" (see Young 1970, pp. 969-1011).
This is the Nigerian story all over again.

Such is our thinking. Embedded in the way we conceive of
modern life, in our sense of history and its evolution, in our sense
of politics and democracy, in our belief in nationality and the prom-
ise of individuals under liberalism, is the article of faith that

primordialism will give way to assimilation, to democracy, science, and development. Nationalism is the transition. Founder-leaders and charismatic presidents pull diverse "nations" together to make one.

We also believe in the remnants of the more antique and the hand made. How dreadful that the Peruvian Indians in the Altoplano throw away their beautifully woven blankets, their magnificent clay pots, and with them the inheritance of the Incas, in exchange for cheap plastics. (It doesn't matter that the culture of the Incas itself was thoroughly destroyed.) It is like intellectuals to be nostalgic about handicrafts, especially when they do not live under the conditions of life prevailing in the Altoplano. They want to preserve primordial culture without the thing itself, to encourage African craftsmen to turn out modern copies of ceremonial masks or to have Soviet Uzbeks dress up in costumes and perform in dance troops presented, at least until recently, under the universal auspices of Sol Hurok.

The irony is that we want to preserve primordialism as a form of nostalgia. We hang on to the culture of modernity as the essential alternative to it. The evolution of mankind is one long Promethean struggle, the outcome of which is its own universality. That is our prophetic vision, whether described in an epic way by Marx or in the dry language of industrial democracy. Clark Kerr (1960, pp. 348-50) describes the logic of industrialism as "a great magnet which is drawing all human life to it and ordering the orientation of this life. Whether a society has been patrilineal or matrilineal, whether responding to the Protestant ethnic or the Bantu ethic, or whether it goes through a prior commercial revolution or not, it ends up following the logic of industrialism."

To realize this ideal only requires remedial action. Discrimination and primordialism go together; the greater the one, the greater the other. Nonprimordial marginals, such as slum dwellers living in the barriadas of Peru or the villas miserias of Buenos Aires disappear when they get a job. American blacks are better off than the Indian untouchables (Harijans). Caste, the most extreme discriminatory primordialism, is so powerful that the untouchables are unable to participate in politics and unable to effect changes in their own condition (see Verba, Ahmed, and Bhatt 1971).

The logic of the liberal solution is compensatory. Primordialism is pathological, but it compensates for what people lack in the material world. The more radical the liberal, the more willing he is to expand social welfare on the principle that those with the greatest need deserve the most, until primordial cripples can walk again.

The pluralist solution, which is representation for compensation, is less demanding than the socialist. Socialism requires not

only the elimination of all such ills, but the acceptance of a high
enlightenment culture by all. Its dialectic is to wed the best of the
classical tradition of knowledge with the evolutionism of modern
egalitarianism. The liberal solution is to provide for world industrialization, plus a popular culture that demolishes all forms of
privilege and permits those who want high culture to go have it without bothering everybody. What counts is that people participate in
democratic life at all levels. For the liberals, political culture is
the substitute for the culture of the enlightenment.

THE THREE-LEGGED STOOL AS A MODEL

The socialists want to return to high culture, to make it available for the masses. The liberal pluralists say this must come
from within the individual, that it cannot be legislated. Both see
primordialism as temporary and passing. Socialists understand
primordialism as a reaction to the thinness of the pluralist solution.
Pluralists see primordialism as a form of compensatory politics.

Let us put the battle between these views in the context of the
revival of primordialism itself and treat the Nigerian example as if
it were a universal predicament. Consider the federal constitution
of Nigeria as a world model. We find a western region (its capital
is Washington) and an eastern region (its capital is Moscow). Call
the third region the third world. How does the principle of the
three-legged stool work? In the western region, pluralism itself
is the solution and extends to the other two. Federalism equals
detente. In the eastern region, one mankind and one language is the
prospect under socialism, but it will take a while. This region
hopes to influence the third world, where the revival of primordialism is a way of rejecting hegemonic modernizing constraints imposed by both West and East. This primordialism, manipulating
the eastern and western region, replicates the politics of the three-
legged stool on a world scale.

To the extent that the third-world strategy works, the two
other regions compete for the support of the third. The latter,
seeking its own "authenticities," uses inflamed and passionate
attachments and the revival of traditional symbols. It arouses sen-
sibilities and holds in contempt the thinness of assimilationism.
Primordialism pays off. It is both genuine and in a pay-off competition between the two industrial regions, at one and the same time.
It is this that we call the Egyptian strategy, since it has worked so
well for Egypt in the Middle East. Primordialism justifies grievance, and grievance justifies aggressiveness and provides authentic
outraged pride.

Now consider the following hypothetical scenario. To prevent being drawn into a global regional conflict, the first two regions come to an agreement. They want more than a marginal detente while they continue the competitive game of doing each other in. The stakes are too high. Oil and power are not enough.

They decide to eliminate the Egyptian strategy. Since the Egyptian strategy is designed to obtain as much as possible from both West and East while escaping domination by them, it depends on tension and conflict between the two. However, since that strategy can be used wherever primordialism can be generalized into large and significant groupings, it becomes too costly.*

By imagination, let us assume that the United States and the USSR decide to put their detente into practice through the United Nations. Together they insist that under UN auspices the Middle East be declared a single development region. Developmental support will be provided by the United States and the Soviet Union. They tell the Arabs to call it quits on the subject of the Palestinian refugees, on the grounds that the Arabs have been able to get rid of about a million of their own unwanted Jews by packing them off to Israel. In turn, the United Nations establishes a federal Middle East government. Libya and Egypt become the western region, while Lebanon, Syria, and Saudi Arabia constitute the eastern. Israel is a "middle belt." Arab oil, Egyptian technology, and Israeli expertise make a hundred deserts bloom.

The prospect boggles even the primordial mind. Not arms but assistance; not war but development; not a sword but peace. The Middle East becomes as it was in Biblical days. It is flowing with milk, honey, and oil. Everybody is happy. The Jews learn Arabic. The Muslims recall that Judaism is one of the foundation stones of Islam. Henry Kissinger, now back at Harvard, is invited to attend a conference of East-West technical experts in Jerusalem. He receives a telephone call from Anwar Sadat inviting him to stop off in Cairo to give advice about setting up a school of higher studies in high diplomacy, one appropriate to an Arab country but not too primordial. Sadat sends a car for him. Speeding across the Sinai desert, the car makes good time. It passes over the Suez Bridge built with U.S. and Soviet aid. Kissinger does not even need time

---

*This did not happen in the Sudan, where conflict between the northern Arabs and the southern Nilotic Christians resulted in thousands of dead, nor has it yet been employed in Ethiopia, where Eritrean Muslims are fighting Coptic Christians. It did not work in Uganda when General Amin expelled the Asians. For this reason a detente becomes imperative.

for prayers. Sadat meets him on the other side of the Canal and the two talk. They are trying to make Cairo by tea time. Just outside of Cairo a mutual aid construction company is fixing the road. Sadat tells his driver not to stop. Suddenly a Jewish Ibo runs in front of the car with his arm raised. He is short and ugly. He wears shorts. He shouts at Sadat, "Stop! Where the hell do you think you are going?" The car stops. The fellaheen pick up picks, shovels, and so on. The rest is history.

CONCLUSION

Will primordialism disappear with development? Will its revival in industrial society prove to be transitory? We are back where we began. Yes and no. Each type of primordialism is likely to appear and disappear. (Now you see the Ibo, now you don't.) Each type changes its meaning. The best solution lies in a highly participatory pluralistic system in which no groups are penalized excessively; however, we know from a variety of studies that the least well educated, those with least status, participate least in politics. We also know that political socialization mostly takes place in the schools and that most political learning is accomplished in the late teens. Hence those who are badly socialized and low on the status scale are the least able to do something for themselves. One way of dealing with relatively inert populations is to arouse them by primordial identification and appeals.

There is a remedial solution, but few of us are willing to face up to it; that solution is to pay the compensatory cost required to reduce primordialism at home and abroad. Moreover, where such efforts have been undertaken the results have been poor, much poorer than anticipated. No simple remedialism will do. It is an all-encompassing, all-embracing problem.

If that poses one impossible situation, our more general conclusion is even worse. It has to do with the character of enlightenment. Not even the faintest echo of the Greek or aristocratic ideal can be heard in the land, so blended is it with utilitarian and populist considerations. The result is an assimilationist culture, which is like weak tea. A case can be made for primordialism, if only as an adventure in the richer depth of primordial metaphor.

What can we conclude from all this? Is there anyting in our parables and imaginary stories of far places that is relevant to our own experience? Perhaps. At this point it is at least possible to make the following observations:

1. Assimilationism and primordialism do not stand in any simple either-or relationship to each other. What may be

primordial can be assimilated; what has been assimilated can become primordial.

2. Universalism, especially of the liberal and socialist forms, is either too vulgarized in the first instance or too demanding in the second. In practice, the socialists have squared the circle by keeping the shell of high culture in the photography of its realism; preserving its worn-out style, its Victorianism; and robbing it of content.

3. Pluralism becomes shaky when territorial units correspond to ethnic ones. The result makes cleavage politics out of primordial affiliations and heightens grievances and perceived disabilities rather than resolving them.

4. Federalism, and detente politics, are easy to manipulate by the Egyptian strategy of primordialism.

5. Within an assimilated and pluralist system, the equivalent of the Egyptian strategy is quota politics. Quota representation enables weak factions to manipulate strong ones.

6. Primordialism, when it represents a pathology of discrimination, requires a compensatory response on an allocative principle. Those with the greatest need deserve a disproportionate share of the benefits that is sufficient to eliminate the barriers to participation.

7. Self-perpetuating or pariah marginals are those with the greatest need and should receive the most disproportionate shares, despite resulting difficulties.

8. Primordialism is thick, metaphorically, where assimilationism is thin, but not all primordialism is thick and not all assimilationism is thin. The problem is to identify the kinds of knowledge and understanding that can provide depth for individuals as individuals instead of in terms of their collective affiliations.

9. Development promised too much, and while it has delivered on a good many of its promises, such as limited compensatory support, it brings about as many problems as it solves, and these may exacerbate primordial conflict.

10. The solution is likely to be one of continual confrontation, a perpetual dialectic in which no outcome or end product is predictable, but a pluralist solution is more likely to work than a socialist solution.

Whatever we think of these points, the pendulum between assimilationism and primordialism and between universalism and parochialism will continue to swing back and forth. At the moment, the swing is somewhat in favor of the primordial. The compensatory adjustment that can regulate how far it can go in either direction, and what is necessary to restore a right balance, will not be easy to find. At least the metaphor of the pendulum is better than that of the three-legged stool.

REFERENCES

Avineri, Shlomo. 1971. Karl Marx on Colonialism and Modernization. New York: Doubleday, Anchor Books.

Barnard, F. M. 1965. Herder's Social and Political Thought. Oxford: Clarendon Press.

Begg, H. M., and J. A. Stewart. 1971. "The Nationalist Movement in Scotland." Journal of Contemporary History 6: 135-52.

Bendix, Reinhard. 1964. Nation-Building and Citizenship. New York: John Wiley.

Commission on International Development. 1970. Partners in Development. New York: Praeger.

Dahl, Robert, and Charles E. Lindblom. 1953. Politics, Economics, and Welfare. New York: Harper and Row.

David, John P., ed. 1966. The American Negro Handbook. Englewood Cliffs, N.J.: Prentice-Hall.

Desai, A. R. 1971. "Need for Reevaluation of the Concept." In Essays on Modernization of Underdeveloped Societies, ed. A. R. Desai. Bombay: Thacker and Co.

Fanon, Frantz. 1956. "Racism and Culture." Presence Africaine, nos. 8-10.

Geertz, Clifford. 1973. The Interpretation of Cultures. New York: Basic Books, p. 6.

Jaeger, Werner. 1954. Paideia: The Ideals of Greek Culture. New York: Oxford University Press.

Kerr, Clark. 1960. "Changing Social Structures." In Labor Commitment and Social Change in Developing Areas, ed. W. E. Moore and A. S. Feldman, pp. 348-50. New York: Social Science Research Council.

Marx, Karl. 1963. "Bruno Bauer, Die Judenfrage." In Karl Marx, Early Writings, ed. T. O. Bottomore. London: C. A. Watts.

Packenham, Robert A. 1973. Liberal America and the Third World.
    Princeton, N.J.: Princeton University Press.

Shannon, Lyle, and Magdaline Shannon. 1973. Minority Migrants in
    the Urban Community. Beverly Hills, Calif.: Sage Publica-
    tions.

Stalin, Joseph. 1942. Marxism and the National Question. New
    York: International Publishers.

Verba, Sidney; Bashiruddin Ahmed; and Anil Bhatt. Caste, Race
    and Politics. Beverly Hills, Calif.: Sage Publications.

Weber, Max. 1951. The Religion of China. Glencoe, Ill.: Free
    Press.

Young, M. Crawford. 1970. "Rebellion and the Congo." In Protest
    and Power in Black Africa, ed. Robert I. Rotberg and Ali
    Mazrui, pp. 969-1011. New York: Oxford University Press.

4

**POLITICAL SOCIALIZATION
RESEARCH AND RESPECT
FOR ETHNIC DIVERSITY**
Judith V. Torney
Charles A. Tesconi, Jr.

If there were a law made that every individual had to forget about his or her ethnic background and just concentrate on being an American, would that be a good thing or a bad thing?

> Nine-year-old Lithuanian-American girl: I think it would be a bad thing, because I think that every person should have his own nationality; he could celebrate the things their way. If it was just American then it would be a boring place to live in.

> Ten-year-old Polish-American boy: It would be a bad thing because if you forget about your nationality you won't be able to do those special things in your nationality. Like if you are Spanish, you celebrate birthdays with piñatas, and you wouldn't have pinatas if you were just American.

> Twelve-year-old Italian-American girl: It would be good because everybody would be equal.

> Twelve-year-old Mexican-American girl: I think bad, because you have to find out how you became and how your customs are and then decide if you want to be a part of it.

> Twelve-year-old Italian-American girl: It would be bad. I like being Italian, it's people's identity. This is what American is about.

Fourteen-year-old Chinese-American girl: Good because we're actually all Americans.

Fifteen-year-old Ukrainian-American boy: People should have the freedom to keep their ethnic identity.

Fifteen-year-old Italian-American boy: Bad because even though we should be Americans first, you can't make everyone the same.

Sixteen-year-old Croatian-American boy: It would be bad because America couldn't be as constructive in views and things that she does. Different groups make America unique and strong.

Seventeen-year-old Lithuanian-American boy: I think it would be a bad thing because every nationality has good things to offer, like parts of its culture that enrich people who belong to that nationality. *

The motivation for preserving cultural diversity ranges in these young people from a love of Mexican piñatas and candy to a defense of diversity and freedom of choice as part of the American creed. In this chapter we propose to examine the assumptions of cultural pluralist theory and, more importantly, the content and processes of socialization that are necessary to support, maintain, and enhance a culturally pluralistic society.

SOCIALIZATION AS PRE-ADULT SOCIAL ROLE TRAINING

Socialization has become a major focus of interdisciplinary concern in the social sciences. This concern has in turn generated three major and distinguishable definitions: (1) socialization as enculturation or intergenerational transmission of culture; (2) socialization as the acquisition of impulse control; and (3) socialization as role training or training for social participation (Levine 1973, p. 62).

---

*These excerpts have been chosen from approximately 30 interviews conducted in Spring 1974 with young people of distinguishable ethnic origin from the Chicago metropolitan area.

All three definitions stress the lingering influence in the individual of early experience, the imposition of social reality, and the progressive adaptation of individual development to societal goals. However, our attention will be given to the third definition, which emphasizes the attitudes and behavior associated with roles in the social system.

Before considering the results of particular socialization studies and of the five differing approaches to ethnic pluralism that can be identified, it is important to take note of two critical dimensions of socialization. The first relates to the matter of "socialization agents." This term refers to parents; schools, including teachers, curriculum, and classroom or school organization; peers; and the mass media and the direct and indirect effects of these agents on the attitudes a child or adolescent acquires. Robert A. Levine (1973, p. 105) underscores the necessity of examining the place of socialization agents when he notes the following:

> Every adult individual . . . notices to some degree
> the evaluative and distributive operations of the
> socio-cultural system. From observations of in-
> dividual instances of conformity and nonconformity,
> positive and negative evaluation, success and fail-
> ure, social reward and punishment--in a process
> equivalent to the vicarious trial-and-error or ob-
> servational learning of reinforcement theorists--
> he draws conclusions about which behavioral dis-
> positions are favored and which disfavored.
> These inductive conclusions become part of his
> cognitive structure, joining attitudes, beliefs,
> and values already there and become consistent with
> them to some degree. From this cognitive struc-
> ture as repeatedly modified by social perception
> and his own normative experiences, comes his def-
> inition of the situation in which he sees his chil-
> dren growing up and his prescriptions and pro-
> scriptions for their adaptive performance. . . .
> The adult in his role as . . . socializing agent
> performs the function of feedback from selective
> experience that is performed by reproduction in
> population genetics and by memory in trial-and-
> error learning. In the more differentiated socie-
> ties the storage and selective propagation of infor-
> mation about the environment is institutionally
> specialized and performed by schools, libraries,
> religious and political organizations.

The socializing agent, in this view, is far more than a mere reflector of sociocultural policy.

Levine (1973, pp. 106, 135) also addresses a second important dimension of socialization, namely slippage in the socializing process and the entry of unplanned and often undesired processes and outcomes, as follows:

> The explicit goals of socializing agents are frequent-
> ly not recognized in the behavior of those they train.
> First, the socializers are at best imperfect psycho-
> logical engineers (they do not command the neces-
> sary but as yet ill-known laws of behavior acquisi-
> tion); second, they must operate within the limits
> set by their trainees' pre-existing behavioral dis-
> positions acquired genetically and through "acci-
> dental" events of early experience. . . . Recogni-
> tion of this slippage . . . brings to our attention
> two major sets of variables related to socialization:
> the conscious aims, concepts, and knowledge of the
> socializers and the relationship between unplanned
> and deliberate influences in the child's behavior de-
> velopment. The most urgent objective for empiri-
> cal research on socialization is to understand the
> relation between the planned and unplanned aspects
> of social learning.

Unanticipated influences are important, and so are the un-
planned outcomes of practices, particularly in the socialization of cultural pluralism. A given educational practice, such as a school policy limiting the discussion of controversial issues, may have a series of planned outcomes, such as less conflict in the classroom, but also a series of unintended outcomes, such as a belief on the part of the students that the freedom to express opinion is not universal or important. (See Torney and Morris 1972 for further examples.) This is particularly important, as we shall see shortly, in attempts to socialize for cultural pluralism when such attempts are based upon untested assumptions of cultural pluralist theory.

Political socialization research, that is, studies of the content of and process by which orientations to the political system and of political role behavior are acquired, is the area of research that is most valuable, relative to socialization for cultural pluralism. Concern with political socialization, and the measurement of the out-
comes of civic education in terms of attitudes as well as knowledge, originated about 15 years ago with political scientists who were seeking to understand how established political systems insured the

development of supportive attitudes in oncoming generations. Many
of these early studies established the seemingly elementary point
that political attitudes existed in young people. It became clear from
a variety of research conducted during the 1960s that in fact the process of political learning begins early in life, with experience in
authority relationships, with decision-making processes, and with
interpersonal as well as intergroup conflict or cooperation. Specific
political issues or elections are only part of this process.

Political learning, like all learning, is cumulative. The knowledge children have gained about the social system, as well as the attitudes they have acquired in the past, influence what they will learn
in the present and future. Lee F. Anderson, Richard Remy, and
Richard Snyder (n.d., p. 8) conclude a discussion of the natural
political world of the child as follows:

> Childhood political learning is critically important
> because it presents valuable, never-to-be repeated
> opportunities on which to build a guided and sys-
> tematic political education. During this period in
> children's intellectual, emotional and social devel-
> opment their political selves are still being formed.
> When we postpone overt attention to political educa-
> tion until the high school years, we run a risk . . .
> that our instruction in later years will be less than
> maximally effective. . . .

A close examination of attitudinal research in general and
political socialization research in particular suggests that the years
between seven and twelve may be uniquely important. This is the
period before too many stereotyped attitudes dominate children's
views of the world (Lambert and Klineberg 1967). Moreover, it is
concurrent with a period when the child's cognitive development is
sufficiently advanced to understand a diversity of viewpoints. Although cognitive abilities are continually increasing, by age 13 or
14 the young person is more likely to have a fixed perspective about
himself, his culture, and his country. A number of studies have
found a certain rigidity after this point, perhaps as the adolescent
seeks to stabilize a personal identity and maximize peer relationships.

181506

FIVE APPROACHES TO SOCIALIZATION FOR AN ETHNICALLY
AND CULTURALLY DIVERSE SOCIETY

Great diversity in motivations and orientations characterizes
the approaches to cultural pluralism. Each orientation is grounded
in a different conception of U.S. society and offers different pre-

scriptions for the kinds of attitudes and social role participations
that should result from socialization. The agents of socialization
differ in their definition of the situation in which these children will
grow up. These differences result from their own attitudes and cognitive structures as well as from their experiences with successful
modes of adaptation, to use the terminology of Levine.

The first orientation argues that no attempt should be made to
further cultural pluralism through socialization. This orientation
typically follows from belief in the melting pot as a viable continuing
model for American socialization or from attachment to an Anglo-
Saxon-Teutonic monocultural core-conformity model (Tesconi 1975).

In fact, this orientation is in some respects realized by socialization, which occurs both inside and outside the school system at the
present time. A core concern of U.S. civic education, in some cases
even at the secondary school level, is a monoculturally biased transmission of patriotism and loyalty. This continues in spite of the fact
that by the third grade more than 90 percent of the 13,000 American
children queried in 1972 in a nationwide study of political socialization agreed with the statement, "America is the best country in the
world" (Hess and Torney 1967, p. 26). Even by the age of seven or
eight, American children are deeply attached to their political community, even though they may know very little about it in the formal
sense. One might argue that what is needed is not more stress on
generalized positive feeling for one's country but rather an understanding of the democratic process, of which pluralism is certainly
one aspect.

If either the melting pot or the core conformity model is adopted
or is perpetuated, the role of socialization agents within the school
system will be to reinforce the process of assimilation. If a family
is identified with a recognizable ethnic group, the implication of this
model for parents as agents of socialization is clear. They have the
choice of denying their investment in the realization of their own cultural background in their children or of attempting to maintain and
orchestrate a complex bifurcation--core-conformity of Americanism
at school, and ethnic identity in community Saturday schools and
family traditions.

In any case this first orientation which is one of monocultural
assimilation, is presented primarily as a point of contrast with the
other four positions in regard to socialization.

Those who wish to preserve their ethnic heritage, promote
ethnic identification, and raise ethnic consciousness are affected by
a second motivation that shapes socialization practices. The orientation that follows from these motives is frequently connected with
the assumption that the culture connected with the heritage of an ethnic group is a valuable resource for future generations and for society

in general and that therefore those who are about to become adults should be instructed in their respective ethnic heritages and taught to value them.

Another source of motivation for the groups expressing these aims is a disdain for the history of the schools as agents of cultural homogenization in American society. There is anger on the part of many of the proponents of ethnic consciousness-raising about the denial of their cultural heritages that they underwent as children and that they see continuing in the formal public schooling of their children. It is not so much that these ethnic group members see themselves as victims of prejudice, as it is that they see themselves robbed of their heritage by a monocultural homogenization process that requires attachment to an assumed cultural standard.

Those whose socialization programs are motivated by concern for the preservation of their ethnic heritages can be distinguished by a particular set of intended or planned socialization outcomes: increased ethnic consciousness, enhanced self and group esteem, appreciation of tradition, and sense of community. As indicated previously, however, unplanned or unintended consequences must be considered. Socialization processes motivated by ethnic consciousness and preservation may generate a defensively high level of self-esteem that denigrates and/or ignores other groups that are different. There is some evidence that what ought to be aimed for is a moderately high level of self-esteem, neither so high that individuals become convinced of the unique value of their own experience in ways that move them to regard those who differ from them only as inferiors, nor so low that individuals see little of value in themselves or their cultural heritage that can be communicated to others.

Another unplanned and undesirable outcome of extensive ethnic consciousness might be a lack of the flexibility necessary to operate in a society with universalistic demands, as well as in a community with particularistic demands. The socializing agents in the educational system who attempt to raise ethnic consciousness and self-esteem face a situation that is more complex than the situation faced by the proponents of monoculturalism. If the schools undertake the promotion of the heritage of a single cultural group, they face complaints from other groups. Sometimes even the parents whose heritage is being considered in the school curriculum complain, because they are convinced of the value of monoculturalism in getting ahead. It is interesting to note that during the interviews with the young people quoted on the first page of this chapter, several of the parents who were not actually present in the room but were listening would enter the conversation to defend assimilation processes. In their opinion ethnic identification, which their children were discussing in positive terms, was only a handicap.

A third approach, intercultural education, arises from some of the same angers concerning the monocultural emphasis that are expressed by those who favor ethnic consciousness-raising. However, it has also been promoted by those who train Peace Corps volunteers, business executives, or others to work in other cultures. Instead of stressing a single-membership ethnic group, this approach stresses the commonalities of ethnic groups and the similarity of intercultural communication between domestic ethnic groups to international communication skills.

The planned or intended positive outcomes of those who take this approach stress increased intercultural competence, including empathy, the ability to take the role or viewpoint of another person, the acceptance and trust of those from other cultural groups, and the ability to interpret customs and nonverbal behavior in differing cultural styles. The role of self-esteem is important as a prerequisite to successful intercultural experience rather than as an end in itself. The assumption is that before an individual can profit from training designed to improve intercultural communication, he or she needs to have a self and group esteem that is relatively undamaged by monocultural homogenization and be relatively open to other people and cultures.

The prerequisites of self-esteem and interpersonal trust are primarily in the province of family socialization agents, while the specifics of intercultural competence are more likely to be in the province of the school.

> In particular we find much evidence to recommend school efforts to create an intercultural dimension in childhood education: We define the term "intercultural" generically to include international as well as domestic second culture experience, since many of the objectives are identical. . . . By the term "dimension" we mean more than adding a few units on Africa and Asia, Mexican-Americans and Polish-Americans, while the regular curriculum remains monocultural. . . . In social studies and language arts, in music and art, the intercultural dimensions are created by incorporating data and experience from appropriate domestic and "foreign" cultures (Carpenter and Torney 1973-74, p. 20).

Relatively little research is addressed to this orientation, and thus it is difficult to assess the possible latent influences and unintended results. However, one possible unintended consequence could be a turning away of individuals from their own ethnic roots. Though

some may see this as desirable, a consequence of choice rather than
of coercive assimilation processes, it is not an outcome intended by
those who advocate intercultural socialization processes.

Those whose primary aim is neither ethnic consciousness-
raising nor intercultural communication skills, but rather the eradi-
cation of ethnic and racial prejudice, represent a fourth approach.
Their focus is on the active realization of democratic values in society as a means of combating racial and ethnic prejudice.

In 1972 and 1973, two major publications reviewed the literature related to this orientation. H. J. Ehrlich (1973) presented a
massive survey of sociopsychological studies of prejudice, with suggestions for socialization practices that should help to combat it.
Robert A. Levine and Donald T. Campbell (1972) have attempted to
distinguish, on an ethnographic basis, societies that have relatively
high and relatively low levels of ethnocentrism.

According to this orientation the planned positive outcomes of
socialization programs include reduced authoritarianism and stereotyping of ethnic groups, heightened tolerance, and the realization of
democratic values in behavior. These objectives bear many similarities to the democratic citizenship objectives measured by the
National Assessment of Educational Progress and by the International
Association for the Development of Educational Achievement (IEA)
Civic Education Project, data from which will be reviewed in a subsequent section of this chapter.

A problem associated with this approach is the absence of democratic pluralism in many aspects of our social system. After all, the
socialization agents in school who carry out this approach have little
influence upon the social system at large. What good does it do, one
might ask, to socialize youngsters in schools according to this orientation if the society in which they will live does not take democratic
pluralism seriously or in other ways makes prejudice and discrimination adaptive rather than maladaptive?

A fifth perspective may be viewed in some ways as inclusive of
ethnic consciousness, intercultural communication, and increased
tolerance. This perspective is derived from a somewhat more explicit theoretical base, which is cultural pluralism theory.

The term cultural pluralism is as controversial today as it was
in the 1950s, when Horace Kallen (1956, p. 46) sought to clarify its
meanings some five decades after he had introduced the term. He
pointed out that disputes over its meaning were, as they still are,
scientific, creedal, or both.

> The creedal modes project some species of totali-
> tarianism--racial, sacerdotal, communist, fascist
> or other. The scientific modes postulate some sort

of monistic sociological theory employing concepts
of organism and other models frequent among social scientists. Scientific may transpose to creedal,
and vice versa, whenever a working hypothesis,
subject to revision according to the testimony of
events and the alterations of time, is transvalued
into a doctrinal system always and everywhere the
same; or when such a system is released into a
working hypothesis altering as it works.

Kallen recognized that the wide-ranging sociopolitical implications of the term would attract much attention and criticism.
After all, in all its senses cultural pluralism speaks primarily to
the way in which a society should be organized and the manner in
which oncoming generations should be socialized.

Despite a relatively long history as a theory of how a democratic society works and a growing body of literature calling for the
incorporation of cultural pluralist theory in all institutional sectors,
particularly those that serve as major agents of socialization, there
is no comprehensive, systematic analysis of this theory and there
has been little direct testing of its assumptions and attendant promises. Indeed, the effects of living in a culturally pluralistic society
upon the developing as well as the adult human are for the most part
unknown. Milton Gordon pointed out (1961, p. 275) what has remained essentially accurate in spite of the wider use of the term cultural pluralism and its increasing role in the formation of education
policy. "No close analytical attention has been given either by social
scientists or practitioners of intergroup relations to the meaning of
cultural pluralism, its nature and relevance for a modern industrial-
ized society, and its implications for problems of prejudice and discrimination."

Nevertheless, the demands for promoting greater pluralism,
which are heard largely in terms of ethnic group consciousness, grow
louder every day; and the promises of cultural pluralism theory, in
spite of the fact that they are based on untested assumptions, are
used to legitimize these demands. Furthermore, the untested assumptions and their attendant promises are often turned to as a
first-line defense, to mute those who suggest that renewed interest
in ethnicity may serve to threaten the modest gains made by blacks
since the mid-1960s.

Several interrelated assumptions underlie cultural pluralist
theory. We shall look at five major ones, most of which relate

directly or indirectly to socialization processes and goals.* We use the term "assumption" in its fundamental sense; it refers to matters taken for granted. Horace Kallen's principal insights and many of those coming from the latter-day advicates of cultural pluralism, emerged from an examination of their own ethnic experiences. He tested these insights as hypotheses with his own and other ethnic conferees, with people who prized and acted upon their own ethnicity. Long before the so-called radical or third-force historians and social scientists, he acted on the principle that the only reality was that which emerged from phenomenologically tested experience.† Thus our use of the term "assumption" will be viewed as pejorative usage by many. However, since we have long been involved in efforts calling for the celebration and perpetuation of ethnicity, we are acutely aware of the lack of supportive evidence surrounding the claims and promises of cultural pluralism theory.

FIVE ASSUMPTIONS FOR WHICH EVIDENCE IS NEEDED

The first assumption of cultural pluralism theory is that membership in, and attachment to, primary ethnic or cultural group life and socially encouraged involvement in this group life promotes in an individual those characteristics we usually associate with a healthy personality type. As Kallen (1956, p. 25) put it, the more culturally pluralistic a society, "the freer, the richer, the more civilized, is likely to be the personality which lives and moves and nourishes its being among the diverse communions." Identity that is rooted in prideful primary ethnic or cultural group attachment is assumed to lead to respect for and receptivity to different others.

This must be counted among the least controversial assumptions of cultural pluralism theory; yet, it presents some questions which must be answered. Although few of us would take issue with the claim that an identity rooted in strong primary group ties leads to a sense of place, belonging, and security, does it follow that

---

*Our analysis of these assumptions has been influenced by Thomas Green 1966. "Education and Pluralism: Ideal and Reality" (Twenty-sixth Annual J. Richard Street Lecture, Syracuse University School of Education.

†We would like to express our appreciation to Professor Eliezer Krumbein of the University of Illinois, Chicago Circle, for bringing this to our attention.

respect or even mere tolerance for different others naturally results?
(This point was suggested earlier concerning those who are committed to the ethnic consciousness orientation. Here our stress is upon
the need for the testing of an assumption about the promised positive
effects of several aspects of cultural pluralism theory.) Moreover,
given the possibility that today's heightened awareness of and pride
in ethnicity is a function of coercive assimilative pressures, what
happens when these pressures are eliminated, when an individual's
membership and attachment to primary ethnic or cultural group life
is socially encouraged? Could it be that the heightened awareness
and pride would no longer be necessary and/or would disappear?

Cultural pluralists are quick to note in these regards that a
variety of groups can coexist with tolerance and mutual respect
without difficulty so long as an open and fluid social order allows
for maximum freedom of association. Conflict and intergroup hostility come as the result of efforts to introduce rigidity into the social order or when the bases of group membership are defined so as
to eliminate fluidity in intergroup contact and membership. Hence,
while cultural pluralist theory values and encourages ethnic and cultural group affiliation, it insists upon fluidity within and between
groups. This brings us, however, to a second assumption which
raises even more questions.

This assumption relates to the principle of freedom of association for individuals and groups. Although cultural pluralists insist
upon the importance of primary ethnic or cultural group membership,
they also insist that such membership must not be rigidly binding or
involuntary. Freedom of association is implicit in cultural pluralist
theory. The individual must be free to move out of and into groups,
"engaging in open or hidden communion with societies of his fellows,
every one different from the others, and all teamed together, and
struggling to provide and maintain the common means which nourish,
assure, enhance, the different, and often competing, values they differently cherish." Attachment to this democratic ideal moves the
cultural pluralist to assume in his theory that personalities that are
characterized by tolerance and openness to "different others," and a
truly democratic society, are dependent upon the opportunities of individuals to encounter and interact with a variety of culturally different others. As Kallen (1956, p. 25) argued, the more groups an individual can encounter, join, or leave, and the more varied their
forms and functions, the more civilized the individual is likely to be,
and this is also true of society as a whole.

However, cultural pluralists must consider the possibility that
inter-group fluidity in the context of assimilative pressures and/or
in the absence of enduring "old world," or any culturally rooted,
bases for ethnic or cultural group identification, could lead to

(indeed, according to some authorities has led to) assimilation. This possibility, alluded to earlier in regard to the intercultural orientation and its approach, poses a serious question for cultural pluralism advocates: What does freedom of association and intergroup fluidity do to those ties which bind one to a primary group?

It should also be noted that the valued principles of freedom of association and intergroup fluidity are dependent upon structural pluralism, that is, pluralism within the institutional sector. Many writers have suggested that pluralism in the institutional sector has contributed to a modern day form of privatism that results in individuals absenting themselves from the public world and that holds out the possibility of frightening social and political control over behavior (Tesconi 1974, pp. 129-39). How much pluralism in the institutional sector is the cultural pluralist willing to tolerate? What does he or she think about the possible connection between privatism and institutional pluralism?

Before these assumptions can obtain an adequate test, several additional questions present themselves. For example, what characterizes "fluidity" in group membership? How is it achieved? What happens to the membership of primary groups when individuals move out of some primary groups and into others? What happens to the individual? Could it mean, for example, as Thomas Green (1966, p. 21) suggested regarding a related phenomenon, that "the Jew has less identity as a Jew, the Catholic less as a Catholic, and even the Episcopalian less as Episcopalian?" Furthermore, cultural pluralist theorists are not always explicit in their discussion of the notion of freedom of association as it applies to what might be considered political groupings or functional as opposed to organic groupings. Research findings relating to such matters as tolerance with regard to ethnic group attachment and tolerance as a function of intergroup mobility organic or otherwise must be identified and related to cultural pluralist theory. As Robert K. Merton (Merton and Rossi 1950, p. 187) pointed out, there is need for a close study of the processes in group life that sustain or inhibit orientations to nonmembership groups, thus perhaps leading to a linking of reference group theory and current theories of social organization, including cultural pluralist theory.

Related to the freedom of association principle is a third assumption of cultural pluralist theory which, as pointed out by Thomas Green (1966, p. 11) holds that there is no single way of life that can without question claim to be the best and that a humane society must afford room for many competing and oftentimes conflicting ways of life. This assumption comes very close to the heart of the theory of democratic pluralism. If there is no one way of life that can without question claim superiority over any other, how does one go about

resolving competing and conflicting values? What are the criteria
for such judgments? If we are to live by the social philosophy of
cultural pluralism, it is necessary to create some effective principles and means for resolving conflicts in values and goals.

These questions illustrate the fundamental problems. They
suggest a need to identify the aspects of the cultures of particular
groups that should be maintained in a society that claims to operate
on the basis of cultural pluralist theory. As it stands, the third
assumption seems to suggest that this is an impertinent question;
but surely we can conceive of aspects of particular group cultures
that might be considered unworthy of perpetuation. In this light,
then, social philosophers and social scientists must ask, as in the
case of "fluidity" noted earlier, what elements are included in the
term "culture" in cultural pluralism.

A fourth assumption and attendant claim of cultural pluralist
theory, as noted by Green, is that it is valuable to have many ways
of life in contact and in competition, that such competition leads to
a balance or equilibrium in the social order. Again, these convictions are also close to the core of the political theory of democratic
pluralism. However, the notion of equilibrium in democratic pluralist theory implies that coexistence is a question of power; specifically, a fair and equal distribution of power. Thus friendly contact and
open competition among and between groups can only take place when
equilibrium is present and when no culture or cultural group seeks
to destroy any of the others. How can this point be reached if reaching it demands intergroup contact on a fair and equal basis and if, in
turn, "a fair and equal basis" is by its very nature dependent upon
equilibrium?

A final major assumption, at least for the purposes of our
analysis, bears directly upon the processes and goals of socialization. This is the assumption that loyalty to a larger society, a
"nation," is a function of, and dependent upon, socially sanctioned
loyalties rooted in a multiplicity of diverse ethnic and cultural groups.
It is this assumption that leads cultural pluralist theorists to the notion that a society will be rich, unified, healthy, and nourished to a
fuller life to the extent that it is fashioned out of genuine human groupings. Kallen (1956, p. 47) points out in this regard that a nation can
be unified "only as a union on equal terms of sovereign and independent diversities alone whose agreement could make and keep it thus
one. . . . The oneness they turn to must . . . start from plurality
and can live only as the associative pattern which this plurality con-
sent to." In short, a healthy society must be based on a mosaic of
autonomous groupings reflecting the underlying differences of the
population.

Morton Grodzins, in The Loyal and the Disloyal (quoted in Wolff 1968, pp. 135-36), presented this assumption:

> Groups, large and small, play a crucial, indepen-
> dent role in the transference of allegiance to the
> nation. For one thing, they are the means through
> which citizens are brought to participate in civic
> affairs and national ceremony. . . . Individuals,
> in short, act for the nation in response to the
> smaller groups with which they identify them-
> selves. . . . Their loyalty to smaller groups in-
> sures their doing it. . . . So it is that loyalties
> to smaller groups supply the guts of national en-
> deavor even when that endeavor has no meaning to
> the individual concerned.

The cultural pluralist advocate seeks to further this argument by claiming that during a period in which the isolated and privatized individual must confront the immense processes of the state and massive organizations of our society, ethnic and cultural groupings can serve as important if not crucial mediating institutions (Tesconi 1975).

Within the context of these assumptions, cultural pluralist advocates claim that as an operational social philosophy cultural plural-ism would prevent the dangerous social and personal disorganization that follows when culturally diverse individuals are pressured to re-ject their primary group ties, including ties to ethnic groups. It is these assumptions, furthermore, that lead cultural pluralist theorists to assert that a fusion of primary ethnic group loyalty with loyalty to a larger cultural entity, such as society at large or the "nation," and the assumption of responsibilities therein can only come about when the primary group is able to enjoy all of the social freedoms that come to those who express basic loyalty to the larger society. In short, democracy for the whole and attachment to the whole comes only with democracy for, and socially encouraged attachment to, the constituent parts.

Several questions relative to the existing supportive evidence for these claims present themselves. Clearly some of the questions and research suggested in reference to the first four assumptions, particularly those addressed to the third, apply to validation of the fifth assumption. Beyond these we must ask if loyalty to the "nation" does indeed follow from group loyalty. If so, how does it come about? Alternatively, it could be that in a time of mass society the human need for a sense of community can be assumed to be so great that it gradually dissolves the bonds of some to the national territory and of others to the common culture that unites diverse groups into a nation state. In short, the bonds that tie groups together at a "national" level may dissolve in a mass society with the help of intensified primary group consciousness and membership need.

In order to draw the implications of cultural pluralist theory for socialization, it is necessary to recognize the importance of self-esteem and identity, particularly in relation to the primary group from the ethnic awareness perspective; the emphasis on communication skills, rather than mere attitudes; and the powerful idea of the generality of intercultural competence from domestic to international situations using the intercultural approach. The approach of cultural pluralism takes from those who would eliminate prejudice a stress upon active democratic values, especially tolerance for diverse opinions and universal awareness of the threats to the democratic process. The approach of cultural pluralism and novel situations, including interpersonal contacts, and the ability to balance group loyalties of very complex types.*

Our analysis up to this point has been intended to emphasize the great need to examine the political socialization research literature relative to the justifiability and validity of cultural pluralist theory and the assumptions that inhere in this theory. This requires that we address several related issues: the sense of political community; a cross-national analysis of cultural pluralism and of adolescents' intercultural tolerance; the role of schools, parents, and television in socialization; and the role of language learning in intercultural orientations.

SOCIALIZATION FOR A SENSE OF COMMUNITY

The role of a sense of community is accorded an important place in cultural pluralist theory. What is known about younger children and their sense of community is based less on primary group community than on a sense of membership in the national political community. R. W. Connell (1971) points out that the ideas

---

*In social psychology the literature on perceived similarity and attraction (Byrne 1971) during the past several years has documented that individuals in reacting to other persons whom they have only a brief opportunity to meet will be more attracted to persons who are perceived as similar to themselves than to persons who are perceived as different in attitude toward a range of issues. This lack of preference for diversity seems to be a basic human characteristic, expressed in a variety of settings.

of young children about potential external enemies posing a threat to their countries are related to primitive diffuse fears that the nice, safe places of their own lives will be disturbed. This causes an intensification of support for the total national system and the status quo. As a result of these basic fears, nationalism becomes strong and resistant to change.

It is probable that these processes are operating in the United States. Positive attachment to a national community is established early, largely with the aid of national symbols. Since the child's initial identification with his or her country is associated with little information about it, symbols provide important concrete links.

When children were asked to select from a set of pictures "the two best pictures to show what our country is" the Statue of Liberty and the American flag were the model choices at all grade levels, third through eighth.* When the children were given the same set of pictures but asked to choose the two that best depicted our government, the statue and flag were seldom chosen: the president, Congress, and voting were much more popular. Elementary school children seem to make a relatively clear distinction between their country and its government, and their sense of political community is established and reinforced by national symbols. Support for the political community is also fostered through consensual pressures from many agents of socialization. One of the reasons socialization to political community is so effective is that the child naturally tends to perceive the world in terms of undifferentiated global evaluations, such as that one's own country is good but that certain others, such as the communist countries, are bad. In factor analytic studies of the attitudes of children in elementary school, the factor of evaluation is much more closely tied to other factors than in the case of older children. (See Merelman 1971; Oppenheim and Torney 1974.) The linkage between good-bad judgments and other attitudes is that which is characteristic of younger children.

There also seems to be a unified wholeness to children's evaluation. In other words, the child's fantasy appears to be that everything must remain just as it is or the whole system is in danger of falling apart. In his family the child may believe that one evil thought on his part can cause great harm to a parent. In school the first- or second-grader realizes with some awe the possible consequences of any misbehavior. Young children tend to believe that all laws were made long ago and that laws should not be changed. In some children

---

*These data are reported in greater detail in Hess and Torney (1967). They are taken from a survey conducted in 1962 of 13,000 American elementary school children.

this attitude may be maintained into middle childhood and expressed in the belief that any conflict of opinion poses a basic threat to society. For a child who makes such assumptions, any form of political dissent is a failure by the system to hold total consensus and is therefore bad. Joseph Adelson and R. P. O'Neill (1966, pp. 295-306) concluded from a study of ten-year-olds that they have a "pervasive incapacity to speak from a coherent view of the political order." This means that they find it difficult to grasp exceptions to rules or alternative kinds of social organization. R. W. Connell (1971) claims that increased understanding and ability to comprehend the political order appears somewhat earlier than this period.

> When children realize that there are disagreements over courses of action, they are able to take sides, and they sometimes do this around the age of ten. When they realize the instrumental character of political action and the fact that different courses of action are supported in order to realize different goals, they have grasped the nature of debate over policy. . . .
>
> Issue conflict in this sense is commonly mastered about the age of 12, and about this age there is a great expansion in the child's awareness of issues and propensity to take sides on them. By middle adolescence conflict over policy is central to the whole idea of politics (pp. 49-50).

A lack of tolerance for legitimate protest or for the competition of group loyalties results from the belief that the system fails as a whole if threatened in any part. Support for dissent or diversity of opinion is not present even in some high school students. The elementary school undoubtedly bears some of the responsibility for failures of socialization toward this kind of perspective. Elementary school children require a great deal of help in understanding what a pluralistic system is, in learning to value its diversity, and in comprehending how a system operates and persists over time. Criticism and the resolution of conflicting ideas are part of democratic pluralism. An understanding that alteration or conflict among some social elements will not necessarily destroy the whole system, could at least be encouraged, if not actually taught, in schools and would be an important aspect of socialization for cultural pluralism.

The continuation into middle childhood of the view of a unified political system that cannot tolerate change or criticism without collapse may be traced to adults who believe that any criticism of the status quo allowed in a school text or by a teacher is likely to warp the values, especially nationalism, that the children have absorbed.

However, the research indicates that for younger children the strength of nationalistic feeling is already so strong that discussions of controversial national policy will not disturb it. For brighter children the denial of conflict and criticism may actually convey the latent message that something must be wrong with the system, since everyone is so eager to allow only safe facts to be exposed. One responsibility of the elementary school should be to teach children not only the maintenance functions of a democratic system but how the parts of that system operate through accommodation, change, and diverse group pressures.

It is also a problem to teach children the distinction between support for a national system and support for its principles. In a study of American children, C. Andrain (1971) found that two-thirds defined Americans as "people who have the beliefs of this country." There was an increase with age in the association of national pride with civic process ("having the most representative form of government in the world"); this was in contrast to what Andrain called "primordial values of blood and soil." One can only wish that Andrain had not viewed civic process and primary group ties as alternative modes of orientation but had determined instead how they complemented each other.

American elementary school children have a quite vague idea about democracy, though their ties to it are strong. Although the definition "a democracy is where the people rule" is accepted by children, the following statement by a sixth-grade boy illustrates that the complexities of the process involved are beyond his grasp.

> Oh, in the United States the people are supposed
> to rule the government--well--I--the people make
> up the government. They are not the officers; the
> government supposedly rules, but the people have
> command over the government. . . . Well, I'd
> say really the people rule, because the people have
> charge over the government; it's just an organiza-
> tion that the people are trying to keep order. So
> really the people would rule, but that is kind of
> complicated because the government rules over
> the people, and the people tell the government.
> It is kind of mixed up, but it's a good set-up, but
> yet there's no real good rule. Everybody has
> power; that is, everybody's power is limited.
> Well, it is like an organization; if the majority
> doesn't like this--why then--it doesn't go. If the
> majority does, it's all the majority--the majority
> rules--nobody rules--but the majority rules (Hess
> and Torney 1967, p. 76).

This understanding of democracy by a sixth grader parallels the description by Andrain (1971, p. 237) of the presentation of democracy in social studies textbooks:

> A populist interpretation of democracy is pre-
> sented. Democracy means government by or-
> dinary people, popular control of the government,
> equal opportunity for all people, and election of
> representatives. The pluralist versions of democ-
> racy, the view that democracy involves a conflict
> and competition among groups--are subordinated
> to the populist interpretation.

Children's attitudes rather closely correspond to those expressed in characteristic textbooks. For example, they do not generally recognize the role of pressure groups in influencing laws. The average person was ranked by sixth, seventh, and eighth graders as having an influence on the laws that was equivalent to or greater than that of newspapers and rich people. The roles of political parties tend to be similarly vague in the views of children.

Not only are children unlikely to state party preferences before the seventh or eighth grade, but among those who did state such preferences there was little relationship to other attitudes such as candidate preferences. Again it is clear that children do not value conflict and dissent as important to the growth of the democratic system. They believe that everyone should agree, including the Democrats and Republicans, and fail to perceive the dramatic issues, other than candidate choice, that divide the two parties. *

This lack of stress upon parties in children's political attitudes runs parallel to the material presented in their textbooks.

> The major point to be made about the treatment
> of the organization and operation of American
> political parties is that this material is generally
> very skimpy and strictly formal. Only two of the
> twenty-five guides discuss the role and importance
> of political parties. In fact, if one were to assume
> that children learn only what the texts and guides
> tell them, the children who use the . . . texts that
> contrast the Russian one party system with the
> American two party system . . . during their

---

*All of these generalizations about pressure groups and parti-
san attitudes are taken from Hess and Torney (1967).

> study of Russia would learn this fact of the U.S.
> Government for the first time. . . .
>
> None of the texts discuss major ideological
> disagreements in the nation since the Civil War.
> The only text that mentions political parties dis-
> cusses the ideological disagreements between
> Jefferson and Hamilton that give birth to them
> but attributes their present importance to pro-
> viding a check on the power of those who run
> the government (Goldstein 1972, pp. 20-21).

It appears from these data concerning young people's understanding of democracy, pressure groups, and political parties that
not only cultural pluralism but democratic pluralism is receiving
somewhat inadequate attention in the schools. This is important
because cultural pluralist theory can only be operationalized in a
society that takes democratic pluralism seriously.

THE IEA CROSS-NATIONAL SURVEY OF
POLITICAL SOCIALIZATION

The research reviewed in the previous section dealt with young
people's attachment to the national political community, their attitudes toward democratic pluralism, and some implications for socialization for cultural pluralism. It is unfortunate that there has
been so little research done on the socialization of attitudes toward
cultural pluralism. In this context it should not surprise us that
there is almost no comparative cross-national literature on the topic.
One exception, recently published, is the IEA Civic Education Project.*
The International Association for the Evaluation of Educational
Achievement in Stockholm has collected data on the outcomes of education in six subject areas. The Civic Education data include responses to cognitive tests and attitudinal questionnaires from more
than 30,000 students (ten-year-olds, fourteen-year-olds, and pre-
university students) in nine countries (Finland, West Germany, Ireland, Israel, Italy, the Netherlands, New Zealand, Sweden, and the
United States). The number of fourteen-year-olds tested in each
country is given in Table 4.1.

_____

*Data on the development of attitudinal measures may be found
in Oppenheim and Torney (1974). The findings are reported in
Torney, Oppenheim, and Farnen (1975).

TABLE 4.1

Sum of Respondent Weights by Country and Population
(fourteen-year-olds)

Country	Population
Federal Republic of Germany	1,317
Finland	2,401
Ireland	848
Israel	1,048
Italy	939
Netherlands	1,696
New Zealand	2,010
Sweden	n.t.
United States	3,207

n.t. = not tested.
Source: Judith V. Torney, A. N. Oppenheim, and R. F.
Farnen (1975), Civic Education in Ten Countries (New York: John
Wiley).

Typically the sampling plan required two-stage stratified
probability sampling. In the first stage schools were selected from
a nationally stratified frame, with a probability proportional to their
student-body size. In the second stage students were selected randomly from within the chosen schools, with probability inversely
proportionate to the size of their schools. Sampling errors were reduced by stratifying the schools by factors such as size of school,
type of school, and region (urban or nonurban) served by the school.
The data were collected in 1971 and included information from teachers about pedagogical practices as well as student and principal
questionnaires.

An important part of the IEA work was the comparison of the
students' home backgrounds with the schools in order to explain the
variations among students. With the replication of IEA surveys
across countries, it was hoped that certain characteristics of the
schools and teachers would emerge repeatedly as related to achievement. The regression analysis in civics was done as the regression
analyses had been done in other subject areas, separately on each
age group in each country. In each of these age-by-country groups,
separate regression analyses were run on each of three outcomes,

in civics cognition, anti-authoritarianism, and participation in political discussion. These two affective outcomes were selected, using
information from partial correlations, from approximately 20 possibilities.

In order to allow for as much comparability as possible across
each subject area, IEA has developed a standard plan for regression
analysis. The predictors are grouped in blocks. Block 1 consists
of family-background composite (occupation, education of both parents, number of books in the home), the size of family, and the age
and sex of the student. Block 2 is made up of the type of school and
the type of track or program in which the student is enrolled. Block
3, which is closely related, contains the specific attributes of the
schools and teachers that are expected to have some influence on the
outcomes. In civics this block includes such variables as the grade
in which social studies instruction is begun in school, the number of
hours the teachers prepare, the frequency of use of standardized
tests, the amount of teacher training in civics and related subjects,
the teachers' acceptance of in-class discussion of issues, the amount
of independence of opinion reported by the students as encouraged in
the classroom, and the stress on patriotic rituals in the classroom
as reported by the students. This third block is termed the learning
conditions block. Block 4 consists of additional questionnaire variables, including student aspirations, interests, and activities; this
is called the kindreds block. Block 5 is a measure of general word
knowledge, while block 6 is a measure of cognitive civics performance.

The results of the regression analysis anti-authoritarianism
will be presented in conjunction with our discussion of the relative
impact of different sources of socialization.

Some data that were related more specifically to intercultural
tolerance and perception of diversity and conflict were also obtained
from these students. As indicated in Table 4.2, when the responses
are averaged for the four items concerning racial and religious tolerance, the highest mean scores among fourteen-year-olds are
achieved by those in the Netherlands and the lowest by those in Israel.
American fourteen-year-olds rank sixth out of the eight countries in
intercultural tolerance. One possible explanation for the low support
for tolerance among the Israeli students is the existence of a state of
war; it is more difficult to understand the low position of students in
the United States.

A second piece of information gathered from these students
was their perception of the existence of conflicts that political institutions either exacerbate or are unable to solve. This conflict index
is derived from a measure of the perception of the realization of
various values by different institutions: how society works. High
scores indicate that the students believe that congresses, elections,

TABLE 4.2

Survey of Fourteen-Year-Olds: Intercultural Tolerance,
Perception of Political Conflict, and Cultural Pluralism

Country	Intercultural Tolerance[a]		Perception of Political Conflict[b]		Haug Index of Cultural Pluralism[c]
	Mean	Rank of Mean	Mean	Rank of Mean	
Federal Republic of Germany	4.5	4.0	6.6	1.0	2
Finland	4.5	4.0	5.3	4.0	1
Ireland	4.3	7.0	4.4	5.0	0
Israel	4.2	8.0	4.3	6.5	3
Italy	4.6	2.0	4.1	8.0	1
Netherlands	4.7	1.0	5.6	3.0	2
New Zealand	4.5	4.0	4.3	6.5	1
United States	4.4	6.0	5.7	2.0	3

[a]The higher the mean averaged response the higher the intercultural tolerance. Mean averaged score is based on the following four items:

1. Hotels are right in refusing to admit people of certain races or nationalities: (A) strongly agree (coded 1); (B) agree (coded 2); (C) no opinion (coded 3); (D) disagree (coded 4); (E) strongly disagree (coded 5).

2. People of certain races or religions should be kept out of important positions in our nation: A through E response as in item 1.

3. No matter what a man's color, religion, or nationality, if he is qualified for a job he should get it: (A) strongly agree (coded 5); (B) agree (coded 4); (C) no opinion (coded 3); (D) disagree (coded 2); (E) strongly disagree (coded 1). A through E response as in item 3.

[b]The higher the mean average response, the more the students perceive that elections, congresses, and political parties create disagreements rather than solving them.

[c]This index was assigned to each country on the basis of social indicators of linguistic, racial, and religious heterogeneity; existence of sectionalism and interest articulation by nonassociational group.

Source: IEA survey as reported in Judith V. Torney, A. N. Oppenheim, and R. F. Farnen (1975), Civic Education in Ten Nations (New York: John Wiley); index of cultural pluralism is by Marie Haug, "Social and Cultural Pluralism as a Concept in Social System Analysis," American Journal of Sociology, p. 299.

and political parties do more to create than to solve disagreements; they do not indicate anything about the perception of pressure-group conflict. Students in West Germany, the United States, and the Netherlands perceived relatively high institutional political conflict, while students in Italy, Israel, and New Zealand perceived more domestic institutional harmony.

A further piece of information that can be related to both of these scores is an index of the cultural pluralism of each country derived by Marie Haug (1967). She rated each of 114 societies on linguistic, racial, and religious heterogeneity, the existence of sectionalism, and interest articulation by nonassociational groups. The countries where IEA tested fourteen-year-olds are all below the mean of these societies on cultural pluralism, but they do vary from 0 (Ireland) to 3 (Israel and the United States).

If the country rankings on perception of institutional political conflict among fourteen-year-olds are compared with the cultural pluralism index, it is evident that the countries for which the greatest amount of political conflict is perceived are scored 2 or 3 on the societal index of pluralism, that is, the United States, the Netherlands, and the FRG. The only country with a pluralism index score of 3 in which students did not perceive domestic political conflict was Israel. There is other evidence from the IEA survey that Israeli adolescents perceive great consensus among all groups of citizens in the face of outside threat. We may conclude that cultural diversity within the range represented by these countries appears in most cases to be reflected in the perception of greater political diversity and conflict by fourteen-year-old students.

If the standing of these countries on the index of cultural pluralism is compared with intercultural tolerance on the part of adolescents, an interesting pattern emerges. The United States and Israel rank sixth and eighth (respectively) on intercultural tolerance; these are also the two most pluralistic societies on Haug's index. Ireland, ranked seventh on students' intercultural tolerance, was the least pluralistic on Haug's index. All of the countries that had medium rather than extremely high or low scores on the cultural pluralism index had students with relatively high intercultural tolerance, ranked first through fifth out of eight countries. These data suggest a fascinating curvilinear model to describe the socialization of cultural pluralism. A society that has very little diversity in language, race, or religion will find it difficult to socialize its students to basic tolerance because of their lack of experience with diverse peoples. The low intercultural tolerance exhibited by the Irish fourteen-year-olds could be explained in this way. The curvilinear model would also account for the lower intercultural tolerance that was found among those growing up in countries with great diversity

(Israel and the United States). Unless students in this very pluralistic situation are provided with extensive educational experience to equip them to cope with this diversity, they will be overwhelmed by it and low intercultural tolerance will result. Students being socialized under conditions of moderate cultural pluralism will have high intercultural tolerance, perhaps even where specific educational programs are not provided. Of course, this model must be held tentatively until more evidence is available.

Cultural pluralism as a societal fact represents a resource, for those countries that can develop effective socialization practices, but it also represents a problem, for those societies that choose to ignore the intercultural dimension of education. If this model is accurate, systems in which a moderately high level of cultural diversity exists can only succeed in creating interculturally tolerant students with considerable educational effort.

LINGUISTIC DIVERSITY, CULTURAL DIVERSITY, AND SOCIALIZATION

Although there is very little socialization research that deals specifically with linguistic communities, the linkage between linguistic diversity and cultural diversity is an important one. The factor that set many first generation immigrants in the United States apart from their children was inability to speak English.

The most striking discovery in a previous interview study was that children, when asked how other countries differed from their own country, placed great stress upon language. This factor was mentioned spontaneously by more than 70 percent of the children interviewed at all ages from six through twelve. For example, these responses (quoted in Torney and Morris 1972, p. 20) were given by an eight-year-old boy:

> I: How are people in other countries different
> from you?
> R: Most talk Mexican.
> I: Anything else?
> R: Most talk different from us.
> I: Do you think it would be better if everyone in
> the world were American?
> R: Yes, because I want them to talk normal, the
> way we do.

This example of ethnocentrism shows a child who feels that his group's way of speaking is the only normal one. He is unable to take the perspective of those who belong to different linguistic communities.

Part of the basic investigation of socialization to cultural pluralism must focus on the relationship of the experience of language to the acquisition of social attitudes. The development of verbal ability in children has been extensively linked to the development of cognitive processes. The speaking and hearing of language appears to have a discernible influence on socialization also. Perhaps children need exposure to a language other than that learned as mother tongue in order to be interculturally competent. M. A. Riestra and C. E. Johnson (1964) report evidence that the study of another language appears to increase positive attitudes toward those who speak that language and toward the culture it serves. The early years of education may be a particularly important time for beginning integrated cultural and linguistic studies.

Although the dimension of language has not been fully explored in its influence upon children's attitudes, some psychologists have studied the reactions of children to speakers of different languages. This phenomenon is of particular interest in countries in which bilingualism is a national problem, such as Canada, Israel, and the Philippines. The technique, called "matched guise," uses tape recordings of bilingual speakers, first in one language, then in another; they are rated by subjects who have been instructed to look for personality traits reflected in the voices. This assessment seems to elicit facets of attitudes and stereotypes that differ from those brought out by standard attitude-rating forms. Some authors suggest that language-rating allows a more private reaction than direct questioning about national characteristics. For example, speakers with Scottish accents were rated in one study as more generous than those with English accents, in spite of the common stereotype derived from other attitudinal measures that the Scots are tighter with money (Cheyne 1970, pp. 77-79).

The findings of Lambert and Klineberg (1967) are important to the study of attitude development and education in middle childhood. They found that a preference for English over French is characteristic of English Canadians of all ages but only of older French Canadians. Among French-speaking subjects there are important shifts occurring at about age 12 toward "feelings of ethno-linguistic inferiority." Language is clearly more than a mode of communication; in some senses it is also a mode of socialization. One appropriate beginning point for an educational effort to foster cultural pluralism would be the introduction of integrated linguistic and cultural studies in the elementary school.

THE AGENTS OF POLITICAL SOCIALIZATION:
SCHOOL AND FAMILY

A discussion of the agents of political socialization is one of the most enduring hallmarks of political-attitude studies in young people. Herbert Hyman, in his review of the literature in 1959, stressed the influence of the family upon political attitudes, in part because political party affiliation was assumed to be the most important type of attitude the child might acquire and because family sources were known to be crucial there. Hess and Torney (1967) spoke strongly about the influence of the school. In that study the average attitudes of eighth graders were very close to the average attitudes of their teachers. This did not allow for the exclusion of influence from other sources, however, since teachers and parents hold many attitudes in common.

There was little evidence for any strong influence of civics curricula in the 1974 study of high school seniors by M. K. Jennings and R. G. Niemi. Civics courses seemed redundant for many students. Overall their conclusion about the influence of the schools was as follows: "Taking any single dimension of school life, its reverberations on adolescent political orientations are customarily modest. When these dimensions are combined, however, they suggest that the school has significant though not overwhelming importance." Lee Ehman (1969) reported that the atmosphere in the classroom was more influential than the actual curriculum content in influencing political attitudes.

The attribution of responsibility to different socialization agents has a number of ramifications for policy making. Should schools take on more responsibility for improving social or political education programs, or is the home influence so strong that the schools would be ineffective even if they were to make a concerted effort? The IEA Civic Education survey (Torney, Oppenheim, and Farnen 1975) can make a unique contribution to the debate, since it provides extensive information about school practices obtained from teachers, a classification of schools and programs, a measure of general verbal ability, and also student self-reports of attitudes.

Although home background, sex, and age are important predictors of civics knowledge and democratic values support, they do not in any sense overdetermine attitudes. Schools with students from less privileged home backgrounds do not have insurmountable handicaps in fostering democratic values. School variables, both those of general quality or academic orientation and those of current learning conditions in the form of practices reported by teachers, play a considerable role. However, it is clear that these practices and learning conditions are part of a large and interdependent system. The alteration of any single school variable, as in teaching more about a particular subject or in stressing memorization less, is unlikely to have a discernible impact upon the acquisition of democratic values unless this alteration is supported by other changes in the climate and objectives of instruction.

A somewhat unexpected IEA finding was that although the determinants of support of democratic values and cognitive achievement in civics were relatively similar, they were quite different from the determinants of participation in political discussion. Out-of-school characteristics were especially important in explaining the variance in active civic interest, according to these data. Also, the knowledgeable student in these countries was not necessarily the most active participant in discussion. Activity and knowledge do not show a strong correlation, and they are predicted by different factors. The schools may encourage political participation and predispose an individual to take an active rather than a passive role, but real and sustained participation probably depends on a complex set of out-of-school factors and the support systems provided for individuals as young adults.

The IEA study indicates that there is considerable similarity in the goals of civic education of these countries and in some of their related practices. There are, however, variations in the relative impact of some socialization agents. The impact of home background and socioeconomic status on democratic values tends to be relatively high in the United States, for example. Without a data base in more than one country, it is unwise to generalize about the intended or unintended effects of socialization.

The data on socialization agents and the studies reported here concern matters only indirectly related to socialization for cultural pluralism. However, two conclusions deserve attention. First, the students' attitudes are not so fixed by the time of school entry that educational experience can have no impact. Second, socialization for cultural pluralism must involve a complex of school, school-related, and community support systems if it is to be successful.

RESEARCH ON THE INFLUENCE OF
TELEVISION ON CHILDREN

Television, especially commercial television, is a source to which socialization research has paid insufficient attention. Children in the period of preadolescence and early adolescence are at a critical phase for understanding the political and social world. This is especially true because of the malleability of their world view. This same age period is also important from the point of view of

children's use of television. Dorothy Flapan (1968) investigated the
interpretation girls placed upon a simple story present in a movie,
done as it might be on television. By the age of nine these children
were able to report communication fairly accurately and to project
feelings and thoughts onto adults whose actions they had observed.

M. L. DeFleur and L. DeFleur (1968, pp. 77-89) reported that
children who frequently watched television were better informed
about the occupations portrayed on the programs than were less frequent watchers. There were no differences in information about occupations not frequently depicted.

These studies, as well as two major and more general studies
of television watching done in England and the United States, confirm
the importance of unintended messages and of incidental learning
from television.

Most studies report that public affairs programming does not
rate high in children's interest compared with situation comedy,
crime, and sports, though its ranking improved at the high school
level. (See Schramm, Lyle, and Parker 1961.) However, studies
of political attitude development that ask children to report the
sources of most importance in forming their attitudes find that the
media rank high.

Trond Alvik (1968), in the Norwegian study discussed earlier,
found that television was the source cited most often by children,
particularly in their information about war. When war was seen in
a reciprocal framework, that is, from the point of view of both sides,
this was usually on a level and in a context that suggested that parents
or some other adult had helped the child to decipher the information
presented by the media. Wallace E. Lambert and Otto Klineberg
(1967), in their study of the attitudes of children toward foreign
people, found that the mass media, particularly television and the
movies, were the most frequently reported sources of information
about foreign people for children in developed nations, that is, in the
United States, Canada, West Germany, and Japan. In the less developed nations in their sample, which were Bantu, Brazil, Israel,
Lebanon, and Turkey, parents and friends were of greater importance.

Herbert Hirsch (1971) gave a questionnaire to all students in
the fifth through twelfth grades in Knox County, Kentucky, a poverty-
level area in Appalachia. The students were asked the following
four-part question: "Where do you get most of your information
about what's going on in (a) your home town, (b) your home state,
(c) the United States, (d) the world?" The group ranked television
first on all questions; second was radio; third were newspapers;
fourth was school. At lower ranks were parents and friends. This
ranking pattern held for all the age levels. The media were ranked

especially high as sources for national and international news.
Hirsch suggests that the impact of television is, to use his term,
more latent than manifest. He defines manifest communication as
material that presents special political views. He refers to the presentation of world events and the portrayal of popular culture and
other elements that involve incidental or observational learning as
latent communication. His evidence for this distinction is primarily
speculative, however.

A strong piece of evidence regarding media impact on children's
attitudes is offered by Connell (1971), who interviewed 92 Australian
children. He did not ask the children to summarize and rank their
general experience with sources of information, as did most of the
studies cited above; rather, for each political opinion or set of
opinions the child expressed in response to an interview question,
he asked why the child believed that or where the opinion came from.
His summary table, derived from many responses, showed that television was the most frequently cited source of information on the
Prime Minister of Australia, the President of the United States, the
Leader of the Opposition, and Vietnam. It was cited less often than
school and family sources as providing information about the Queen.
Many of the ideas about political figures commonly expressed by his
group could be traced to television.

It was once assumed that media communications influenced
leaders of opinion, who in turn influenced other; the current research
suggests that children get information from the media and then seek
interpretation of this information from an adult. This parallels
Alvik's description of adults as decipherers of information for young
people.

In addition to the direct media influence, unintended as well as
intended messages are part of television programs. Pictures, music,
and voice quality combine to communicate in very powerful ways and
as much by implication as by direct statement. For example, a
farmyard scene shown while news about farm legislation is discussed
will surely evoke a different reaction than pictures of angry farmers
meeting to demand higher prices. In addition to the potential double
effect of its messages, there is often a great contrast in the communications children receive from television from those that they get at
school. Let us examine several topics in social studies in which educational objectives and the media presentations seem particularly
congruent.

Sense of History

Most educators would agree that giving children some sense of
history, some sense of the continuity of past, present, and future

events, is important for their understanding of political events and the interactions of groups. When history is studied in schools the aim is to understand the underlying causes of events. Too often, however, the relationships of past events to the current scene is not carefully explored, and the student is seldom given help in understanding that the actions of contemporary groups may reflect historical circumstances. History as taught in school too often exists only in the past; television news broadcasts, in contrast, move abruptly from one contemporary news scene or story to another and fail to develop any themes of causality or continuity. The news seldom has a past or future dimension. Although their faults are different, school courses and television broadcasts both fail to help the student to understand present events in terms of their historical antecedents or to project current social trends into the future.

The Existence of Conflict and Means of Nonviolent Resolution

A second aim of most educators is to teach children that issues exist over which individuals and groups disagree, but that the means for resolving these conflicts, such as negotiation, are to be preferred and that conflict makes a valuable contribution to democracy. Unintended communication through the selection of topics, both in school materials and in television programming, contributes to the students' misunderstanding of conflict. In 1971 a survey was made by Robert D. Hess (1972) of randomly sampled paragraphs from social studies texts written for nine- and ten-year-olds in schools in the United States. Less than 20 percent of these paragraphs mentioned these four major social problems: race and ethnic relations, distribution of income, political negotiations and processes, and ecological problems.

> Less than one percent of the seventeen thousand paragraphs gave the reader the impression that race and ethnic relations . . . involve conflict and stress. Less than one percent discussed distribution of income in any way that suggested economic inequality or exploitation. The guides generally totally avoid dealing with social class and show no awareness that . . . some Americans are poor (or even that people have different amounts of wealth) (Hess 1972, p. 20).

The fact that explicit statements about conflicts or problems are extremely rare in these texts permits the message to come through that conflicts between individuals and groups do not exist. If we were to believe these texts we would think that racial injustice and economic inequality might once have been problems but now have been solved.

The selectivity that has operated, at least in the United States, in deciding what is newsworthy enough to be shown on television communicates a message to children that is almost diametrically opposed to that communicated by the school texts. The kinds of international or foreign events that an American child is most likely to see on television news programs are those concerning war or other episodes of violence. The community groups pictured are usually involved in protesting government policy. The representation of a benign society that is communicated to students by textbooks is contradicted constantly by the news that appears on television and in other media of communication.

An International or Intercultural World View

In the case of a third objective, which is to give children a picture of the world as composed of many cultures and a picture of the interdependence of the people in it, the school and the television both seem to have laudable aims that are not always effectively communicated. In addition to the news programs, which we have already discussed in terms of their emphasis on international violence, films about travel are probably the most frequent television exposure that young people have to other countries and the cultures of other peoples.

In travel programs a common way of mobilizing viewer interest is by showing exotic and unusual aspects of other cultures. This may result in comments such as those recently obtained from interviews with young children, who when asked how people in other countries were different from themselves mentioned such exotica as "people in Africa eat ants" and "in Japan they bind the children's feet." A recent travel film shown on local television also provided several examples of unintentional condescension. The film began with several scenes of the narrator in a Norwegian bed with his feet sticking out from under what was described as a typical Scandinavian comforter, "always too long or too short, too hot or too cold." Presumably this was designed to amuse the viewer; in fact the implication was that Scandinavians do not know how to make comfortable bedding. The narrator went on to compliment the Norwegians for "being on our side in the war" and to describe Norwegian food with the added comment "of course, I like shrimp better the way we fix it in the good old U.S.A." These assumptions about another country, its furnishings, and its foods do not contribute to a view of the world in which human diversity in custom and opinion is valued. However,

there have been a number of excellent programs dealing with the immigrant experience and intercultural relations within the past two
years.

To summarize, gaps exist between the history of the past as
it is taught in school and the fragmentary views of the present that
appear on television, between the formal election process as it is
taught in civic education and the community protests presented on
the media; between conflict-free social studies texts and current affairs broadcasting, in which violence is an everyday matter and conflicting attitudes are conveyed in powerful terms. The ability of a
student to resolve these conflicting points of view depends in large
part upon his or her level of cognitive development.

Children will interpret material from the media, as well as
from other sources, in a way appropriate to their cognitive developmental level and previously acquired information. When material
is to be designed particularly for use with children, it should be presented in such a way that the information can either be assimilated
to existing cognitive schemes or assimilated with only a slight accommodation. Individualizing the message to correspond to the
child's readiness is possible in some school settings, but this is
more difficult with mass media, the programs of which are designed
to appeal to a broad segment of the population and not particularly to
be understood by one who looks at the world through the cognitive
prism of an eight-year-old. This is particularly true of current
events programs, which are usually designed for adult audiences,
which it is assumed operate at an adult cognitive level.

It is also important to realize that contradiction between what
the child sees in the media and what his or her classroom experience
has been may in fact be helpful. Piaget's theory states that children
may move forward in their cognitive development when there is contradiction between the material gained from one source of perception
and that gained from another source. The existence of mismatch
brings about the active cognitive process of accommodation. The
child may accommodate his internal cognitive structure to cope more
effectively with the world, without aid from teachers or parents.
However, the schools could help by dealing explicitly with contradictions between what the student can read in a textbook about ethnic
minorities and what is in the newspaper about intergroup conflict,
what is heard in the classroom and what is seen on television.

Even this relatively small amount of research dealing with the
communicative media as agents for socialization has important implications for the school as an agent of socialization in general and
as an agent for cultural pluralism in particular. This research suggests that television is an important and potent source of information.
However, children have little opportunity for resolving the contending

and sometimes conflicting information gleaned from television and other agents of socialization. This is unfortunate, because an opportunity is missed for the maintenance of diversity in general and socialization for cultural pluralism in particular. If, as political socialization research indicates, an attachment to cultural pluralist ideals is dependent upon an ability to accommodate to different values or life styles, educating youngsters in ways that help them decipher the information received from the media and resolve contending learnings is especially important.

CONCLUSION

Most of the discussion in this chapter has dealt with political socialization research, as contrasted with what might be called research on socialization for cultural pluralism. The reason for this is clear. The research that is specifically concerned with attitudes toward cultural pluralism, particularly in preadults, is scanty. This is especially true in regard to the assumptions of cultural pluralist theory detailed earlier. We have attempted, however, to summarize the political socialization research, which provides indirect evidence relative to these assumptions. However, if cultural pluralism is to serve as a descriptive and explanatory ideal rather than as a proselytizing one, it must be made more specific. What this means, among other things, is that numerous in-depth studies that deal with the assumptions of cultural pluralist theory are needed.

Cultural pluralism as a social fact can be a resource for a society, and it appears to be particularly essential to those societies that seek to achieve democratic pluralism. It appears, however, that the utilization of cultural pluralism as a positive resource is dependent upon certain socializing activities carried on by the school, in concert with other institutional sectors of society. Appropriate and valid socializing activities in this regard, however, are dependent upon research findings that are not yet available. Such findings must be forthcoming, or it is likely that cultural pluralism will become increasingly dysfunctional for American society.

REFERENCES

Adelson, Joseph, and R. P. O'Neill. 1966. "Growth of Political Ideas in Adolescence: The Sense of Community." Journal of Personality and Social Psychology 4: 295-306.

Alvik, Trond. 1968. "The Development of Views on Conflict, War, and Peace among School Children." Journal of Peace Research 5: 171-95.

Anderson, Lee F., Richard Remy, and Richard Snyder. n.d. "Improving Political Education in Elementary Schools: Challenges and Opportunities." Position paper of American Political Science Association Task Force on Elementary Education.

Andrain, Charles. 1971. Children and Civic Awareness. Columbus, Ohio: Charles Merrill.

Byrne, Donn. 1971. The Attraction Paradigm. New York: Academic Press.

Carpenter, John A., and Judith V. Torney. 1973-74. "Beyond the Melting Pot to Cultural Pluralism." In Children and Intercultural Education, Annual Bulletin of the Association for Childhood Education International, p. 20.

Cheyne, William M. 1970. "Stereotyped Reactions to Speakers with Scottish and English Regional Accents." British Journal of Social and Clinical Psychology 9: 77-79.

Connell, R. W. 1971. The Child's Construction of Politics. Melbourne, Australia: Melbourne University Press.

DeFleur, M. L., and L. DeFleur. 1968. "The Relative Contribution of Television as a Learning Source for Children's Occupational Knowledge." American Sociological Review.

Ehman, Lee. 1969. "An Analysis of Selected Educational Variables with the Political Socialization of High School Students." American Educational Research Journal 6: 559-80.

Ehrlich, H. J. 1973. The Social Psychology of Prejudice. New York: John Wiley.

Flapan, Dorothy. 1968. Children's Understanding of Social Interaction. New York: Teachers College Press.

Goldstein, R. J. 1972. "The Elementary School Curriculum and Political Socialization." In Political Youth, Traditional Schools, ed. B. Massialas, pp. 14-33. Englewood Cliffs, N.J.: Prentice-Hall.

Gordon, Milton. 1961. "Assimilation in America: Theory and Reality." Daedalus 90, no. 2 (Spring).

Green, Thomas. 1966. "Education and Pluralism: Ideal and Reality." Twenty-sixth Annual J. Richard Street Lecture, Syracuse University, School of Education.

Haug, Marie. 1967. "Social and Cultural Pluralism as a Concept in Social System Analysis." American Journal of Sociology 73, pp. 294-304 (November).

Hess, Robert D. 1972. "The System Maintenance Function of Social Development in the Schools." In Proceedings of 1971 Invitational Conference. Princeton, N.J.: Educational Testing Service.

_____, and Judith V. Torney. 1967. The Development of Political Attitudes in Children. Chicago: Aldine Publishing Co.

Hirsch, Herbert. 1971. Poverty and Politicization. New York: Free Press.

Hyman, Herbert. 1959. Political Socialization. Glencoe, Ill.: Free Press.

Jennings, M. K., and R. G. Niemi. 1974. The Political Character of Adolescence. Princeton, N.J.: Princeton University Press.

Kallen, Horace. 1956. Cultural Pluralism and the American Idea. Philadelphia: University of Pennsylvania Press.

Lambert, Wallace, and Otto Klineberg. 1967. Children's Views of Foreign People. New York: Appleton-Century-Crofts.

Levine, Robert A. 1973. Culture, Behavior, and Personality. Chicago: Aldine Publishing Co.

_____, and Donald T. Campbell. 1972. Ethnocentrism: Theories of Conflict, Ethnic Attitudes and Group Behavior. New York: John Wiley.

Merelman, Richard. 1971. Political Socialization and Educational Climates. New York: Holt.

Merton, Robert K., and Alice Kitt Rossi. 1950. "Reference Group
    Theory and Social Mobility." In Continuities in Sociological
    Research, ed. R. K. Merton and P. L. Lazarsfeld. New York:
    Free Press.

Oppenheim, A. N., and Judith V. Torney. 1974. The Measurement
    of Children's Civic Attitudes in Different Countries. New York:
    John Wiley.

Political Knowledge and Attitudes, 1971-1972. 1973. National
    Assessment of Educational Progress report number 03-55-01.
    Washington, D.C.: U.S. Government Printing Office.

Riestra, M. A., and C. E. Johnson. 1964. "Changes in Attitudes
    of Elementary School Pupils toward Foreign Speaking Peoples
    Resulting from the Study of Foreign Language." Journal of
    Experimental Education 32: 65-73.

Schramm, W. L., J. Lyle, and E. B. Parker. 1961. Television
    in the Lives of Our Children. Stanford, Calif.: Stanford Uni-
    versity Press.

Tesconi, Charles A., Jr. 1974. "Schooling and the Privatization
    of Experience." McGill Journal of Education 9, no. 2 (Fall).

_____. 1975. Schooling in America: A Social Philosophical Per-
    spective. Boston: Houghton Mifflin.

Torney, Judith V., and Donald A. Morris. 1972. Global Dimen-
    sions of U.S. Education: The Elementary School. New York:
    International Studies Association.

_____, A. N. Oppenheim, and R. F. Farnen. 1975. Civic Educa-
    tion in Ten Countries. New York: John Wiley.

Wolff, Robert Paul. 1968. The Poverty of Liberalism. Boston:
    Beacon Press.

5

RESPECT FOR PERSONS AND ETHNIC PREJUDICE IN CHILDHOOD: A COGNITIVE-DEVELOPMENTAL DESCRIPTION

Florence B. H. Davidson

Historically it has been difficult to gather even the simplest information on the racial and ethnic attitudes of school children. Ethnic prejudice is said to be a well-researched area of social psychology, but nevertheless the data on school-aged children are sparse and suspect. Theories of childhood prejudice have been built upon data that has been collected in a manner too unsubtle or circumscribed for the many variables that contribute. The 1974 nationwide survey by the U.S. Office of Education had to be canceled in midstream because its too-direct questions had aroused opposition from schools and parents; nor has any research been undertaken that emulates the sociological scope of the studies by J. Porter (1971) and M. E. Goodman (1954) on preschoolers.

Two of the studies reported here had collection of descriptive data on the ethnic attitudes of seven- to thirteen-year-olds as their first goal. A cross-sectional study probed the attitudes and underlying values of 146 children in three grades in city and suburban schools; a similar longitudinal study also included background information on 22 suburban fifth grade classmates observed over a three-year period. As their second goal, the studies sought understanding of the often-neglected role of cognition in prejudice and/or in respect for other people.

The second goal comes from a more difficult problem in the study of prejudice, which is that exclusive preoccupation with eliciting the phenotypic negativity or superficial prejudices to be examined can produce research conclusions that lack human context. Such conclusions do not seem to relate to children as they are seen happily playing or seeking mastery of the environment outside the laboratory. For example, in some research by Harris, Gough, and Martin (1950), the "less tolerant group" of eight- to twelve-year-olds was said to "have a cynical, distrustful opinion of others [and be] . . . fearful of being exploited or duped." Their conclusion, that "one must attend to the total personality as well as to specific attitudes," implies that the children need therapy.

In the 1940s and 1950s, when many of the important studies were carried out, it was held that prejudice is a personality trait and that early childhood defines personality. Knowledge about further child development was lacking. The influence of the view that prejudice is an unconscious trait reduceable only by therapy (Sanford 1956) is still strong. M. E. Goodman in 1964 referred to a study by B. Kutner (1958) as her basis for assuming that "true prejudice begins as early as seven years of age." Kutner's "clearly prejudiced" group had simply acquiesced to ethnic stereotypes provided by their teacher, but he concluded after cognitive testing that "prejudice permeates all aspects of behavior and is an integral part of personality." J. Porter in 1971 repeated G. Allport's (1954) speculation that prejudiced children go through a phase of undifferentiated negativity in grade school. One of Porter's sources was a study by Trager, Radke, and Davis (1949) that concluded that the prejudices of seven-year-olds are "partly crystallized." They observed that children of seven are able to offer a philosophical rationale; however, the nature of the rationale and its fixity were not actually investigated, nor were older children studied. Hence it must now be asked whether children have fixed prejudices or beliefs that are "crystallized" in the same sense as those of adults.

A second theory, that prejudice is almost entirely imitative of its cultural context, appeals to common sense but is also discouraging to educators. Goodman (1964) wrote that, "this view predominates in the work of social psychologists, as well as sociologists and anthropologists who have seriously studied the matter." School personnel typically interpret this social learning view, as well as the psychoanalytic stress on early childhood, to mean that parents hold most of the chips. A less static paradigm of prejudice that includes cognitive-social development and the child's increasing ability to reason and respect others should encourage educational efforts.

HYPOTHESES

The work of Lawrence Kohlberg (1963) describing the development of distinct moral stages during childhood makes it feasible to explore children's ability to form judgments about "human nature" or people in general, judgments that would predispose the children toward respect or lack of respect for others. In Kohlberg's usage, moral means just; thus the child's concept of justice should depend upon the cognitive ability to estimate what others deserve or what kind of respect to give them. Respect for persons is the basis of morality; therefore it is postulated in the present research that stages of moral development can be described as coterminous with stages of respect for persons.

It is assumed in this chapter, as in Kohlberg's research, that moral values constitute a finite or limited set of variables pertaining to universal issues such as affection, punishment, and contracts; that these variables or values are organized in each mind with some internal logic; and that their usage, organization, and meanings during childhood are restricted by limitations in experience and cognitive development. Kohlberg's theory of the development of moral judgment parallels J. Piaget's theory of general cognitive development (1926). As the child matures, his or her modes of reasoning and sets of value assumptions can become successively more adequate. If the child is bothered by inconsistencies that appear between social thinking and the experience gained while interacting with people and trying to solve unfair situations, the child will be inclined to reorganize his or her thinking at a higher stage to accommodate new insights.

In cognitive-developmental psychology, a stage theory requires invariance of the sequence, internal organization of each stage, qualitative differences among stages, and universality in their applicability (Kessen, 1970), but it does not require that all children progress at a similar rate or reach all of the stages. Such rigor of definition began with the work of Piaget. Although he turned away from studying social development to devote himself to the stages of physical cognition, Piaget identified many parallels between impersonal and social reasoning. In the longitudinal studies by Kohlberg, the structures of social thought, including the rules by which thinking is organized, appear to evolve in the same way as awareness of mathematical operations evolves in the studies by Piaget.

Researchers such as M. Feffer and V. Gourevitch (1960), Swinson (1966), Cowan (1969), and Colby (1972) have compared perspective-taking in the physical and social realms. R. Selman (1973) found social role-taking stages necessary but not sufficient for correspondingly higher stages of moral judgment. To begin to be moral, the child must coordinate the perspectives of two persons, and later he or she must take an objective view beyond those of all the interested parties. At the age of seven the cognitive bases for these processes have not yet appeared. Thus respect for other persons and groups must of necessity be inadequately defined by a child of seven.

Selman (1973) states that role-taking as a series of logical structures involves a predicational logic, one predicated on the nature of persons. This is different from the propositional logic of Piagetian stages, which is independent of domain. The present research constitutes a preliminary investigation of children's stage-specific assumptions about the nature of persons. Such assumptions underlie stage structure and presumably affect both the desire to take the role of another in a moral dilemma and the final moral judgments. Attitudes toward ethnic groups may in part depend upon the underlying structure and content of the assumptions about people that make up each stage. Therefore a correlation between ethnic attitudes and moral stages was postulated for this research. The higher the stage, the more positive should be the attitudes toward other races and ethnic groups.

Four other hypotheses and topics of exploration follow upon this major one.

1. If the rationale for prejudices and the quantity of their expression typically changes with moral stages, they cannot be said to be fixed during childhood.

2. Positive relationships will exist in childhood between being analytic, being tolerant, and being at a higher moral stage.

3. More prejudice will be found among city children than among those in the suburbs, and the nature or quality of this prejudice will be different.

4. Prejudice will be associated with an absence of moral-stage progress in the well-studied children of the longitudinal group. The causes of this lack of progress can be preliminarily investigated.

METHOD

Subjects

In 1970-73, 18 white and four black classmates were studied intensively from ages 10 to 13 to discover personality, IQ, family, and school factors in moral judgment and prejudice that might be overlooked in the larger cross-sectional study carried out simultaneously. These students attended a suburban school that has a 3 percent black enrollment. The black children are bused from Boston by a voluntary program called Metco. In 1975, at age 15, they are being interviewed further for a clinical report that will cover the relevant background variables. For the present report they provided indications during testing of qualitatively different kinds of prejudice that could be checked against behavior.

The cross-sectional study involved testing for prejudice and
for moral maturity, 53 additional children from the same suburb and
48 children from a medium-sized industrial city. All of these children were aged 7 to 13 and were in three grades of school, second,
fourth, and seventh. There were 27 boys and 26 girls from the
suburb and 22 boys and 26 girls from the city. The classrooms providing children were chosen by school principals on the basis of the
presumed flexibility or willingness of their teachers, but about two-
thirds of the city children were not located through the 13 different
schools they attended. The city testing was begun with randomly
available groups at a large (600 children) inner-city day camp during
the summer. The numbers of subjects were made to correspond to
the numbers tested in the suburbs by locating in two schools, 15
children whose parents agreed to allow testing. Parental permission
was required by the city schools but not by the suburban schools.
The day-camp sample may have been overweighted with poor children,
since the camp is low-cost; however, the reputation of this camp also
attracts the lower middle class. The sample of 15 additional children was approximately 50 percent upper middle class.

The total sample of 176 was completed by 53 sixth grade boys
from a wealthy and nonintegrated suburb. Their moral maturity had
been tested for another project, which had tapped all 53 boys in their
grade. In the present study they served only as a confirmatory sample, to test the relation between prejudice and moral stage.

In the total group 20 children were black, 12 were Jewish, and
5 were Oriental. Of the city subjects, 13 percent were on welfare.
While 35 percent of suburban parents were professionals, slightly
over half of both city and suburban parents were lower middle class,
as classified by father's occupation. The city and suburban schools
in this instance had the same per-pupil expenditures, and the two
schools providing one-third of the city children had outstanding
physical plants. Teacher salaries and backgrounds were comparable;
however, the teachers' expectations for the children and the actual
student populations were very different in the two places, casting
doubt upon the application of traditional social class designations to
school children. Most children in the suburbs seek to please each
other in middle-class ways. City children show their feelings more
directly and do less explaining. The different effects of peers upon
each other in the two places seems to contribute more to behavior
than does father's occupational status.

Instruments

All the children, in groups of four, played a specially devised
dice game called "Comments" upon a modified Parcheesi board. A

"man" representing a pictured American racial or ethnic group attempts to reach "home," overcoming social obstacles not designated,
and thereby becomes a "full American." The groups pictures are
oriental, black, Irish, Italian, Jewish, Indian, Puerto Rican, and
Mexican. Some game spaces were painted various colors to signify
that a free comment about one or another of the ethnic groups would
be required should the dice throw so fall. Since the investigator had
been called a "social studies consultant," her work was explained as
"recording how children react to a possible new curriculum." Parents were told that only good information on children's attitudes
could lead to good curriculum.

The children showed pleasure and frankness in play, with their
self-consciousness about revealing prejudices decreasing as the
game absorbed their attention. This spontaneity, shown in pretesting, led to an important assumption, that children who evidence
tolerance, openness, or moral progress are not merely hiding
negativity that would appear in the absence of the investigator. Behavioral observations did not contradict this assumption, and there
was an impressive consistency of attitude shown in the game and in
the private interviews.

An interview schedule for a subsequent occasion was constructed
from the comments collected in pretesting at two age levels. Attention was given to making the interviews parallel for each age and to
choosing comments that were representative of all the more provocative remarks offered at that age, both positive and negative. Each
remark was introduced with: "One of your classmates while playing
the game said. . . . What do you think?" Specific information
about recent or frequent fights with schoolmates was also sought.

During a second private interview, each child was presented
with Dilemmas III, IV, and X from the Kohlberg Measure of Moral
Maturity. Additional data collected on the longitudinal subjects included Iowa Achievement Scores; Stanford Binet IQ's; protocols on
the "Tasks of Emotional Development," a projective picture test by
Cohen and Weil; and results of parent, teacher, and child interviews
on family attitudes. Parental permission for this study of the longitudinal group was obtained.

Coding

The responses to the game and to the probing interview were
coded as one. The total comments of each child were numbered and
tabulated on a blind sheet, then analyzed by two raters to produce
percentages of: ethnically negative, positive, and neutral remarks;
open and tolerant remarks not oriented to rigid norms and not

necessarily pertaining to ethnicity; and remarks showing directional thinking, either analytic or informational as opposed to stereotypic, anecdotal, or pronouncing (or "annunciatory," in Piaget's term).

The ethnically negative remarks seemed to be of three different types. Those that were the most openly hostile were almost always from children with an admitted tendency to fight, while remarks that seemed teasing were paired with the tendency to be stereotypic or "annunciatory." Indirect or aversive, and often patronizing, prejudices were also noted.

The Kohlberg Measure was scored according to the issue method described in the scoring manual (unpublished), by two independent raters trained by Kohlberg. In this method, either a pure or a major-plus-minor moral stage score is assigned to each issue appearing in each dilemma, to each issue appearing across dilemmas, and then to each dilemma as a whole. This permits checking one estimate of the child's intended meanings against another, allowing the basic assumptions to be better understood. For every subject a scoring grid with 24 cells (8 issues and 3 dilemmas) is obtained. A weight of 3 is assigned to each score at a single stage; 2 to each major score that is part of a mixed score; and 1 to each minor score that is part of a mixed score. The moral maturity score is the sum of the weighted percentages of usage of each stage. Weighting consists of multiplying each percentage obtained from the cells of the scoring grid by the number of the stage used.

The rater agreement on negativity and tolerance was .78; on directional thinking .84; and on stage of moral maturity .82.

RESULTS

There are five major findings from the two studies. First, moral stages were inversely related to the numbers of ethnically prejudiced remarks. The correlations between stages and percentages ranged from -.52 to -.73 for six groups, significant at the .001 level. Many more negative remarks were offered by the low-stage children at all ages. IQ did not make a significant difference in the correlations found on the longitudinal group, which were -.73 at age 10 and -.71 three years later. (See Table 5.1.) The same correlations with IQ partialled out were -.64 and -.63 (p = < .001). This indicates that prejudice is not fixed in childhood, since rationales change.

The second finding covers the lesser cognitive correlations that were investigated. As Table 5.1 shows, a significant positive relationship existed between openness or toleration and a higher moral stage.

TABLE 5.1

Correlations of Moral Stage and IQ with Other Variables
(longitudinal group; N = 22)

	Moral Stage in Fifth Grade	Moral Stage in Seventh Grade	Stanford Binet IQ
Moral stage			
Fifth	1.00	.79[a]	.60[a]
Seventh	.79[a]	1.00	.55[b]
Percent of ethnic negatives			
Fifth	-.73[a]	-.71[a]	-.46[b]
Seventh	-.64[a]	-.71[a]	-.41[b]
School achievement			
Fifth	.61[a]	.36[b]	.70[a]
Percent of directed thinking			
Fifth	.25	.39	.50[b]
Seventh	.44	.45	.49[b]
Percent of tolerant statements			
Fifth	.51[b]	.71[a]	.40[b]
Seventh	.15	.51[b]	.15

[a] $p = < .001$.
[b] $p = < .01$.
Source: A study conducted by the author, as described in the text.

Tolerant attitudes, measured independently of ethnic attitudes but including some of them, also predicted moral-stage change in the longitudinal group. In the top half of the group the relationships between tolerance and moral-stage levels are much more regular than in the lower half, where inconsistent social and personal values as well as personality problems might cause development to be uneven. The Fischer's Exact Test was performed on the top half of the group in tolerance. The result, $P = .008$; $p = < .01$, indicates that predictions can be made from the percentage of tolerance shown in grade five to the amount of change in moral stage during preadolescence (by grade seven). The correlation between tolerance and change for all the longitudinal subjects was .43 (p = < .02). This shows the importance of open attitudes at the outset of adolescence to a result of moral growth and ability to respect.

Directed thinking, or the ability to be analytic and make pertinent observations, did not correlate significantly with moral stage. Perhaps at an early age the style of relating mainly to friends, with a minimum of analysis of issues, permitted supportive or critical responses to produce some new ideas. Moral growth similar to that resulting from analytic thinking occurred among the stereotypic thinkers. Although this conclusion refers only to children of low-stage morality, it is contrary to hypothesis.

Given these results, how important is directional thinking to social and moral development? Age and place results may interact. The growing differences shown in Table 5.2 between the tendencies of city and suburban children to stereotypic and/or nonanalytic responses indicate that adolescent differences should generally be greater than earlier differences. This conclusion must be tested. If city adolescents are far more prejudiced than those in the suburbs, it may be because stereotypic thinking and general nonverbalness in adolescence does not permit a moral logic to develop that would encourage them to view prejudice as mistaken. City children at both nine and thirteen keep half their non-information-giving comments on a stereotypic and feeling, or "annunciatory," level. Suburban children at thirteen offer five times more social reasoning than stereotypic comments.

TABLE 5.2

Types of Spontaneous Comments in City and Suburb
(in percent)

Type of Comment	At Age Seven		At Age Nine		At Age Thirteen	
	City	Suburb	City	Suburb	City	Suburb
Physical information	30	41	12	16	3	1
Social information	48	34	38	39	29	28
Stereotypes and feelings	7	9	26	18	37	12
Social reasoning	15	16	24	27	41	59

Source: A study conducted by author, as described in the text.

The investigator's impression was that suburban children offer information to avoid discussing embarrassing issues of prejudice, especially at age nine, to a greater extent than do city children. However, Table 5.2 shows both groups transitional at age nine between a preponderance of informational and explanatory remarks.

The third finding of the study is that prejudices or negative remarks made up 36 percent of the total ethnic remarks made by all the city children while playing the game and being privately interviewed about others' statements made during the game, and 13 percent of the suburban remarks. Tables 5.3 through 5.5 show how these are distributed. Between ages seven and thirteen, prejudiced remarks decreased 10 percent in the city and 50 percent in the suburbs.

TABLE 5.3

Moral Stages in Suburb and City
(N = 93)

Grade and Moral Stage	Percent in Suburb	Percent in City
Two		
One	29	82.0
Two	71	18.0
Four		
One	35	69.0
Two	40	12.5
Three	25	18.5
Seven		
One	6.6	12.5
Two	53.3	62.5
Three	26.6	25.0
Four	13.3	0.0
All grades totaled		
One	23.8	51.2
Two	50.0	32.6
Three	21.5	16.3
Four	4.8	0.0

Note: Average moral stages in grade two were 1.7 in the suburb and 1.0 in the city; in grade four, 1.9 in the suburb and 1.6 in the city; in grade seven, 2.5 in the suburb and 2.1 in the city; and for all grades, 2.1 in the suburb and 1.7 in the city.

Source: A study conducted by the author, as described in the text.

TABLE 5.4

Racial and Ethnic Attitudes of Three Age Groups of Children in Suburban Schools
(by grade; in percent)

Attitude	By Whites			By Metco Blacks in Same Classes		
	Second (N = 13)	Fourth (N = 19)	Seventh (N = 33)	Second (N = 3)	Fourth (N = 2)	Seventh (N = 5)
Toward blacks						
Negative	23	21	18	51	38	30
Neutral	62	68	74	22	18	47
Positive	15	11	8	37	44	23
Toward whites[a]						
Negative	0	4	9	7	33	33
Neutral	91	84	80	93	47	50
Positive	9	12	11	0	20	17
Toward Jews						
Negative	12	6	12	0	3	10
Neutral	81	80	63	83	97	84
Positive	7	14	25	17	0	6
Toward others[b]						
Negative	21	19	9	35	31	15
Neutral	53	55	67	18	42	85
Positive	26	26	24	47	27	0

[a] Irish, Italian, and so on.
[b] Spanish-speaking, oriental, and native-American.
Source: A study conducted by the author, as described in the text.

TABLE 5.5

Racial and Ethnic Attitudes of Three Age Groups of Children in City Schools
(by grade; in percent)

Attitude	By Whites			By Blacks		
	Second (N = 8)	Fourth (N = 15)	Seventh (N = 12)	Second (N = 3)	Fourth (N = 6)	Seventh (N = 4)
Toward blacks						
Negative	56	61	31	31	28	14
Neutral	15	19	53	27	53	54
Positive	29	20	16	42	19	32
Toward whites[a]						
Negative	6	0	23	71	74	57
Neutral	82	85	49	29	26	43
Positive	12	15	18	0	0	0
Toward Jews						
Negative	33	39	28	12	18	42
Neutral	67	55	72	83	82	58
Positive	0	6	0	5	0	0
Toward others[b]						
Negative	23	26	21	42	39	35
Neutral	38	53	61	37	45	42
Positive	39	21	18	21	10	23

[a]Irish, Italian, and so on.
[b]Spanish-speaking, oriental, and native-American.
Source: A study conducted by the author, as described in the text.

Table 5.3 shows the average moral stage at each grade in city and suburb and the percentage of ethnic negativity associated with each moral stage. The average moral stage of the city group increased at the same rate as in the suburbs, about one stage over the five-year span, but initial differences in moral stage were maintained. In the longitudinal group, change was approximately two-thirds of a stage over three years.

The city child of ten resembles in moral logic the lower-middle-class suburban seven-year-old. The average suburban grade school child at 10:2 is at moral stage 2.1, while the city child at 10:3 is at moral stage 1.7.

The fourth finding is not the result of hypothesis testing, but it appears that there are three types of prejudice expressed by children, the aversive, the aggressive, and the developmental. This is a tentative finding, since the types overlap and the ambiguities in coded data did not warrant statistical checking. In the suburbs, children, like adults, avoid confronting their dislikes; there is an avoiding type of prejudice that was not seen very frequently in the city children studied. Among city children, aggressive and hostile prejudices were easily expressed and even seemed to be expected. A remark by a seven-year-old, "I never met any Jews. But the big Jews, I heard they come after you. They're bad," bears a relation to the more typical assertion, "Blacks fight more." Blacks, for their part, called attention to the meanness or hostility of particular white students or of white people in general. Aggressive prejudice is correlated with a tendency to fight, especially among suburban children.

The typical prejudice of the suburban child is patronizing and also careful to avoid open blaming or hostility. A ten-year-old girl put it as follows:

> You shouldn't break the law if you could ever get it
> changed. So I don't know if I would help a slave.
> You should go give some talks in the slave markets,
> to end slavery. But there's always troubles, you
> can't stop them, like hunger and slaving. So do
> your little bit. Slaves aren't really doing any good.
> They aren't saving lives, or really helping people.
> One or another might become somebody, if he could
> choose to, like a surgeon. So they should be free,
> in case they might choose to. . . . Martin Luther
> King didn't go too far, so everybody was sad at his
> death.

The third type of prejudice is childish, exploratory, and often teasing. It can be called developmental, since it disappears in the

suburban group in proportion to age whenever more of the analytic
and fewer of the stereotypic, pronouncing, and self-referrent statements are made. This type of prejudice also exists in the city,
where even more teasing comments are heard, but the lack of a decline in stereotyping as compared to reasoning between nine and
thirteen, as shown in Table 5.2, makes developmental prejudice
difficult to identify. The lack of expectation that verbal and social
reasoning skills will be developed in school and the influence of
lower-class speech on the continued use of stereotypes need to be
investigated.

The final conclusion is that developmental prejudices appear
to be correlated with lack of moral stage change in the small longitudinal group. In three cases stage change occurred dramatically
at age thirteen when anxieties about personal effectiveness lessened.
At this point prejudices, including "blacks are dirty" and "Jews
swear a lot, " were disclaimed. All three were boys who had be-
haved immaturely. One had suffered from anxiety after hospitaliza-
tion, and two had relatively unsupportive or uncommunicative homes.
Case histories in preparation show a strong relationship between a
child's description of parental effectiveness in outside jobs and the
child's interest in societal change, as in the issue of prejudice.
Moral stage change may be affected by the same parent-image factor, among many others.

DISCUSSION

A prejudice represents a judgment, albeit a prejudgment. A
prejudgment can be changed by a better rationale, but at a given
time the person's prejudices relate to a basic construction of interlocking values that is no more logical than his or her cognitive-social
development allows. The Kohlberg Test is a measure of the maturity
of the structures of the logic of fairness, which in this context means
the fundamental value judgments and rules by which thought is organized. The correlation between thought structures and the more
transient content of ethnic prejudice is partial but interesting in that
it ties absurd and irrational prejudice to a conscious and presumably
"fair" judgment pattern. This pattern can be described and even
influenced.

The most fundamental and parsimonious explanation resulting
from this research into prejudice is that the gratuitous content of
its expression is built upon a discernible logic that fits descriptions
of moral judgment. The other factors that have long been associated
with prejudice, which are parental example, personality traits, social class, intelligence, ego abilities, and education, are subsidiary

to this judgment factor and must not be allowed to confuse its importance. In 1953 Gordon Allport made a relevant statement, as follows:

> The prevailing dictum that motivation is always a matter of "tension reduction" or of "seeking equilibrium" is . . . scarcely consistent, I think, with all the known facts. This prevailing atmosphere of theory has engendered a kind of contempt for the "psychic surface" of life. The individual's conscious report is rejected as untrustworthy.

Fortunately, there is an inborn motive to seek mastery of the environment and its troubling problems, well described by R. White (1959), which impels even children toward social understanding and mastery of moral logic. Children are particularly concerned about questions of fairness that impinge on their own lives. The frequent cry of "No fair!" reveals a concern that can be capitalized on in education.

Prejudice cannot be called crystallized, because the formal structure of its moral rationale changes. The change is based on the widening logical capacity and the widening capacity to imagine others' motives that occurs in all children. An increased capacity for respect is the basis of morality. It decreases prejudiced attitudes. For example, "insult teasing" is a time-limited type of childhood prejudice associated with stereotypic thinking and "annunciatory" egocentric tendencies. Aggressiveness and other causes of prejudice are also potentially reducible by cognitive development. The continuing tendency to prejudice in some children, especially those of the core city group, is perhaps no more fixed or necessary than the continuing low moral stages associated with poor life conditions.

Such life conditions affect educational outcomes. Even in a city that is generous in its educational expenditure, the teachers from past experience have low expectations of receiving carefully reasoned verbal responses from thirteen-year-olds, as well as from seven-year-olds. The children use language to reinforce group values, even when "why" questions are asked about social problems. It is interesting to note that little progress in abstract social reasoning in the spontaneous situation of the prejudice testing (game and interview) had been made by age thirteen, and the percentage of stereotypic answers to probes about what classmates had said dropped far less than in the suburbs. Like younger children, city adolescents abbreviate statements, make many jokes, and assume that their context is shared even by an "outside" investigator. An

impulsive human contact is more valued than an abstract statement.
Illustrative anecdotes are offered in place of arguments that could
more closely specify meanings. This use of speech must have an
effect, as yet unmeasured, upon moral reasoning and prejudice,
nevertheless, the favorable effect of the city child's empathy on his
moral reasoning should not be overlooked. That empathy has some
power to compensate for abstract reasoning is suggested by the lack
of correlation between directed thinking and childhood moral stage.

Childhood Stages of Respect for Persons

The following abbreviated account of the stages of children's
respect for persons may make the complex structural relations between attitudes of prejudice and their underlying values somewhat
more clear. These descriptions are based upon the local results of
this study. Only items 1 through 5 pertain in all the descriptions of
the stages to Kohlberg's universally applicable stages.

Very young or low-stage persons define respect as obedience.
Those at Stage 2 equate it with egalitarian attitudes that stress
mechanical balancing. At the conventional Stages 3 and 4, children
show interest in the idea of respect for people in general and mutuality as the basis of relationships, but they exclude arbitrarily
disliked persons and "enemies" from consideration. In Kohlberg's
work, mutual respect as understood at Stages 5 and 6 is the attribution to the other of a personal value equivalent to that of the self,
making judgment of the person involve more than judgment of outer
particulars or even of his or her totality of actions. Universal
principles of ethical conduct are then seen to be necessary. The
present study of children had no subjects at Stages 5 and 6.

Stage 1

A child's view of the interactions of people at Stage 1 is based
on concrete and superficial qualities that are immediately apparent.
The characteristics of this stage are as follows: (1) one person's
perspective can be taken at a time, and usually the perspective
chosen is that of the authority; (2) the motives of others are not
considered; (3) people are valued according to their possessions,
power, size, and numbers, while labels (such as "bad man") are
concretized; (4) respect is obedience to authority rather than promotion of the welfare of others, since only the powerful have such
responsibility; (5) the consequences determine whether choices are
good or bad, and punishment automatically follows an act disrespect-
ful to a person not "bad"; (6) powerful authorities such as God and

the government are assumed to be behind many chance-appearing events; (7) it is believed that persons or groups should be coerced, since authority is needed for safety; (8) disrespect and prejudice are based on either a stereotype accepted from a quasi-authority or an imputation of dangerousness; and (9) there is little differentiation of hypothetical individuals from the labeled groups to which they belong.

The central characteristic of Stage 1 is its reference to authority or to the ultimate consequences of interpersonal actions and not their intrinsic fairness or unfairness. "Respect is obey your parents, or obey the police, the judge and the President. And your teacher," says Deb, age nine. Fear may enter the description of respect as part of the orientation to consequences and punishment, but affection is not referred to as relevant to good behavior, even by children from affectionate, nonpunitive families.

The importance of concrete authority and reified labels appears in the following answer from a bright ten-year-old to the question, "Should a slave be helped to escape from the pre-Civil War South?" "If a slaveowner mistreated his slave, and the slave came to me, I'd make him my slave. A slave was a slave, and that's the way it was. I wouldn't feel sorry for him, because his owner had paid for him. So he was a slave. A slave has a master."

Conclusions are usually stated as if there were no choices. In adopting almost any view of an authority and assuming that others should also, the child denies his own and the others' personhood. The fundamental dignity of being a defender of one's own interests is lost. "The slave can't escape. He has to go back, even if he has a good reason," says a black ten-year-old.

Stage 1 conclusions begin with organically based cognitive limitations at the age of seven, but what can be said when they are retained in adolescence? It may be that a threatening environment renders authoritarian views adaptive. Prejudice is then natural, because one result of low awareness of personal choice-making is low conscience orientation. This in turn gives the freedom to use the pejorative stereotypes available in a given environment, omitting considerations of individual differences and nonauthoritarian notions of respect.

"Jews, they come into a town and take over the golf courses. I've known that from my uncle. So I say, 'Get out of here, you Jew,' when I see some hippie." These are the words of Jim, a suburbanite, age ten, who seeks power through verbal and other assault, accompanied by teasing charm. The complex problem of the cause of the retention of low-stage thinking versus normal-stage change is pointed up in that while none of Jim's tests at ten showed interest in taking the viewpoint of another person, the self confidence and even self respect (revealed in his charm) that he

gained through successful fighting seemed to be moving him to the
more gang-or-friend-oriented Stage 2 by age 13. Stage 1 is essentially simplistic, and discrepancies between its logic and the logic
of a value system that affirms the worth of self-assertion produce
new insights, leading to a change in stage. This can occur at age
seven or later.

Stage 2

At Stage 2 an uncritical self-respect seems to result in attention being more focused upon the concrete aspects of practical living.
The right choice is equated with the smart and self-pleasing one.
Respect for others, while still impersonally and mechanically understood, is described as permission for peers or groups to pursue
their own aims. The power of authority is diluted by a new awareness that everyone has competing claims. The value judgments
typical of this stage are as follows: (1) since others have individual
goals and the right to pursue them, so does the self, which can use
others if they allow it; (2) lack of understanding of motives leads to
a pseudo-liberality that states that "all people are equal" and that
authority can be opposed; (3) respect means noninterference with
the intentions of others; (4) fairness is balancing individual interests
according to what seems smart or useful rather than by any abstract
"good"; (5) justice is treating the other as one has been treated;
(6) caring is a pragmatic helpfulness, making repayment; (7) because
evaluation of others remains egocentric, assumptions are often
unique or idiosyncratic; (8) subsuming human rights under the wills
of individuals permits stereotyping; (9) the laissez-faire attitude
about the values of others can promote indifference as a seeming
virtue.

Lew first heard the interviewer repeat his classmate's statement, "Many Indians have different beliefs than ours," when he was
at Stage 1. He replied then, at age ten, "You ought to try to change
them, or they might try to scalp you, because they wouldn't like
you." Three years later, at Stage 2, he said, "Let the Indians
wear or think whatever they want. After all, they sold New York
to us. If they want to start trouble, let them; maybe it's a protest."

Movement to Stage 2 seems to be contingent not only on greater
awareness of personal effectiveness but also on a new ability to observe the subjective planning of others and a realization that the
goals of others do not coincide with one's own.

The child also comes to realize that all people are aware of
each others' subjectivity. This startling insight should evoke the
implicit moral question, If everyone's plans are different, and all
people have equal value, whose plans can fairly prevail? Such a

question does not arouse interest when posed by the investigator, and the answer is abortive: "What wins is fair, because each person can press for his own ideas."

Two examples of the inadequacy of Stage 2 conclusions follow. To the question, "What do you think about the problems of mixing the races in schools?" a thirteen-year-old black girl replied, "I think each case should be decided by what the people there would like. Whatever they feel like." To the question, "Your classmate said, 'Mexicans sneak over to get jobs in this country.' What do you think?" A ten-year-old replied, "Why sneak? We should let everyone in. But we should feed our poor people first. Then if the Mexicans came, it would be their own fault for coming here, if they starved and we ran out of money."

Although respect is not spontaneously mentioned or described, the concept closest to it is a formal egalitarianism, a stressing of the right to liberty of all people. Freedom from interference by others is central, but links between formal and effective freedoms, such as the necessity of equal opportunity, are not seen. "All are equal" becomes a mere cliche.

Some children do attempt to reconcile opinion differences, especially as they grow older, and between seven and nine they shift from information-giving to exploratory reasoning. However, the reasoning employed is selective and superficial. The use of reciprocals is one of the first achievements of concrete operations (Piaget 1926); and since concrete operations were found to be necessary but not sufficient for Kohlberg's Stage 2 by D. Kuhn (1972), the mechanical egalitarianism and balancing of Stage 2 social relations is of interest. "If one does it, another can. Indians in the city can look slobby if the people do. They have their own ideas, but they can trade," said a thirteen-year-old boy.

Stereotypes are used less frequently than at Stage 1 because there is increasing awareness of the external aspects of individuality and the variability of goals. However, assessment of people based on any simultaneous awareness of even such evident variables as sex, age, work-role, or popularity is seldom undertaken. Questions are resolved impulsively. The new unimportance of the good-bad dimension of Stage 1, as compared to the ability to operate pragmatically, frees the Stage 2 child from a responsibility for idealistic solutions. This may be useful for gaining a sense of self and the possibilities of self during childhood.

However, Stage 2 can be maladaptive, in that it is still egocentric and provides no rationale for the mutual solutions of problems that are truly shared. Its instrumental hedonism leads to conflicts of interest and fighting over petty disagreements. The data show most clearly that fighting leads to further anger, fear, and prejudice;

yet fighting is thought of as a source of justice, as when a suburban Stage 2 thirteen-year-old thoughtfully advocated "a war and then a peace treaty" as the fair solution for race riots.

The maladaptiveness of an extreme Stage 2 position appeared clear in this area of race relations. Militancy can be instrumentally hedonistic. The simplistic justifications that have been offered for black militancy had their counterpart in the troubled discussion by some city children of a club called White Power.

There was also a white suburban boy with an IQ of 130 who remained at Stage 2 through age 13 by cultivating indifference. This attitude was expressed by him as follows: "Segregation is not right, I guess. But I'd go along with the whites, because I know them better. I wouldn't worry about people I didn't know."

It is necessary to conclude that both the prejudice of anger and the more typical prejudice of indifference are easily promoted by Stage 2 values.

Stage 3

As a prerequisite to Stage 3, the child must be old enough to understand that his own motives and feelings can often be detected by others and that the view of another as seen by him can also be anticipated by that other (Selman 1973). When this maturation occurs, it is possible for the typical balancing or trading of excuses at Stage 2 to evolve into offers to try to understand motives, which would initiate concern for empathic understanding. This would lead to a Stage 3 reorganization of values. A new conception of relationships based on pleasing one another or "being good" is the core of Stage 3.

Taking the perspective of another person promotes a deeper understanding that in turn leads to a further desire to maintain shared expectations and approval. As the limitations of the selfish egoism of Stage 2 for producing fairness become apparent, many children generate reorganized prescriptive statements that assume new values, as follows: (1) they may say that respect, like praise, should be given for others' good motives; (2) they may say that the seeking of approval and mutuality keeps people together; (3) caring for others, now assumed to be "normal," leads to trust, enjoyment, and often general optimism, in their opinion; (4) Golden Rule altruism, an ideal self, and an awareness of conscience evolve from the "good person" orientation; (5) good sentiments in family relations tend to be substituted as a model for the superficially objectified "all are equal" idea of human rights; (6) in order to prescribe collective norms and ideals for society a leap is made from the dyad to the universal; (7) conforming cooperation or recourse to benevolent

authorities best solves social problems; (8) global sympathy tends
either to mitigate prejudice or to produce a shallowly changeable
evaluation of minority group members; (9) nevertheless, ethnic
group stereotypes are given credence as being "majority" views;
and (10) an obligation to make a display of concern for others is recognized, but decisions affecting intergroup relations tend to be based
on personal feelings and in-group views.

One suburban boy's answers to the question "Do you like to
fight?" changed from "Nobody's going to do it for you" at Stage 2 to
the following Stage 3 answer three years later.

> I don't fight anymore. I never did much. You have
> to be respected by acting good, not in the way of
> being tough. But other kids are suckered in by that.
> There's a few like that in every school, a few who
> can't make friends, and who want to try it the tough
> way. Especially black people. They get friends by
> acting tough. . . . I don't dig that system too much.
> It's not much of a friendship, and it's not necessary.

The change shows an increase of optimism in assumptions about
human nature and consequent criticism of what now seems immature.
Yet there are still, at thirteen, glaring defects in his empathy.

At Stage 3 respect is more than cold justice and is less related
to naked power. The knowledge that persons have reasons for what
they do allows them to be given the benefit of the doubt. This opens
the way for persons, and not individual acts, to become the basis for
an evaluation of a life as moral and good. "Respect means someone
you can look up to." However, sentiments of niceness or meanness,
rather than objective criteria of character, determine who is good.

The values of Stage 3 are rooted in the enjoyment of others.
This seems to lead naturally to the idea that conformity to simple
prescriptions for virtue and niceness can solve social problems. It
should be enough simply to fulfill the good expectations of others; but
if problems persist, egocentric pronouncements are often brought
forth. The in-group (friends, white people, black people) must be
maintained, and collusion in covering each other's weaknesses is
considered correct. A ten-year-old stated this as follows:

> It's half and half, whether you should pretend to like
> someone. A lot of pretending is just from fear,
> they are afraid to say they don't like them, that is,
> the Negroes. I'll be friendly, but not hang around
> if I don't like someone. That way, if you look like
> you care a little bit, nothing bad is going to happen,
> because they will care about you, if you're polite.

There is considerable concern about prejudice in the suburb among the Stage 3 children; but concern about prejudice does not mean that personal negative prejudgments are eliminated, since the typical conformity to majority views introduces a potential contradiction. Rationalization is used to resolve contradictions. The following equivocal remark by a nine-year-old suburban boy was scored as showing underlying negativity or aversive prejudice: "Nobody likes black people. There must be a reason. Prejudice is wrong, if you are a nice person, you don't show that you don't like them. There's a lot of things they could do to make it easier. They got to think about that, not just us."

The disadvantages of Stage 3 are its susceptibility to rationalization, preventing idealism from bringing about effective social reform; its lack of rationale in seeking "niceness"; and its idealizing of people. The complex political, economic, institutional, and psychological causes of social problems are ignored or not understood. Sympathy is found to be easier than a comprehending empathy or sharing of outlook. Approval-seeking among friends is narcissistically satisfying, making arrest at Stage 3 common even in adulthood. Idealism about people may lead to a sense of shock at their aberrations, which in turn justifies blame and punishment. At Stage 3 there is neither a firm theory of human character nor a set of principles of morality that could maintain a more consistent and "unshockable" trust. A patronizing approach to people who are less fortunate is common; but prejudice is less apparent than at earlier stages and it is evidently mitigated through the enjoyment of people that is simply presumed as the basis of morality at this stage.

Stage 4

The beginning of formal operational thinking in adolescence can initiate a new need to define the social world and systematize it abstractly. Gaps in understanding of human nature are now filled by hypotheses, and more precise models of the social world are constructed. What seems to initiate the change from Stage 3 to Stage 4 is the need for a more formalized and widely applicable system of moral values that can take into account new hypotheses about the variability of human character and new knowledge of the institutional and impersonal workings of society. Of course, this societal orientation is more likely to be lacking in city children whose families feel little leverage over their own lives. Goal-directedness in the outside world promotes Stage 4 considerations.

The most noticeable change is the appearance of rule-seeking. At Stage 4 there is a search for explanations or rules to tie together the disparate social elements and sentimental aspirations of Stage 3.

A single hypothesis or system of relations at this stage, but not at Stage 5, seems to serve better than pluralistic and often unrelated solutions to moral problems. The external dictates of religion, an ethical system, or more typically "the law of the land" can serve as an instrument of conventionally accepted logic to unify solutions to questions of justice.

In terms of respect, the particularities of Stage 4 are as follows: (1) conscious respect and esteem are the basis of friendship (2) a third-person perspective introduces more objective fairness, and exchanges should be reciprocal and of value to each party; (3) human life is called good because of its moral dimension; (4) the obligation is to a specified moral code above personal relations, and concern about dishonor can supersede concern about disapproval; (5) claims of justice, rights, and equality are subordinated, if necessary, to the fixed expectations of society; (6) responsibility exists for consequences to others rather than simply for avoiding bad acts, but responsibility is limited by rules; (7) the socially productive results of a sense of duty (hard work, education) are respected; (8) conflicts between moral law and the legal system cannot be clearly resolved, but the legal system usually predominates; (9) respect for authority is subsumed under mutual respect; (10) prejudices or, more typically, sentiments of antiprejudice are based on the search for "objectivity," impersonal definitions, and emphasis on categories and conventional ideas; and (11) realistic interest in the thoughts and feelings of others leads to judgments that may be harsher than when influenced by Stage 3 trust.

The role-taking ability progresses to the extent that the Stage 4 adolescent can imagine the point of view of a generalized or neutral observer. A new awareness of society as a structured whole leads to the assertion of its right to make demands on individuals. Complex hypotheses are constructed about hypothetical social networks; but further aspects of formal operational thinking, such as transcending the reification of social institutions and offering philosophical hypotheses about the various assumptions on which societies might be built come at later stages.

The ability to take the point of view of a neutral observer leads to the formulation of criteria for respect. These recognize the socially productive results of "character" and a sense of duty. "Caring" seems increased. The Stage 4 person redefines and codifies a previously intuitive appreciation of the Golden Rule. A thirteen-year-old boy gave the following example. "You have to be respected by acting in a way that people will see you care about others; you hold back a little, you don't just go swaggering around saying everything you hate."

A tendency to stereotyping can result from the emphasis on categorization and definition at Stage 4. A girl of 13 gave the following opinion of a law against euthanasia:

> This law must be to prevent doctors from bad judgments against Catholics, because Catholics believe that it is only God's job to take life. The law must represent that there are different religions and beliefs. But such a law to protect Catholics from doctors seems unfair to the rest of us. I think Catholics should have their own countries and laws.

The following is another example of Stage 4 thinking: "The people on welfare are just pretty lucky that we give them that. What did they do to deserve it? The least they can do is to stay in school."

Notions of in- and out-groups are still important, but personhood is now well defined. Nevertheless, persons of other nations are easily ignored, and thus rendered nonpersons, by the rule-obeying mentality. Divisions of national boundary limit the respect owed to people's needs, as illustrated by the interview below with a thirteen-year-old suburban boy.

> Interviewer: Should poor Mexicans be allowed to come here to work in our fields?
> Boy: If they couldn't get a job there, we could show we care, but our President's job is to take care of the U.S. citizens. We have to take care of jobs for our poor.
> Interviewer: What if our poor are better off than their poor?
> Boy: The President has to go by our laws, and by the definition of his job.

Chauvinism can result from extreme Stage 4 thinking. A view of people that defines them by their place in the social system promotes inattention to the importance of trust-maintenance in psychological and moral development. The simplistic reduction of the complexity and richness of human nature to a moralistic definition of goodness can be overly coercive and prevent growth beyond conventionality.

Stage 4, like the other preprincipled stages, has its circular reasoning, which can serve as a defensive shield against compassionate suffering or the existential anguish described in modern philosophy. Avoiding principled thinking and being content instead to simply share the thinking of others also avoids the self-denial demanded by a truly higher-stage morality.

Reliability and Validity of the Stages

The kind of reliability that ensures that the answers represent
an individual's best thinking and not fluctuations of test situations,
which might, for example, favor older children, in this case depends on the investigator's rapport and the persistence of the question, "Why do you think that way?" When possible the investigator
took care to know the children first, either as director of the inner-
city day camp or as the counselor in the suburban schools in which
the testing took place. Good reliability with Kohlberg's measure is
attained only when testers and scorers understand the limits of
stage structures and probe to clarify first responses.

As for the validity, the criterion concepts for the stages and
their invariance logically derive from Kohlberg's theory, which
states that structural change is an active process of transformation
of already existing thoughts that no longer seem to fit experience.
Stage consistency is demonstrated in this research in that over half
the scores in each test were at a single modal stage. As in other
studies (Turiel 1966; Rest, Turiel, and Kohlberg 1969), there is a
normal distribution of major and minor scores to adjacent stages
only. The statements showing children's structural thinking at each
stage and the spontaneous remarks about ethnic attitudes have face
validity as obviously connected to each other. However, statements
in the descriptions of stages labeled as inferences made by the
present investigator must be noted.

Predictive validity for the Kohlberg test could refer to moral
behavior, but Hartshorne and May (1928) have shown that moral behavior is situation-specific, unstable over time, and nondevelop-
mental, that is, showing no regular relationship to age. Kohlberg
claims only a loose correspondence between moral judgment and
moral behavior. Prejudice as here measured, however, is not only
an instance of behavior but also a form of judgment, and therefore
it is closer to moral judgment than such behaviors as cheating or
taking part in a protest.

Implications for Change

It seems safe to conclude that where there is a reinforcing
environment that is aggressive or insecure, the circular reasoning
of a low stage will be strengthened and its primitive assumptions
about people in general will be retained, thus interfering with
progress to the next stage. The child stressing the defensive properties of the particular values of a stage presumably reduces the
occurrence of idea conflict, which would lead to questioning of the
adequacy of these values in the same manner as an external environ-

ment containing only familiar ideas reduces the probability of challenge and change. Socioeconomic conditions that threaten children
underlie prejudice.

All children from 7 to 13 are capable of ethnic prejudice, because they are not yet principled in morality. Most do not show
prejudice for lack of immediate cause. Some are moving toward
becoming principled, while others remain at low stages of morality.
The values of the preconventional Stages 1 and 2 are more supportive
of prejudice than those of the conventional Stages 3 and 4. Only the
values of the principled stages, Kohlberg's Stages 5 and 6, insist
upon respect for all persons (Kohlberg 1963; Lovin 1973). In a preliminary study of adults in the North and South, Jaquette and Carrick
(n.d.) found no prejudice at Stages 5 and 6.

It follows that intergroup education should foster moral change.
It should be neither primarily information-giving, as in the typical
black studies, ethnic history, or Indian lore courses, nor primarily
aimed at emotional experience, as in the "T-group." A more developmentally sound aim for intergroup education intended to reduce
prejudice is the stimulation of moral stage change through rational
discussion. Serious dilemmas that challenge students to seek more
mature conclusions about any moral problems may or may not include the unfairness of prejudice. The consideration of moral problems seems to produce moral stage change (Blatt 1963) without the
burden of any specific accusation of racism or prejudice. Positive
respect for all persons is achieved in measurable stages.

APPENDIX A: THE WORK OF KOHLBERG

In Kohlberg's theory of moral development (1963), the child's
identity is a critical and basic organizer of attitudes. Moral judgments are the outcome of a constructive process in which the child
is trying to organize, regulate, and understand the social environment. At each new stage the child integrates his or her own experiences with his ideas more adequately. There is an inherent
logic in the progressive differentiation and integration of moral
judgments, which produces a genuine developmental sequence of
stages.

Kohlberg's stages of moral development have been verified by a
20-year longitudinal study of 50 American males age 10 to 16 who
were interviewed every 3 years. All of the subjects went through
the same sequence of stages. Although the rate of development and
the terminal point of the adult stage are different for different individuals, the nature and the order of the stages of moral thought are
the same for all.

Support for this order of stages is found in the age trends in various cultures and social classes, the patterns in the correlations of overlap between the stages, and the results of longitudinal studies of individual development (Kohlberg 1963). The universality of the stages and their order has been confirmed in a number of cross-cultural studies. Some of the age trends in American culture are as follows:

> Stage 1: Obedience and punishment orientation (found at age six and after). Egocentric deference to superior power or prestige, or a trouble-avoiding set. Responsibility with reference to outside standard.
>
> Stage 2: Naively egoistic orientation (may begin about seven). Right action is that instrumentally satisfying the self's needs and occasionally others'. Awareness of relativism of value to each actor's needs and perspective. Naive egalitarianism and orientation to exchange.
>
> Stage 3: Orientation to approval and to pleasing and helping others (may begin in pre-adolescence or later). Conformity to stereotypical images of majority or natural role behavior. Judgment by intentions.
>
> Stage 4: Authority and social order maintaining orientation (often begins during adolescence). "Doing duty" and showing respect for authority and maintaining order for its own sake. Regard for earned expectations of others.
>
> Stage 5: Contractual legalistic orientation (usually a post-adolescent stage). Recognition of an arbitrary element or starting point in rules or expectations for the sake of agreement. Duty defined in terms of contract, general avoidance of violation of the will or rights of others, and majority will and welfare.
>
> Stage 6: Conscience or principled orientation (very rare). Orientation not only to actually ordained social rules but to principles of choice involving appeal to logical universality and consistency. Orientation to conscience as a directing agent and to mutual respect and trust.

This theory of the development of moral judgment parallels Piaget's theory (1926) of general cognitive development. As the

child matures, his or her modes of reasoning and sets of value
assumptions become successively more adequate. If the child is
bothered by inconsistencies while interacting with people and trying
to solve unfair situations, the thinking of the child will be reorganized at a new stage to make it possible to deal with them.

The six stages form an invariant developmental sequence, in
which attainment of a higher stage is dependent on the attainment
of each of the preceding stages. Each represents a reorganization
of the thought structures to create a more advanced level.

Morality is often thought of as a development of conscience, of
an internal motive or monitor for decisions that affect other people.
Conscience, however, is only one of ten major issues or institutions
used to define the stages. The other issues include law, civil rights,
authority, and economic property. Each of these institutions is
understood in a new way at each stage, according to the way people
are valued and respected. To illustrate, here are the conceptions
of civil rights of Johnny, a bright middle-class boy. He is responding to the following dilemma: "Before the civil war, we had laws that
allowed slavery. According to the law, if a slave escaped, he had to
be returned to his owner like a runaway horse. Some people who
didn't believe in slavery disobeyed the law and hid the runaway slaves
and helped them to escape. Were they doing right or wrong?" This
dilemma involves the issues of conscience, of law, and of civil
liberties. Johnny answers the question this way when he is ten:
"They were doing wrong because the slave ran away himself, they're
being just like slaves themselves trying to keep 'em away." When
asked, "Is slavery right or wrong?" he answers, "Some wrong, but
having servants aren't so bad because they don't do all that heavy
work."

Johnny's response is Stage 1, a punishment and obedience
orientation. Breaking the law makes it wrong; indeed, the badness
of being a slave washes off on his rescuer. People are often "bad."
He does not yet have concepts of rights.

At age 13 he is asked the same question. His answer is mainly
a Stage 2 view that people who defend their own interests are doing
the right thing (instrumental relativism). He gives the following reply:

> They would help them escape because they were all
> against slavery. The South was for slavery because
> they had big plantations and the North was against it
> because they had big factories and they needed
> people to work and they'd pay. So the Northerners
> would think it was right but the Southerners wouldn't.
>
> If a person is against slavery and maybe likes
> the slave or maybe dislikes the owner, it's okay for

him to break the law if he likes, provided he doesn't
get caught.

At age 19, in college, John has a Stage 4 orientation to maintaining a social order of rules and rights. He then answers as
follows:

> They were right in my point of view. I hate the ac-
> tual aspect of slavery, the imprisonment of one man
> ruling over another. They drive them too hard and
> they don't get anything in return. It's not right to
> disobey the law, no. Laws are made by the people.
> But you might do it because you feel it's wrong. If
> fifty thousand people break the law, can you put them
> all in jail? Can fifty thousand people be wrong?

John here is oriented to the rightness and wrongness of slavery itself and of obedience to law. He doesn't see the wrongness of
slavery in terms of equal human rights but in terms of an unfair
economic relation, working hard and getting nothing in return. The
same view of rights in terms of getting what you worked for leads
John to say about school integration: "A lot of colored people are
now just living off of civil rights. You only get education as far as
you want to learn, as far as you work for it, not being placed with
someone else, you don't get it from someone else."

When last interviewed at age 24, John had not reached Stage 5.
There is hope, however; some subjects have moved from Stage 4 to
Stage 5 in their late twenties.

APPENDIX B: THE NEED FOR MORAL EDUCATION
TO MAKE ETHNIC PLURALISM WORK

Our review of the development of reasoning during childhood
makes it clear that the presumption that ethnic attitudes are fixed in
early childhood is unwarranted. Even if phenotypically they might
appear unchanged, which is not established by a review of the research, the remarks of many children in the study just described
show that the underlying reasoning does change. The accepted view
in psychology, that early attitudes determine later attitudes, deserves further investigation for three reasons provided by this

---

This appendix was co-authored by Florence B. H. Davidson and
Lawrence Kohlberg.

research: the children interviewed before age 13 show uncertainty
about their own rationale for intergroup attitudes and change it later,
even when their attitudes do not become much more fair, as in the
cases of many of the city children; they verbally deny dependence on
parents and others as valid sources and clearly experiment with
ideas themselves; and when healthy attitudes of respect are sought
by survey questions, most cases show an evolution of the rationale
provided for the judgments of persons and groups in the direction of
taking more viewpoints and widening the logic by which the judgments
are made.

Although in environments favoring prejudice the late adolescents and adults often take Archie Bunker's stand that there is no
need to submit their prejudices to any rational system of human
values, the young are less likely to show dogmatism. They can be
challenged during the process of education. In the "game" portion
of the final study reported here, the children often lightly admonished
each other on statements that seemed to one or another too biased.
"Boy, you sure got a couple of prejudices!" "You can't hate old
Italian ladies for having big noses."

While it is well known that attitudes such as ethnic prejudice
have many determinants, such as environment, personality, intelligence, ego strength, education, and socioeconomic status, and
that the same determinants also affect the rate of progress and the
end-point of progress through the moral stages, nevertheless there
is theoretical and practical importance to the relationship discovered
between moral stage and amount of prejudice. As we have noted,
studying attitudes apart from their underlying rationales is mislead-
ing. This relationship to moral stage shows that the emphasis in
remediation may be placed upon the development of basic values that
represent clear thinking and moral maturity. This should prove
more productive than previous intergroup relations models of
information-giving, such as black studies and Indian lore, and sensitivity training, such as T-group and gestalt confrontation, which
raise the hackles of the prejudiced before the process begins. Both
of these models are really only suitable for interested volunteers.
Attempting to stimulate self-change in respect and rationality
through listening to peers in moral discussions need not be focused
directly upon ethnic prejudice and can appeal to many.

One of the problems of public education is caused by its desire to be accountable to parents and taxpayers by staying out of
controversial areas and by teaching for existing tests, so as to
demonstrate successes and recognize failures. However, social
and moral development are too important to ignore, and they are
hardly tapped by either IQ or achievement tests. The realization
that cognitive-social development can be mapped and stimulated

makes a new curriculum possible. We have been content to stress factual information in the social studies and to separate "affective" and "regular" education, to the detriment of both. What is needed is awareness that more socially mature and caring men and women will come from an educational system that is oriented toward concern for social justice, a system that raises questions without specifying a particular educational content for their answers.

In this kind of education it is necessary to go beyond value clarification. Value-clarification procedures have usually been based on the assumption that all values are relative. As summarized by Engel (1970), this position would have the following implications:

> In the consideration of values, there is no single correct answer but value clarification is supremely important. One must contrast value clarification and value inculcation.
>
> This is not to suggest, however, that nothing is ever inculcated. As a matter of fact, in order to clarify values, at least one principle needs to be adopted by all concerned. That principle might be stated: in the consideration of values there is no single correct answer. More specifically it might be said that the adequate posture both for students and teachers in clarifying values is openness.

While we also stress openness and the avoidance of inculcation, we do not agree with Engel that all values are relative nor that children should be taught value relativity. For example, a dictatorship is philosophically not the most fair form of government, even though the majority of the people in a given nation may believe that it is. That all values are relative to their society is an unsound doctrine. In terms of our research, there are culturally universal values. The order of the stages is also universal, because their structures of thinking increasingly approximate a rational philosophy and encompass more viewpoints in conceptions of social justice.

Although we believe that relativism is an incorrect philosophic view, the educational objective of stimulation of moral stage development cannot be called indoctrinative. In the first place, it is nonindoctrinative because it is not addressed to transmitting a specific value content but rather to stimulating a new way of thinking and judging. In the second place, it is nonindoctrinative because it is not imposing something alien on the student. Movement to the next stage is movement in a natural direction, in the only direction the student can go. In the third place, it is nonindoctrinative because the core of the theory is that a sense of rights and justice cannot be

taught but can be stimulated to develop. The objection to indoctrina-
tion presupposes that all children have a sense of rights, but such a
sense of human rights actually comes about only through the process
of moral development that we seek to stimulate.

If developmental moral education is nonindoctrinative in its
objectives, so must it be in its methods. These need not be very
different from the methods of value clarification. Filmstrips have
been published for grade school children that have stories ending in
discussion questions about what would be fair. A discussion method
based on verbal dilemmas was first proposed by Blatt (n.d.) for
slightly older children. This relies for its effects upon the kind of
argument among the students that evokes a sense of disequilibrium
about their own positions and a consequent movement to a more
comprehensive one.

Confrontations are usually between students at adjacent stages.
Laboratory studies by Rest, Turiel, and Kohlberg (1969) have demonstrated that adolescents comprehend all stages below their own
and sometimes the next stage above and that they prefer the highest
stage they can comprehend. When adolescents were exposed to all
stages, the most change occurred in response to exposure to the next
stage up. This is a viable technique, because most classrooms contain students at three stages.

The techniques and skills of inductive moral education require
training teachers to lead discussions. The means have not been
evolved by which the teachers could recognize various levels of interest or ability at role-taking in the classroom and perceive whether
preadolescents were moving in the direction of formal operational
thought. Empathy remains unmeasurable. These skills are needed
for promoting the high stage of morality that would preclude prejudice.

Opportunities to practice moral discussions and learn the empathic skills that are already demanded by their profession could
enlarge the teachers' understanding of ethnic problems. Counselors
with therapeutic skills or listening skills should be passing these on
to teachers for their work with children and families. This could
lead to the desire for and creation of a more just "community
school," in which sharing of governance tends to raise the moral
level. We are experimenting with stimulating empathy and inference-
making by teaching peer-counseling in high school. We have also
begun some work on a "just community school" within a public high
school in Cambridge, Massachusetts.

In addition to verbal discussion and activities designed to encourage empathic and listening skills, a curriculum that incorporates
social service activities and involvements can help build the ego
strength necessary for progress to higher moral levels. Lack of a
sense of personal agency, of an ability to shape one's own life, is

part of a vicious circle from which no attempt to alter bad conditions
is begun.

When thirteen-year-olds were asked what could be done to improve ghetto life, suburban adolescents answered with reasoned but
distanced analyses, while a typical city child said laconically, "Get
that guy back from the moon. Maybe he will tell us what to do."
This was probably an expression of frustration about the government
preference for spending money on the space program rather than on
the cities, but by itself it galvanized no classroom support for movement to a higher moral stage. The child, feeling words to be useless, made little attempt to be cogent.

Activites outside the classroom, especially those making use
of empathic skills, such as teaching younger children or serving old
people, give adolescents a needed way of being useful in the real
life of their communities.

A direct attempt to alter expressions of prejudice in school can
not be considered out of place. Since about 1947 the climate of public opinion in this country has turned strongly against prejudice
(Simpson and Yinger 1958), and children tend to admire proponents
of this sensible view. However, teachers should not approach this
task moralistically; they must recall that most young people are not
yet at Stage 3 and may not take motives into account. This they
must be gently and inductively encouraged to achieve. A typical
mixture of attitudes based on limited understanding is the following
from a nine-year-old white city girl:

> Busing is a waste of time on the bus, and it's for no
> use. They might get to like each other, the mixed
> kids, but not that much. They would play in differ-
> ent places; they always do here. I don't know why
> the blacks do that. They are really incredibly tough.
> They stick together, and you always hear, "After
> school I beat you up." I like them because they really
> make their way. You have to give them that. It's
> not so easy to be black, as I know, because with my
> dark skin some people think I am.

Because there is no intergroup education in the school, this
girl's questions will go unanswered, and her open attitudes will
have no opportunity to influence the more closed ones of some classmates. Her teachers typically will withdraw from the authoritarian
attitudes of the children, the overgeneralizing, stereotyping,
ridicule-poking attitudes that are often blamed on parent failure
rather than on the inevitably oversimplifying nature of immaturity.
Even the racial put-downs arising from concern about social status

that are all too adult, need not be threatening. Children are probably more thoughtful and more responsive than has been assumed, and new ways to stimulate moral growth and the growth of that delight in others that is entirely natural must be found.

REFERENCES

Allport, Gordon. 1954. The Nature of Prejudice. Cambridge, Mass.: Addison-Wesley.

Blatt, Moshe. n.d. "The Effects of Classroom Discussion Programs upon Children's Level of Moral Judgment." Ph.D. dissertation, University of Chicago.

Cohen, H., and G. Weil. 1971. Tasks of Emotional Development: A Projective Test for Children and Adolescents. Lexington, Mass.: D. C. Heath.

Colby, A. 1972. "Logical Operations in the Development of Moral Judgment." Ph.D. dissertation, Columbia University.

Cowan, P. 1969. "Social Learning and Piaget's Cognitive Theory of Moral Development." Journal of Personal and Social Psychology 3.

Davidson, Florence B. H. 1974. "Respect for Human Dignity and Ethnic Judgments in Childhood." Ph.D. dissertation, Harvard University.

Feffer, M., and V. Gourevitch. 1960. "Cognitive Aspects of Role-Taking in Children." Journal of Personality 28.

Goodman, M. E. 1964. Race Awareness in Young Children. 2d ed. enlarged (1st ed. 1952). Cambridge, Mass.: Addison-Wesley.

Harris, D.; H. Gough; and W. Martin. 1950. "Children's Ethnic Attitudes II: Relationship to Parental Beliefs concerning Child Training." Child Development 21.

Hartshore, H., and M. May. 1928. Studies in Deceit. New York: Macmillan.

Jaquette, D., and P. Carrick. n.d. "The Effects of Moral Judgment on Minority Group Stereotyping in a Northern and Southern High School." Term paper, Harvard College.

Kessen, W. 1970. "Stage and Structure in the Study of Children." In "Thought in the Young Child," eds. W. Kessen and C. Kuhlman, Monographs of Sociology for Research in Child Development, Series 83, vol. 27.

Kohlberg, Lawrence. 1963. "The Development of Children's Orientation toward a Moral Order." Part 1, Vita Humana 6.

Kohlberg, L. and R. Meyer. 1972 (summary, 1974). "Development as the Aim of Education." Harvard Education Review 42.

Kuhn, D. 1972. "The Development of Role-taking Ability." New York: Columbia University.

Kutner, B. 1958. "Patterns of Mental Functioning Associated with Prejudice in Children." Psychological Monographs 72.

Lovin, R. 1972. "The Universal Perspective and Moral Development." Cambridge, Mass.: Harvard University.

Piaget, J. 1926. The Language and Thought of the Child. New York: Harcourt, Brace.

Porter, J. 1971. Black Child, White Child. Cambridge, Mass.: Harvard University Press.

Radke, M. 1950. "Children's Perceptions of Negro and White Social Roles." Journal of Personality 29.

Rest, J.; E. Turiel; L. Kohlberg. 1969. "Relations between Levels of Moral Judgment and Preference and Comprehension of the Moral Judgment of Others." Journal of Personality 37.

Sanford, N. 1956. "The Approach of 'The Authoritarian Personality.'" In Psychology of Personality, ed. J. McCary. New York: Logos.

Selman, R. L. 1973. "A Structural Analysis of the Ability to Take Another's Social Perspective: Stages in the Development of Role-taking Ability." Paper presented at the meeting of the Society for Research in Child Development, Philadelphia, Pennsylvania, March 1973.

Simpson, George; and J. Milton Yinger. 1958. Racial and Cultural Minorities. New York: Harper Brothers.

Swinson, J. 1966. "The Development of Cognitive Skills and Role-
    Taking." Dissertation Abstracts 26, 4082.

Trager, H.; M. Radke; H. Davis. 1949. "Social Perceptions and
    Attitudes of Children." Genetic Psychology Monographs 40.

Turiel, E. 1966. "An Experimental Test of the Sequentiality of
    Developmental Stages in the Child's Moral Judgments."
    Journal of Personal and Social Psychology 3.

White, R. 1959. "Motivation Reconsidered: The Concept of Com-
    petence." Psychology Review 66.

6

CHILD DEVELOPMENT
AND RESPECT FOR
CULTURAL DIVERSITY
Irving E. Sigel
James E. Johnson

Most would agree that an educational system that limits its objectives to the instilling of intellectual mastery of the traditional three R's is in no position to usher in the twenty-first century. Events since the end of World War II have shown the necessity for seriously addressing problems concerning human understanding and sensitivity; the compelling need to study these problems has been illustrated as drastically as the deficiencies in U.S. scientific studies were illustrated by Sputnik in the mid-1950s. Global interdependence has become a reality, making it imperative that U.S. educators broaden their goals to include vital and meaningful psychoeducational experiences designed to foster greater harmony among nations and among the diverse ethnic, racial, socioeconomic, and religious groups within our own pluralistic society.

In a pluralistic culture such as ours, the need to help children accept others who are different from themselves continues to be a problem. The current and eventual well-being of our nation may depend in no small way on how successful we are in preparing the next generation to learn to live, to let live, and to recognize the rights of persons and groups to express their identities in their own ways within the framework of our society.

The task facing the educator is far from easy. It is doubtful that a simple juxtaposition of groups in a school or in a work situation will automatically improve human relations. Proximity of contact may instead increase social distance and defeat good intentions. At times the old adage that intimacy breeds contempt turns out to be valid because the behaviors of some group members are inimical to the values and coping behaviors of others. For example, in a study done by Irving E. Sigel, four-year-old black and white lower- and middle-class nursery school children were brought together. One

aim was to see how these two racial and two social class groups
would interact in a benign environment. Our observations indicated
that as time went on the children segregated themselves along class
but not racial lines. Middle-class black and white children played
with each other, but lower-class black and white children did not.
Why did this occur? The answer from one middle-class child when
referring to a lower-class child is representative: "He doesn't know
how to play. He always takes things away. He doesn't share." This
pilot study suggested the critical issue: contact is not sufficient but
must be supported by programmatic input by the educator to counter-
act the negative aspects in the situation. In a word the question becomes, How should educators work with integrated groups to promote
positive or at least neutral attitudes among them in contrast to negative and hostile ones?

In common with educational initiatives in general, the developing and implementing of a program intended to facilitate intergroup
understanding must take the child's perspective into account in order
to be effective. Such a program must be in touch with the developing nature of the child's intellect and must be responsive to the child's
ability to comprehend the communications sent his or her way. As
we shall see, the concept of cultural pluralism is a difficult intellectual achievement. Along the way the developing child must first
learn such seemingly obvious facts as, for example, that not all
persons share his or her feelings and expectations, even when confronted with identical situations.

Implied here is the argument that social attitudes and behaviors
are filtered through the child's cognitive status. As we shall show,
cognitive status also influences understanding of others and the ability to emphasize and respect others' individual needs and integrity.
Thus, to be effective, developing psychoeducational programs must
take cognitive features into account. Social and emotional factors
are relevant, to be sure, but they must be considered in a cognitive
framework.

Accepting the necessity of cultural and subcultural interdependence for mutual physical and psychological survival at home and
abroad, adults and children must attain the concept that most ethnic,
racial, and religious differences among people must be dealt with in
a framework common to human and social survival. Group differences should be recognized, but they should be carefully considered
in social decision making. One issue is the degree to which social
group differences are to be considered relevant or not. Skin color
is a group difference that should be ignored, while religious practices may have to be considered. For example, should Catholic attitudes on birth control or abortion be imposed on those who do not
have such religious beliefs? The realization that group differences

can be made positive or neutralized by consideration of the broader context is an important cognitive achievement. A prerequisite for this type of realization, however, is the understanding of the deceptively simple notion that members of groups are also individuals. Although it is impossible to ignore the group, the individual must constantly be kept in mind. The ability to do so requires a certain level of intellectual maturity, as we shall see.

To show the intellectual sophistication required, let us consider the following example. If we take "pride" or "respect for others" as the critical features of membership in certain religious and racial groups, then knowing the group membership of an individual tells us something about that individual even if we do not know the individual. We assume that the individual possesses the critical feature by virtue of the fact that he or she is a member of a group we define in terms of the given feature. For example, if we know someone is Roman Catholic, we may know something about his or her belief system; likewise, if we know someone is a Black Muslim, we may know something of the belief system of that person and something about his or her social habits and goals as well. However, at the same time mature thought demands that we recognize that we do not know how the Roman Catholic or the Black Muslim interprets his or her belief system or acts in relation to it. Moreover, there are a host of other factors that are relatively unrelated to someone's belief system about which we remain ignorant, such as mannerisms, thoughtfulness, and assertiveness. In a word, the name of the belief system is not enough to reveal the individual's character. Therefore it is necessary to function on two levels simultaneously when conceptualizing the other: on the level of group membership and on the level of individuality. The cognitive processes that permit such conceptualization are not immediately available to the young child, and even when they are attained in development, such processes are not enough to assure respect or love for the other. Such an outcome is beyond our scope or specific intention but relates to the involved value systems, as expressed perhaps in emotional considerations.

An understanding of the capability of conceptualizing the other simultaneously on two levels, as a member of a group and as an individual, and of the cognitive processes involved in this ability presupposes an understanding of the way cognition develops and functions among children. To further children's understanding of others, the planned situational arrangement must be set within the context of the ability of the children to comprehend the meaning of the intended product, which is understanding of pluralism.

DEVELOPMENTAL PERSPECTIVE

In recent years it has been increasingly believed that the road to intellectual maturity proceeds in an orderly, stage-like way, that there are qualitative differences among children at different phases of intellectual growth in terms of the mental tools or operations available for organizing and interpreting experience.

Children do not grow intellectually simply by increasing their storehouses of information gained by experience in an additive fashion. Rather, there are distinct ability levels that prescribe the kinds of environmental input the developing child can maximally profit from and the kinds of responses that can reasonably be expected from the child.

An understanding of the implications of the stage concept is critical for educational programming and diagnosis. Children at different stages of intellectual growth differ considerably in their interpretation of experience. For example, preschool children and early elementary school children tend to believe that what they see is real in a literal sense. Thus a young child regards dreams as actual happenings and will insist that the moon moves to follow him or her around. The young child is unable to draw inferences from perceptual input, especially when there is a conflict between perception and reason. Thus, unlike the adult or the older child, the preschooler does not understand that a person is not strong by virtue of his height, and so on.

In other words, one critical consideration to remember is that intellectual development can be described in terms of qualitative changes in the way the child views and interprets the world and that these changes proceed in orderly stage sequences. In gross terms, two stages in intellectual development may be described as egocentric and sociocentric. A child in the egocentric stage possesses a belief that the world revolves around him or her and that all others must be the same in terms of wants, intentions, expectations, and so on, especially when others are in the same situation or when the child is experiencing something emotionally important. In the sociocentric stage the child has the ability to take the point of view of the other and to realize that the other may experience feelings and expectations that may be in conflict with the child's own internal state.

There are many additional ways of depicting the qualitative differences between the egocentric and sociocentric child. For instance, the egocentric child is stimulus-bound, and concrete perceptual cues dominate over covert factors, while the sociocentric child is capable of inference making, which enables reason to win over perceptual forces.

Further elucidation of the qualitative differences in cognitive capability that are inherent in a stage concept of development can be accomplished by a summary account of J. Piaget's theory of intellectual growth. There are other theories, to be sure, but our bias is Piagetian because Piaget provides one of the few comprehensive theories of development of knowledge. For Piaget there are three major stages in intellectual development: (1) sensorimotor intelligence, (2) preoperational intelligence, and (3) operational intelligence.

Sensorimotor Intelligence

Sensorimotor intelligence refers to prelanguage or practical intelligence and has been studied by Piaget (1954) in detail. Roughly during the first two years of life, the infant accomplishes the following kinds of developmental tasks: the attainment of rudimentary knowledge that is the prototype of concepts through sensorimotor actions and coordinations with respect to the environment; differentiation of self from the environment or the beginning of self-object relations; localization of self in space; and the beginning of awareness of cause and effect and of time and space, in part because of the ability to identify the permanence and substantiality of objects.

Much of the intellectual gains during the sensorimotor period are the result of the child's sensorimotor actions on the concrete world of objects. By coordinating sensorimotor actions the child is capable, for example, of precise reaching behaviors that secure an object and bring the object to the child's mouth. Hence basic object relations are mastered and the child is capable of nonsymbolic "reasoning" on a practical plane, which foreshadows later symbolic reasoning. This coordination provides the child with the skills and learned behaviors necessary to adapt to the environment, which is the essence of intelligence for Piaget.

Piaget's term for the learned behaviors of the sensorimotor period is schemata; that is, each learned action, according to Piaget, is an organization of particular behaviors that are relevant to one another. The schemata are acquired through the complementary processes of accommodation and assimilation. Assimilation is the process by which the child alters incoming environmental information to fit his or her already existing intellectual state, while accommodation is the process by which the child modifies his or her intellectual apparatus to meet the demands of the new information. Intellectual development is directed toward a balance of assimilatory and accommodatory processes. Such an equilibrium is never fully achieved, however, for as soon as a steady state is reached in the intelligence of an individual, a change in the environment prompts further modification. Likewise a change in the intellectual apparatus of the individual will lead to further discriminatory actions and perceptions that will change the individual's construction of what might otherwise be constant environmental stimulation. In Piaget's theory this dynamic mechanism of intellectual development is called the equilibration process.

Although the newborn begins life with an undifferentiated view of self and the environment, during the first two years major intellectual strides are made. The child learns that the environment functions on the basis of certain physical properties, such as space, object permanence, and causality. Even as the child moves out of this period of sensorimotor intelligence, he or she is still dominated by the physical attributes of the environment and remains a perceptually dominated organism. At this period the child is preabstract, that is, unable to grasp what is called in biology a "genus-species" relation, or a higher class concept. For example, he cannot yet understand that a cat is in a broad general class, animal. For the child under two the world is experienced not as an integrated picture but as a series of stills coming one after another. More advanced symbolic thinking awaits further intellectual and linguistic growth.

Preoperational Intelligence

At the end of the second year the child has acquired certain intellectual skills that permit him or her to function on a more symbolic level and thereby enter upon a preparatory period leading to full intellectual competence. This stage is called preoperations and is subdivided into a prelogical phase roughly from two to four years, and an intuitive phase, from four to seven years.

Prelogical Phase

In this phase the child is no longer "thinking" and "reasoning" in purely motoric terms, that is, on a practical plane. Instead, the child is beginning to be able to function on a symbolic plane. Early manifestations of this are awareness that something can stand for something else and treating an object as if it were what the child is intending it to represent. This can be observed in the young toddler's pretend play behavior. In other words, the child is demonstrating an ability to differentiate the signifier (that which stands for something) and the actual object, a differentiation that represents the onset of symbolic thought.

Lest one be misled by this momentous symbolic breakthrough, it is well to remember that the prelogical child is still an immature, egocentric thinker. Some tell-tale signs of this immaturity include the following: inability to take the point of view of others; egocentricity with respect to symbolic activities; face-value judgments and unreflective thought; grouping of objects on the basis of single attributes and inability to classify flexibly according to the multifaceted aspects of stimuli; concentration of attention on only one feature of the environment at a time (Piaget 1961).

The child's inability to deal conceptually with the multiple characteristics of objects, such as size, color, width, height, texture, and function, is one reason Piaget refers to the child as prelogical at this time in intellectual ontogeny. Although the concept of an object has already been acquired, and some notion of what a class of objects means, the child is not able to incorporate the attributional diversity inherent in any single object into the formation of single classes. For instance, although the child is capable of classifying men and women as people and pears and bananas as food-- first-level concepts (Welch 1940)--he or she cannot use two attributes of the same object, that is, cannot break up the group of apples into small green apples, large green apples, small red apples, and big red apples.

The prelogical child is still dominated by his or her perceptions. The primitive conceptions are still largely determined by the physical appearance of objects. Unlike the sensorimotor child, however, the prelogical child can approach objects in a symbolic way rather than through direct motoric action.

Intuitive Phase

The second part of the preoperational period of intellectual development is the intuitive phase, roughly from four to seven years. The intuitive child is still egocentric and is still dominated by his perceptions, as was the prelogical child. The intuitive child is unable to make inferences about events when the perceptions are at odds with reason. Relevant here is the time-worn example of the mass of clay that the preoperational child is unable to conserve over transformations along irrelevant dimensions, such as changes of shape. At this point in intellectual development the child's difficulty, according to Piaget, is an inability to decenter, or deploy his attention, on more than one aspect of the stimulus at a time. Consequently, the child places too much importance on one dimension of the stimulus while neglecting other dimensions.

Three fundamental operations emerge during the intuitive phase: the ability to think in terms of classes, the ability to see relations, and the ability to handle number concepts. The child can classify material on the basis of objective similarity. When presented with an assortment of squares and diamonds, with each assortment consisting of two colors, the child can classify on the basis of shape or color but still cannot make multiple classifications utilizing both dimensions simultaneously.

During this phase of cognitive development the child is becoming increasingly able to understand the meaning of similarity and classification and can see relationships such as "Mr. Krause is the father of William." This results from emergent relational concepts such as seriation or the ability to rank objects according to some criterion. The child is said to be in the intuitive phase because he or she is not necessarily capable of verbalizing these newfound classificatory capabilities or otherwise indicating an awareness of them.

In the intuitive phase the child is also beginning to use numbers and to order things in terms of quantity. Because of this increasing ability to disregard certain properties of items and see that a relationship can exist on a numerical basis even though the objects may differ structurally, the child can now count different kinds of things. In doing so the child is able to produce a sum, which is an abstraction. The crucial difference between this phase of intellectual development and the next stage is the lack of reasoning processes or operations.

Operational Intelligence

The operational period of intellectual growth is also divided into two parts: concrete operations, approximately from 7 to 11 years, and formal operations, from 11 to 15 years.

Concrete Operations

The onset of concrete operations is marked by the emergence of certain reasoning processes that appear to be logical. At this point in intellectual ontogeny most logicians would agree that the child is able to think in logical terms. The term "operation" refers to the child's internalized responses or the tools for mentally acting upon objects. Lawrence Kohlberg (1963, p. 16) stated that mental acts are "in imagination the thing or concept thought about in order to reach some conclusion. According to Piaget, a concept or classifi-

cation is not a mere task of labelling a set of stimuli, it is an actual
'piling together' of objects included in a class."

A number of operations have been described by Piaget, such
as the logical operations involved in simple arithmetic (reversibility),
in the organization of items into class hierarchies (classification),
and in the arrangement of objects along a continuum of increasing
values (seriation). One important consequence of the acquisition of
these concrete operations is an increasing ability to deal with number concepts. According to Piaget, the acquisition of the number
concept requires the child to (1) perform reversible operations (that
is, for every mental action or operation there is one that cancels it,
such as $5 \times 3 = 15$ and $15 \div 5 = 3$); (2) develop the logic of class (that
is, the grouping of diverse items into a single classification) and
realizing that classes can have included classes (for instance, the
animal class has a subclass, cats); and (3) comprehend and develop
an understanding of asymmetrical relations (that is, the ability to
rank items in descending or ascending order): the child has to be
able to count one object first and another one second.

Concomitant with the development of concrete operations is the
waning of egocentrism and the emergence of the ability to decenter.
That is, the child is now able to focus attention on more than one
aspect of the situation at a time, is able to coordinate different perspectives, and is capable of making inferences. The child is no
longer ensnarled by his or her own perceptions but instead is able
to reason beyond the physical appearance of things.

Formal Operations

A major limitation of concrete operations is that the child
needs the "crutch" of physically present supports in order to reveal
a facility in logical reasoning. At formal operations, the last stage
in Piagetian theory, the young adolescent no longer requires concrete objects to perform mental acts. Furthermore, unlike the concrete operational child, the young adolescent is capable of "stepping
back" and reflecting on his or her own thought processes. The young
adolescent has finally mastered true abstract thinking and is able to
engage in hypothetical-deductive reasoning and propositional logic.
Although language does not control formal operations, it is needed
for the expression of formal operational thinking. The young adolescent is now able to speculate, form hypotheses, plan scientific
study, test all possible combinations and permutations, and seek
validation in a systematic manner.

To the extent that the Piagetian stages are accurate summary
observations on the course of intellectual development, it is hoped

that the above portrayal of them is not too schematic and that it is
sufficient to demonstrate to the reader that qualitative differences
in intellectual capability do exist. An important realization about
the stage concept is that it represents the different ways children at
different developmental levels characteristically organize and mentally operate on information. A central problem remains, however.
How does the child go about obtaining knowledge and information
about his physical and social world with which to nourish the development of operativity? What role can the adult socializing agent play
in this process? To these topics we now turn our attention.

What Is Learning?

Consistent with the organismic model of man (Reese and Overton 1970), it is our belief that the child is not the passive recipient
of external stimulation but is an active organism that seeks out information. The view that the child is outreaching by very nature has
important implications for educational practice. For one thing, the
educator who accepts this philosophy would avoid depriving the child
of opportunities to participate in his or her own development; instead, the educator would do everything possible to create a climate
in which the child could grow at his or her own pace. At times the
educator may challenge the child to excel to a higher level of development, but only if the child is ready for such stretching. To be
successful in this difficult endeavor, the "agent of development"
must adapt interpersonal communications to suit the current state
of the child's cognitive ability. The ability to make this adaptation
requires sensitivity to the child's ability to understand. To this end
the stage concept of development may be helpful.

In terms of the way the child obtains information and knowledge
about the physical and social world, it is useful to think of the child
as a scientist. The similarity between the scientist and the child
does not rest in any kind of mutual interest in chemistry or physics
but rather in similar processes of discovery. The child as an active
organism develops an idea, expresses the idea in action or verbally,
and then proceeds to act on this and on the resulting feedback from
the environment. At times the child discovers that he or she is in
error, that expectancy is violated. For example, many young children tend to be trusting of adults because most adults are nice to
them and do not harm them. Children then proceed on this belief.
However, parents and teachers may inform the child that all adults
are not trustworthy. The child who accepts this warning as valid
must come to understand that not all adults are the same. This is
probably a difficult concept for many children to learn. How does

the child really know the validity of the warning? The children who
exhibit a strong urge to put the warning to a test may get into trouble,
in which case the experience will teach them of their error. This
example shows that in some cases the adult cannot allow the child
the freedom to use the experimental method and must use protective
measures. Many of the rules and restrictions parents and teachers
enforce are necessary for this reason.

The child and the scientist move about and encounter new experiences, which are interpretable only in terms of previously constructed conceptualizations of the world. In a sense, a changing child
encounters a changing world. In traversing the course of intellectual
development, the child interprets experience in ever-changing ways,
but always in terms of the existing knowledge base and the mental
tools available for processing the information. Thus an oral reading
of this chapter would be incomprehensible to a nursery school young-
ster, but if the words were translated into certain types of activities,
the child would understand something of what is being said. Because
of the variability of what the child can comprehend, which is a function of developmental level, it behooves the educator to understand
on what level the child is, enabling the educator to choose an appropriate communicational device and manner. In sum, then, the
knowledge the child acquires as a function of the adult's articulation
of experience, and the interpretation the child attaches to the adult's
message, varies according to the child's level of competency.

There are two general classes of environmental input in which
the adult is directly involved in terms of the articulation of experience
and its influence on intellectual growth. These are teaching behaviors
and management behaviors. Teaching behaviors require the child to
transcend the concrete here and now and respond on the basis of non-
observable aspects of the situation. These would be asking the child
to infer another's intentions, to reconstruct a past event, or to plan
a future activity. Management behaviors are techniques used by
adults to control and discipline the child. The latter class of behaviors can be used to the same cognitive ends as the former kinds
of behavior. For example, they would include questioning the child
about the consequences of misbehavior on others in order to induce
inference-making about the internal state of others. These two
classes of adult behavior can have important results in terms of the
child's intellectual development; it is critical, however, to take into
account the developmental level of the child when employing them.
It is also important to bear in mind that the child is influenced by
adults in other ways, such as through modeling and observational
learning.

Development of Social and Interpersonal Knowledge

As the child moves through his or her social world, given the cognitive capabilities the child has at any particular moment, social and interpersonal situations that demand "solutions" are encountered. For example, as the child comes into contact with children and adults who have characteristics different from the members of his or her own family, it becomes necessary to construct broader conceptualizations about people in order to adapt to the social environment. It is also necessary to learn certain skills in order to engage in interpersonal relations.

The likelihood of success of any programmatic educational input designed to improve children's understanding and acceptance of different people from various groups is in part contingent upon the developmental considerations relevant to this purpose. To this end, some familiarization with the findings from a relatively recent field within developmental psychology is pertinent. This area of inquiry is concerned with the acquisition, progression, and utilization of concepts about social phenomena, or social cognition. Some of the behaviors studied in the area of social cognition include empathy; role-taking; communicational efficacy; moral reasoning; and the development of prosocial behaviors such as sharing, helping, and altruism. To provide an exhaustive review of the literature in this booming field of child psychology is neither possible nor appropriate for this chapter; the interested reader can refer to the excellent review chapter by C. Shantz (forthcoming).

As we shall see, the findings from the studies dealing with the cognition of social phenomena are generally interpreted according to the formal descriptors of Piagetian theory outlined above. The social behaviors subsumed under the area of this class of cognitive problems are influenced by the child's stage (ability to process knowledge and information) and by the kinds of reactions encountered from others. At this point we shall target three kinds of sociocognitive behaviors for summary review: social perspective-taking, empathy, and altruism. The three classes of behavior chosen are interrelated and are particularly relevant to our discussion of child development and respect for cultural diversity.

Social Perspective-taking

Perspective-taking or role-taking is defined as the cognitive ability to distinguish one's own point of view from that of others and then to assume multiple perspectives. Social perspective-taking is different from perceptual perspective-taking (Piaget and Inhelder 1956) in that social perspective-taking refers to interpersonal relationships, in which the ability to take into account other people's emotions, thoughts, wishes, and intentions is involved. Normal adults are usually quite efficient at such behaviors. Many theorists hold that role-taking may well be the mechanism for the development of most social activity, including competition, cooperation, empathy, communication, prosocial behavior, and moral development. Although normal adults are competent, children younger than six or seven and retarded or severely disorganized adults have difficulty in understanding the viewpoints of others (Chandler 1973; Devries 1970; Elkonin 1960; Feffer 1959 and 1970; Feffer and Gourevitch 1960; Flavell 1968 and 1971; Looft 1972; Mead 1934; Milgram 1960; Miller, Kessel, and Flavell 1970; Selman 1971 and 1973).

The difficulty young children experience in taking perspectives other than their own into consideration is understandable, given Piaget's description of cognitive development. As noted, prior to operational thought the young child is egocentric and is unable to shift from one point of view to another. Under the age of seven the child cannot generally differentiate between his or her own and other people's perspectives and is unable to simultaneously consider the multiple perspectives or aspects of a given situation (Looft 1972). This is particularly true in experimental situations in which the child is required to take into account a perspective in conflict with his or her own (Chandler and Greenspan 1972) or in everyday situations in which the child is emotionally aroused. However, egocentrism as such is not emotional or egotistical; egocentrism is a nonconscious characteristic of the child's cognitive system. It is not that the child will not take the other's viewpoint (egotism) but that the child cannot do so for developmental reasons (egocentrism).

Cognitive and social conflicts, or mismatches between the way the child and others construct the environment, foster conflict, which creates tension. Reducing the tension leads to a waning of the egocentric point of view. Peer group interaction, particularly competition and argumentation, is important in the decline of egocentrism and in the subsequent development of role-taking skills. A major change, then, in role-taking ability occurs at the onset of Piaget's concrete operational stage, when the peer group is becoming increasingly important to the child (at seven through eleven years of age).

Further strides in the progression of role-taking ability are evident in the formal operational child, usually 11 years and older. Formal operations are not constrained by the need to have observables. The child can think in terms of the nonobservables and the hypothetical. In terms of role-taking this is demonstrated by a freedom from the physical appearance of roles, by coordination of a variety of personal and social ideas or images, and by evolution of behavior in relation to the above factors. In addition, the formal operational child is capable of recursive thinking; that is, the type of thinking by which people can imagine that certain others are thinking the same things about them as they are thinking of those others, and so on. Simultaneously, the formal operational child can take into account the belief systems of others and their general attitudes and the ways in which these might be affecting the others in particular instances. An elaboration of the development of role-taking ability up to and including maturity is provided by R. L. Selman (1971, 1972, 1973).

Empathy

Both conceptually and operationally, the concept of empathy has been beset with some confusion in recent years. Much of the problem has arisen over the role of noncognitive factors in the empathic response and over the basis for the empathic response. Some investigators have defined empathy as the capacity to experience vicariously the affective state of the other (Dymond 1950; Feshbach 1973; Feshbach and Feshbach 1969; Feshbach and Roe 1968), while others have conceptualized empathy as the capacity to be cognitively aware of the way others feel (Borke 1971, 1972, and 1973). N. Feshbach refers to the latter as social comprehension and suggests that social comprehension may be a necessary requirement for the empathic response but should not be confused with it. In other words, there is some agreement that empathy involves a response to another person's affective state, but the nature of this response and the basis for it are clouded in controversy. For example, does one respond empathically on the basis of some inference about the other person, the situation the other person is in, or some combination of the two?

A cogent discussion of these issues is provided by R. J. Iannotti and J. Meacham (1974) and Iannotti (1975), according to which, if empathy is regarded simply as an awareness of the other's emotion in a cognitive sense, then it is being used as another term for social comprehension or role-taking with respect to the affective state of the other. When empathy is operationally defined as the ability to select the correct emotional reaction for another in familiar stereotypic situations (Borke 1971, 1972, and 1973), it is identical to a cognitive sense of social norms of how people should feel in different situations. If, however, empathy is defined as a correct recognition of the emotional state of another when that state is different from one's own (Burns and Carey 1957; Chandler and Greenspan 1972; Dymond 1950; Weinstein 1969), then it is being used as another term for emotional perspective-taking. The latter usage is different from the first in that it requires a sociocentric orientation. Neither usage, however, demands any kind of affective reaction to the other's emotional state.

Some researchers hold that empathic response requires some emotional response in the observer to the perceived state of the other (Aronfreed 1969; Feshbach 1973; Feshbach and Roe 1968; Krebs 1970; Mehrabian and Epstein 1972; Mood, Johnson, and Shantz 1973). Theorists who require some approximation between the emotion of the observer and the emotion of the other also differ in their interpretation of the basis for the response of the observer, which for some theorists is the other person's internal affective state and for other theorists is the situation of the other. In the latter case, the observer may be egocentrically responding to the way in which the situation would emotionally influence himself or herself; for instance, a little boy may correctly report that another child at a birthday party is happy because the birthday party makes him happy. On the other hand, an empathic response may involve some decentering or role-taking. This is the case when the observer is responding to the internal state of the other and is attempting to look at the situation from the other's viewpoint. For example, a child emphasizes that another child may indeed be sad at a birthday party, even though the first child was not experiencing the situation in this way but only came to share this feeling with the other child to some extent after witnessing the child in distress.

Developmentally, then, whether the nature of the response is held to contain emotional elements or not, the potential basis for the response changes as the child approaches operational thinking. Before operations the child responds egocentrically to the situation the other is in and can identify with it only on the basis of past experience or familiarity. After operations the child is capable of inferring the affective state of the other by adopting the perspective of the other independently of his or her own perspective.

If empathy is held to involve some affective response to the emotional state of another, then empathy is more than a cognitive skill. In this sense the observer must be capable of and willing to vicariously experience the emotion of the other in addition to being cognitively aware of what it is. If one defines empathy in this way it is easy to realize how empathy may be a motivator for many different kinds of behavior. Empathy can then be viewed as an inhibition of antisocial behaviors such as aggression and as a facilitator for prosocial behaviors, including altruism.

Altruism

A controversial issue in psychology and elsewhere is whether or not an altruistic motive exists independent of self-serving or

self-enhancing needs. The arguments pro and con are lengthy, and
the two sides need not be presented here; the interested reader may
refer to M. Hoffman (1974) for a pro position and to C. Cofer and
M. Appley (1964) for a con position. The purpose here is to present
the possibility that empathy, mediated by cognitive role-taking skill,
provides the motivation for the altruistic response.

Altruism has been defined as any behavior that helps another
without entailing immediate positive reinforcement to the benefactor
(Krebs 1970). Historically the research on this topic has largely resided in the domain of social psychology and has focused on the characteristics of the benefactor and the recipient and on the existence of
possible reinforcement contingencies. For example, many studies
have investigated altruism in terms of the perceived status of the
recipient and the affective state of the benefactor, while other research has addressed the problem in the context of expectation of
reward and observational learning (Berkowitz 1972).

Few studies have examined altruism within a developmental
framework or have addressed the question of what cognitive processes
may be involved. Only recently have investigators begun to give attention to the hypothesis that some characteristics of the benefactor,
specifically the developmental variables, may be involved in the expression of altruism and its prosocial behavioral derivatives (Aronfreed 1968; Hebb 1971; Hoffman 1972 and 1974).

Acknowledgment of the importance of developmental variables
in the expression of altruism is implied by Hoffman (1971, p. 7)
when he states that altruism "rests ultimately on the human capacity
to experience the inner state of others who are not in the same situation." In a later paper Hoffman (1974) discusses the role of the development of empathy or "empathetic distress" in the altruistic motive. He traces the development of the synthesis of cognitive and
emotional factors involved in "sympathetic distress," upon which
altruism is said to be predicated. Whereas the younger child's
"sympathetic distress" is primitively passive, involuntary, and
transitory and leads to actions that are often inappropriate and ineffective, this experience in the older child is typically more objective, more differentiated, and more consistent and very often leads
to appropriate and efficient action.

In summary, a case has been presented for the view that the
three sociocognitive behaviors, which are role-taking, empathy,
and altruism, are interrelated, and the position is taken that a discussion of them is germane to the topic of educational programming
and the development of understanding and to the acceptance of individuals of various social groups. The view has been advanced that
cognitive role-taking underlies the development of empathy, which
in turn is a motivator for such positive social responses as altruism

and, by extension, generally positive approaches toward others from different groups. It is apparent that the development of these behaviors is consistent with Piaget's formal description of cognitive development. Before the advent of operativity or logical reasoning, children seem incapable of assuming the role of the other. This characteristic of their information-processing system limits their ability to empathize and to behave prosocially in deliberate and effective ways. With the decline of egocentrism, young children become able to "put themselves in the shoes of the other," which makes empathy and altruism possible.

Nonintellective factors, we repeat, are also involved in the above progression. Therefore any cognitively based program of instruction that is used as a vehicle to promote greater intergroup and interpersonal understanding and acceptance must recognize a basic limitation. The facilitation of conceptual growth, social comprehension, and role-taking ability does not assure our intended outcomes. However, providing children with these necessary conditions for understanding and accepting one another should considerably improve the probability that these ends will be accomplished.

IMPLICATIONS FOR CLASSROOM PRACTICE

What has been said thus far concerning the natures of cognitive and sociocognitive development has been stated in general terms and is not intended as a complete or an exhaustive account of this very complex set of problems; rather, the purpose has been to provide a developmental perspective and some direction for what is to follow: the critical task of translating theory and information into practice. To accomplish this task we will begin by discussing in some detail a specific but multifaceted cognitive phenomenon, namely the development of classification behavior. We will attempt to show how a delineation of this developmental course can contribute to a teaching strategy directed toward the improvement of interpersonal and intergroup relations.

Classification Behavior: Class Labeling

Let us begin at the most elemental point and take any object—an apple, a pear, ice cream, whatever we wish. Stop for a moment, and think about this object. The apple has many attributes. It has size. It has a particular texture. It has a skin, a stem. It grows on a tree. It has curved surfaces. It has color. It has utility. It has taste. It can be put to many uses; it may be used for food or for

something to throw. Each of these attributes is an accurate designation of part of this thing we call "apple." The pear and the ice cream
can be discussed in the same way, each possessing similar as well
as diverse attributes. Each object possesses a myriad of attributes
denoting various aspects of its structure and function. Too often we
become unaware of these complexities because we tend to focus on
an apple in its primary function as something to eat or as something
red. The same thing is true with most objects, and unfortunately it
is often true when we think about people or groups. We establish a
particular relationship with the object or group and are aware of its
primary role, and then too often we continue to think of it in these
limited terms.

Such an attitude toward complex objects is very economical, in
that it facilitates the establishment of appropriate behaviors and attitudes toward the objects, but it is also a limitation. We develop a
schema of "apple," by which actions and meanings are organized.
When we read or hear the word "apple" a set of responses is elicited
that define a range of associations with the word "apple." The range
of responses and associations is stereotyped, since we often learn
about objects in limited ways. For example, the most frequent associations of the word "apple" are probably "fruit" and "red." Relatively few people think of the apple in terms of its curved surface,
its pulpy texture, or its stem.

We have discussed a familiar concrete object; now let us take
an important social event of the past decade, the war on poverty. In
connection with this particular event, the first thoughts that come to
mind may be associations such as Lyndon Johnson, the 1964 Democratic platform, Head Start, and federal spending. The reader may
select other attributes of this event, each one of which may denote a
class concept; for example, politics, liberalism, or domestic problems. There may be differences in the attributes selected by the
authors and by the reader, but commonalities will also appear because the authors and the reader share a common educational and
cultural experience. Likewise, we could generate a list of attributes
descriptive of different racial, religious, ethnic, or socioeconomic
groups. For example, take the concept "working class." We might
come up with the following labels: persons who earn wages, persons
who are manual laborers, persons with union cards, and so on.
Again the range of possible attributes is long, and not everyone
would agree on them. In effect, the list produced could represent
stereotypic thinking unless qualified by objective knowledge of individual cases.

The cognitive processes involved in identifying a social event
such as the war on poverty or a social group such as the working
class are identical to the ones involved in the illustration with the

apple. What we have done in each case is to identify a set of critical attributes that defines part of the totality. This labeling of attributes we call "multiple labeling."

An awareness of the range of attributes or aspects of any instance is a crucial prerequisite to the development of more complex classification behaviors. If we are able to specify many labels, we can classify instances in many categories. Thus, for example, we can classify the apple under the class "edible" or the class "having a curved surface" or the class "red." We could categorize the war on poverty under the class "federal aid," or "poverty programs," or "domestic problems," or "political action." We could categorize the working class under the category of "wage earners," "manual laborers," and so on.

The number and kinds of instances that can be brought under a particular heading depends on the criterial attribute selected. Thus for the class "fruit," we could include such objects as pears and oranges; but if our criterial attribute was the class "red," we would select additional instances possessing the attribute "red." Similarly, we could construct the class "federal programs," including the Head Start, Title I, and space programs, and we could construct the class "domestic federal programs," including the Head Start and the Title I programs but excluding the space program. If we categorize working class under "persons with union cards," we can include such groups as factory workers, teachers, and college professors; if we categorize working class under "wage earners," college professors would not be included.

Being aware that objects have many attributes is an important step in achieving awareness of the complexity of the environment. It provides the child with a broader range of information about events and reduces the amount of stereotyped thinking. To illustrate, if we think of a Negro only as black, of a Catholic only in terms of religion, or of the mainland Chinese in terms of their politics, we are thinking in terms of only one attribute; but there are many other attributes of each of these social instances. Stereotyped thinking exists when classifications are based on a limited number of attributes. When the child looks upon every object, every event, and every person as containing many attributes, it suggests that no one member is fixed in any particular class but that it can be in any number of classes, depending on the criterial attribute selected. Thus, if the child is looking around the room for all things that are black, he or she may include a person, a bottle of ink, and a shoe. If we now ask him to think of all things that have feet, he may now put the black person, the Caucasian, the chair, and the piano under one heading of objects having feet. In this way the child can learn about the relativity of class membership.

Preferences for Attribute Selection

A number of studies have been made of the bases children use in forming classifications. It has been found that some children show strong preferences for certain criteria of classification. These preferences have been called "styles of categorization," a term that means the consistent employment of particular classification criteria with different kinds of material. In classifying humans, for example, the presence of a certain size, shape, or color of physical features may be the criterial attributes on which classes are built. These are called "descriptive" criteria.

A second predisposition that has been identified is a tendency to classify items according to their functional interdependence, that is, according to the relation of one object to another. We have called this the "relational-contextual" approach. As an example, if a horse and a wagon are included in an array of items, an individual may group these together because the horse pulls the wagon. Other individuals tend to classify on the basis of inferred attributes of items, which we have called "categorical-inferential." In this case every instance in an array is an instance of the class; for example, an apple is thought of as a fruit, and a horse as an animal.

We have discovered that as children get older they make less use of relational-contextual criteria of classification and more use of the descriptive and categorical-inferential criteria. That is, they tend to shift away from relating things on the basis of common functions or interdependence to the more objective type classifications. These changes reflect the child's increased awareness of the complexity of items, as well as the ability to deal with materials on the basis of their objective features. The child relies less and less on his or her own unique subjective experiences as bases for classifying instances.

Apart from the tendency for styles of categorization to change with age, we have found strong personal preferences for particular modes of categorization in both children and adults. The preference for one or another mode is a personal characteristic. We know little about the origins or the modifiability of these classificatory orientations (Coop and Sigel 1971; Sigel, Jarman, and Honesian 1967).

Complex Classification Behavior

We have discussed categorizations based on the ability of children to use a single attribute as the basis for classification. The ability of children to deal in combinations of attributes emerges later, only after they have mastered certain kinds of intellectual tasks. The child must, as we have indicated, be aware that single attributes can be used as the basis of classification, that an object has no fixed position in any one class but can be a member of many classes. This is an illustration of decentration.

When the child understands the logic of single classification, he or she is ready to learn multiple classification. The essential logical processes of multiple classification are addition and multiplication.

The addition or the combining of classes can be illustrated by showing children pictures of tall and short Eskimos and Gypsies. The addition of classes can be illustrated by forming the following classes: (1) people who are tall or short; (2) people who are Eskimos or Gypsies; (3) people who are tall or are Gypsies; (4) people who are short or are Gypsies; (5) people who are tall or are Eskimos; and (6) people who are short or are Eskimos.

Multiplication of classes can be illustrated, using the same pictures. The following classes can be formed by multiplication: (1) tall Gypsies; (2) short Gypsies; (3) tall Eskimos; (4) short Eskimos.

The ability to combine two or more attributes is a very significant one in the logical development of thought. It is a prototype of complex thinking, in which classes are combined and recombined as the needs of the problems dictate. In the process of combining and recombining a group of items, the child has to shift criteria; flexibility is required in the manipulation of multiple criteria.

The significance of the ability to combine attributes was demonstrated in an experiment conducted with second and third grade children. In this study the children were given a task in which objects of observation had two dimensions. Such a task can be described as a matrix task, since one dimension of observation is on the horizontal axis and one on the vertical axis, each subgroup so defined forming an entry in the matrix. In the study a set of blocks was used that decreased in size in both length and width. The schema of the experiment, in a simplified form, can be represented as shown in Figure 6.1. The child's task is to fill the void in the matrix, which requires picking a block that is smaller in each dimension than the preceding block. In order to do this the child must be able to coordinate a decrease in length with a decrease in width. This task is one of logical multiplication, of combining two attributes to form a new classification.

We found that children capable of performing this task were also capable of performing another very important function, which is that of conserving, that is, of holding a characteristic of an item as invariant in the face of transformation. Although there are other indicators of ability to conserve, we found that children who were able to multiply classes were always able to conserve.

FIGURE 6.1

Schema of a Matrix Task

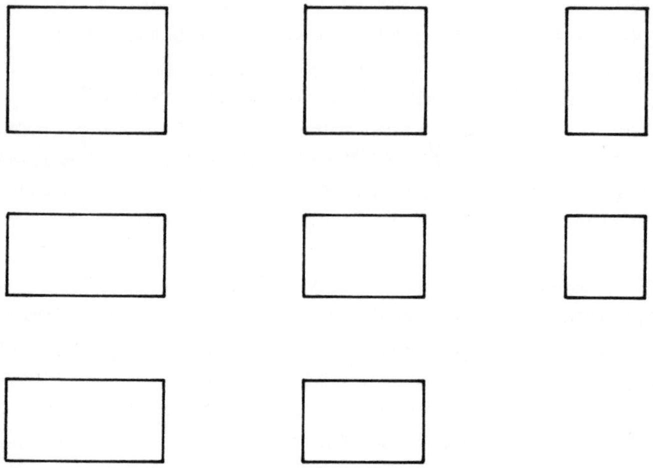

Source: Irving E. Sigel, F. Hooper, and F. Stevens, unpublished data.

For the reader who is unfamiliar with the classic conservation
problem, it can be described briefly. A child is presented with two
balls of clay, equal in size and identical in shape. One of these two
balls of clay is transformed into a sausage or a pancake or a cup,
and the child is asked whether the two pieces of clay are still equivalent. The ability to understand that there was merely a transformation in shape, but no change in amount, is called conservation. In
order for the child to understand this, to see that as the transformed
piece of clay gains in length it loses in width, requires the ability to
combine two attributes, namely length and height, and to realize that
there is interrelationship, that if one measurement decreases, the
other increases. The ability to conserve can easily be seen as relevant to many kinds of logical thought problems in the physical and
social sciences. In economics, for example, dollars can be changed
into other types of currency, with the purchasing power remaining
constant.

Reversibility and Reciprocity

In order to deal with problems of multiple classification and interdependence of attributes such as those just described, the child must be capable of two mental operations, reversibility and reciprocity.

Reversibility is a mental operation in which materials or ideas are reorganized so as to reconstruct the original state or class. In the example of the clay, reversibility is evident when the child is shown to be aware of the fact that when the transformed piece is rolled back into a ball, there will once again be two identical balls. In arithmetic, reversibility is manifest in the proof or subtraction. In classification, reversibility is manifest when the classes are reorganized and then brought back to the original state. Comprehension of reversibility reflects the awareness that instances conserve their identity even though placed in another class.

An example to illustrate reversibility is the case of dollars, which can be changed into yen and then converted back into dollars. The value of the dollar, or the value of the money in question, has been conserved even though it appears in a different form. Also, if the money is changed into other denominations, such as smaller coins or smaller bills, the amount is still the same.

Reciprocity connotes an interaction between objects or events. For instance, in urban sociology a reciprocal relation exists between the frequency of occurrence of crime and neighborhood solidarity and street surveillance. As applied to this specific case, the principle is that neighborhood solidarity is inversely related to the frequency of criminal acts in the streets. An increase in neighborhood solidarity causes a decrease in crime, while a decrease in solidarity is associated with an increase in crime. There is a reciprocal relationship between neighborhood solidarity and crime in the streets.

An understanding of the principle of reciprocity is crucial to scientific and logical thought. J. H. Flavell (1968, pp. 209-10) describes its importance as follows:

> Reciprocity entails not the outright elimination or negation of a factor but its neutralization, that is, holding its effect constant in some way while a second factor is being varied. For instance, where the problem is to study the separate effects of kind of metal and length on the flexibility of a rod, . . . the younger child finds himself at an impasse; he cannot literally negate either variable, i.e., work with a rod not made of some metal and not possessing some length. The

older child uses the reciprocal operation with
great profit here. He takes two rods of different
metals but of the same length (here length is not
negated, but neutralized or controlled--not
lengths per se, but length differences are annulled)
in order to study the effect of kind of metal, and
two rods of a single metal and different lengths to
study the effect of length.

The addition of the reciprocal operation to
the subject's repertory in solving scientific problems brings a general advance in strategy and
tactics: it disposes the subject towards the controlled experiment, that is, the nullification of
one variable, not simply to study one variable,
but to study the action of some other variable
free from error variance contributed by the first.
The younger child negates a variable in order to
study the causal efficacy of that variable. The
older child develops a better strategy: negate or
neutralize (whichever circumstances dictate; both
negation and reciprocity are at his disposal) factor A in order to study the effects of varying factor B; negate or neutralize A and B in order to
assess the uncontaminated action of C, and so on.
Once again we see that the transition from concrete to formal operations is a transition towards
genuinely scientific methods of analysis.

Relationship of Complex Classification
Behavior to Multiple Causality

An important application of the competencies in multiple classification described above is to the awareness of single and multiple
cause-effect relationships. Up to now we have focused on the relationship between instances of a class, the relativity of class membership, and combining and recombining of classes. The same intellectual process as that described in multiple labeling and multiple
classification is relevant to the whole question of multiple causality,
which is a crucial consideration in the social sciences, where events
typically occur as the result of combinations of causes rather than
as the result of a single cause.

Let us backtrack for the moment and consider single causality
(see Laurendeau and Pinard 1962; Piaget 1930). As with multiple
labeling, with causality we can begin by thinking in terms of single

causes. However, as the analysis of causal problems is made, it is soon apparent that no single cause is sufficient to explain any event. This is particularly true in the social sciences, which deal with complex events and complex causation questions. Therefore it is important for the teacher to facilitate the child's understanding that events do not just happen but come about for reasons that are both observable (descriptive) and unseen (inferential). The coordination of attributes to build a new class is a process similar to coordination of a number of causative statements, leading to a description of multiple causation.

Common to these two operations, classification and causation, is the ability to perform logical multiplication, that is, to coordinate two discrete elements, fusing them into a single concept. It is a combinatory action, producing a new criterion by which items can be classified or explained. It is assumed here that the ability to multiply generalizes both to different kinds of classification and to causation.

Examples of Multiple Classifications and Multiple Relations

Let us now see how a specific teaching strategy can be designed for the classroom, based on knowledge of simple and multiple classification and simple and multiple causality. Let us take a unit of study that is common in our public schools, namely the pioneers. The purpose of this unit of study is to show something about the white man and the Indian in early colonial days. Consider first the tepee. What attributes of the tepee can be identified? We can talk about its function as a domicile, its portability, the materials from which it is made, and its shape. We can show the child how each of these attributes applies to this particular tepee. Consider next the log cabin of the pioneer. What attributes does the log cabin possess? We can use the same kinds of criteria, that is, function, portability, materials, and shape.

Let us now take the tepee and the log cabin and discuss some of their similarities. They have a similar function as a domicile. There is some similarity in materials, in that both use some wood. But there are also many differences. One is stationary and the other is portable. One is made entirely of wood; the other is made mostly of skins. One is conical in shape and the other is rectangular. Given these similarities and differences, the teacher can ask the children to examine these objects and explain or think about the significance of each of the attributes that are listed. Let us take, for example, the issue of shape. Why is a tepee conical? What function does this shape serve? It is related to fire; a simple way to make smoke escape is to leave a hole in the top of a conical structure. Why is a log cabin rectangular? This is a simple way to build with logs.

In this discussion we have begun to show how two rather discrete items share certain common properties and also have differences. We focused on similarities and differences. However, thus far we have concentrated on single attributes. We can now include in the discussion other types of domiciles, such as lean-tos and clapboard houses, which were also present in the pioneer communities. We can also include forts, which have some features in common with houses. We can include many kinds of buildings, all of which have the common attribute of domicile but which also have other qualities that permit subclassifications. Then we can place in one group wooden, permanent domiciles, which could be forts, log cabins, and clapboard houses, and in another group portable domiciles, including wigwams, tepees, and lean-tos.

The strategy suggested here is important; it requires that the child, rather than the teacher, discover the attributes relevant for discussion. The multiple labeling and multiple classification are accomplished because the teacher provides the materials and asks the child to discover the relationships. From our research efforts it has become clear that letting the child provide the labels and discover the similarities and differences enables the child to assimilate this information more readily and to achieve an awareness of the complexity of the items. This conclusion is consistent with the Piagetian theory, which holds that assimilation of information leads to alterations in the point of view. Thus, as these new bits of information become categorized in appropriate cognitive schemas, the schemas increase in content. The searching and labeling by the child, who utters and hears himself or herself say "wood," "big," "small," and so forth, provides the context within which significant bits of information are acquired with which to identify environmental phenomena.

Our evidence is sufficiently strong to warrant the generalization that using a discovery-type approach, guided by the teacher, is better than other methods.

When Is a Criterial Attribute a Good One?

Teachers have biases about which criterial attributes are "good." Although various attributes or combinations of attributes may be considered equally accurate and relevant, some are valued over others. An illustration of the evaluation system and its subsequent effect on classification behavior follows.

Two types of tasks were given to a group of experienced social study teachers to demonstrate the relative significance of certain types of information. The respondents were presented with three items, a peach, an apple, and a banana, and were asked to pick any two of these three items and give a list of the ways in which they were alike. Most of the teachers picked the apple and the peach. From all the statements made by the entire group, 17 different attributes were listed. The maximum given by one individual was eight, but every member of the group recognized the presence of each of the 17 and agreed that the objects did contain these attributes. Why did not everyone list all 17 attributes? This was discussed with the group. The reasons given reflected the conviction that certain kinds of responses were banal, unsophisticated, or unimportant. For example, the attribute of having a curved surface, common to both objects, was seen as an insignificant response. In general the use of descriptive statements was seen as a reflection of low intelligence. This observation led to a discussion of what criteria a teacher used to decide if a response was good or not good. There was consensus that abstract ideas are better than nonabstract ideas.

At the next meeting with the teachers, a physical science experiment was described in which a strip of metal was placed over a candle and each end of the metal rose. The teachers were asked why this phenomenon occurred and were permitted to request additional information. They asked such questions as, "How far was the candle from the metal?" "What was the metal made out of?" "For how long was the metal heated?" "Was the heat conducted equally in the metal?" "How long was the candle burning?" "What kind of candle was used?" In other words, a number of descriptive, factual questions were asked. No longer did the teachers consider such questions banal; they realized that these questions could, when properly employed, provide significant bits of information, the totality of which could lead to a desired answer to a question. The upshot of the discussion was that the teachers learned that the "goodness" of various criteria for classification depends on what questions one seeks to answer. Thus, for the botanist the color of the flower may be a crucial criterion for determining its species. For the geologist the shape and size of a rock may be important criteria for classification. For the social scientist similar surface criteria, such as the dates of battles, may or may not be important. The goodness of different types of criteria cannot be determined in general, but only with respect to the particular problem being studied.

CONCLUSION

We have come to the following conclusions. Instances (objects, events, and persons) are multidimensional, possessing many discrete

attributes. Attributes, singly or collectively, can be used as bases
for forming classifications. Classification on single attributes is
easier than classification on multiple attributes; therefore the younger children are able to do it. Through appropriate teaching strategies and demonstrations, children can learn that these single attributes can be combined to form new subclasses; to do this, they must
be able to coordinate two or more attributes. Reversibility and reciprocity are important intellectual operations needed to accomplish
this coordination. Children who are able to combine attributes and
to perform the operations of reversibility and reciprocity, are able
to conserve. The integration or coordination of attributes can be accomplished through the use of discovery procedures. Labels of any
kind may have a utility, which depends on the problem to be solved.
Labels selected by children reflect their preferences; but the reasons
for such preferences and the degree to which the preferences can be
modified are yet to be discovered.

Use of Multiple Classification to Teach about Others

Classroom teaching methods can be selected that enable the
child to accomplish two things simultaneously, to develop a strategy
of discovery and to acquire information. The kind of illustration
given previously, about the houses of the pioneers, can be translated
very easily into any number of examples, using ethnic, racial, religious, or socioeconomic group exemplars. For example, a teacher
can present to grade school children the names of three children
said to live in Europe: Jack Lucido, Mary Smith, and Jack Kommarowski. The children can try to guess what countries these three
children are from. Suppose the children guess that Jack Lucido is
from Italy, Mary Smith from England, and Jack Kommarowski from
Poland. The children are then asked in what way any two of these
children are similar and in what way any two of them are different.
Suppose that most of the group pick Jack Lucido and Jack Kommarowski as alike. At the most mundane level, they state that each has the
same first name, that they are both boys, and that presumably both
go to school. Such an exercise indicates to the children in the class
that Jack Lucido and Jack Kommarowski, despite differences in nationality, have certain features in common.

The teacher could then lead the children in a discussion of the
significance of the similarities between Jack Lucido and Jack Kommarowski. They have the same first name because they come from
two countries in which this name is used. They are both boys, which
suggests that it is accepted that first names reveal gender in the two
different countries and that there is no reason to believe that the

association of first name with gender is any different in the two countries. That they are both from Europe and both go to school indicates the importance placed on education in both countries and also hints at a similar level of technological and economic development and similar value systems in the two countries, and so on. This illustration shows that from a simple comparison many questions can evolve and many interesting discussions can be pursued, all helping the child understand people from different groups. In his reading and thinking the child will now consider commonalities as well as differences in making ethnic comparisons. The teacher can extend this exercise, comparing Jack Lucido and Mary Smith, and Mary Smith and Jack Kommarowski; the children can make a three-way comparison of commonalities and differences. The exercise, of course, can be extended by considering exemplars from different racial or religious groups, such as a Catholic, a Jew, and a Black Muslim. Perhaps the technique may be applied to the comparison of the similarities and differences among poor, middle class, and rich children living in an American city. The possibilities are boundless.

Through experiences of this kind, the child can learn about the relativity of relationships, the ways in which classes can be combined and recombined, the ways in which items in a class can be selected for a number of rational reasons, and above all that every instance is a complex of many attributes. In the process the child learns more about various groups of people, how people are both alike and different. This sharpened conceptual understanding should hopefully result in heightened understanding and empathy.

The attributes selected by the teacher and the ways in which they are used depend on the goals of the curriculum. If we are interested in studying customs and self-pride in different groups, for example, then certain differences in attributes may be more important than the similarities in these or other attributes. If we are studying the impact of certain cultural phenomena on two people, certain similarities may become very important. In selecting significant attributes and analyzing commonalities and differences, and thereby evolving classification schemes, the child acquires practice in performing logical operations.

Such an approach is not limited to persons or groups but can also be applied to events. Take, for example, three very disparate events, the defeat of the Spanish Armada, the American Revolution, and the capture of Saigon by the communist insurgents. Here are three events that occurred at different points in time and at different places on earth. What are the commonalities? What are the differences? What can we learn from such an examination? The complexity of each of these instances is enormous, and of course there are only limited kinds of information that it would be important to select. We can readily ascertain some significant differences and similarities that could provide the child with a perspective that would further the goals of social science education. For example, in each of the following three instances, the threat of major powers to inferior powers was overcome: the British defeated the Spaniards in 1588; the Americans finally defeated the British in 1781; and the Vietnamese threw out the Western powers in 1975. The commonalities among the British, the Americans, and the Vietnamese in these cases were their presumed military and economic weakness, their relatively unsophisticated political and economic systems, and their strong desire for autonomy and independence.

Changing the Styles of Categorization

We have hypothesized that a more flexible use of styles of categorization and a greater understanding of diverse social groups will occur when children are encouraged to seek alternative classifications and when the list of alternative attributes is large. In encouraging expansion of the list of commonalities and differences, the teacher should not at first limit or evaluate the responses but should accept them all as equally valid.

The process of discovery of commonalities through labeling and identifying is crucial. The gains are lost if the teacher sets himself or herself up as the source of such information. Later on the teacher can help the children determine which of the particular labels, or classification criteria, answer some questions or solve some problems better than others. In other words, the criteria for evaluating the quality of the response should be worked out in reference to particular goals.

In addition, teachers should help children draw the distinction between an opinionated statement and one supportable by consensus on the facts. Moreover, a strong emphasis should be placed on the need to acknowledge individual differences within groups. Intergroup understanding ultimately boils down to an understanding of individuals.

The teacher should be sensitive to the children's styles of categorization and encourage the use of those styles being used least. A child who is responding primarily in any one mode, whether descriptive, contextual, or inferential, should be encouraged to work with the other modes. Our judgment about the value of such a strategy is based on research performed using physical science with fourth, fifth, and sixth graders, in which it was found that the children who solved problems most effectively were those who could ask about or perceive relationships on both the descriptive and categorical

levels. The results suggested that the ability to shift from one criterion to another is important in solving classification problems
(Scott and Sigel 1965).

When and how can such procedures for increasing flexibility in
styles of categorization be instituted? Here our conclusions are ex-
trapolated from our research. We found that with certain classes of
material, such as those that can be presented visibly to the child in
three-dimensional form, competencies in multiple classification are
evident as early as kindergarten and first grade. This would suggest that procedures intended to broaden styles of categorization
could be instituted in the primary grades. Content that could visibly
present to the child the possible alternative classification responses
would have to be selected. Later, use could be made of more symbolic representational material such as pictures and eventually words.
In addition, more concrete and familiar content should be introduced
before less familiar abstract content.

In practice, children in these early years have little experience
with procedures of the kind described, which encourage broader and
more flexible modes of categorization. The schools do not encourage
them, but stress "correct" and "incorrect" methods of categorization.
Our evidence seems to indicate that if we could expose children at an
early age to experiences that broaden categorization, thinking in
more original ways would be facilitated. When this teaching strategy
is applied to social-group concepts, a predictable outcome is an increased understanding about others.

Research Implications

The approach and strategy suggested here for facilitating
greater interpersonal and intergroup understanding places a premium
on the child's self-discovery in real-life contexts. Under the guid-
ance of the teacher, the categorization exercises described can hopefully serve as an impetus for conceptual development, improved social understanding, and subsequently a greater probability that children will empathize and respect others from different social groups.

It may be added that the categorization methods can be used in
conjunction with other methods, such as role-taking techniques.
Role-taking could take the form of having children invent narratives
and perform dramatizations based on their descriptions of various
classes of persons and groups. Such activity should serve to further
enhance intergroup understanding, since there are data that indicate
that role-playing contributes to the child's decentration (see Staub
1971). By methods such as these, the educator can achieve greater
harmony between different racial, religious, ethnic, and socioeco-

nomic groups within our pluralistic culture. This is a constructive proposal based on research and theory from child development.

In common with intervention research in general, there is a need for research on both the nature and outcomes of the programmatic input. Concerning the nature of the programmatic intervention itself, a number of possibilities need to be explored. An important research question concerns the usefulness of combining classificatory exercises with other techniques such as role-taking training. One study, for example, could deal with four groups, each having different experiences: classificatory training; role-taking training; classificatory plus role-taking training; and a control group. The feasibility and effectiveness, over all populations and as a function of different samples, of such a program can be ascertained. Perhaps for certain groups particular types of input are most effective. Likewise, the manner in which the input is presented deserves study. For example, would the effects be the same if the medium of presentation were symbolic and distant (on television as opposed to "live")? Such a study would provide information of relevance to the transportability of the program and its accessibility to larger audiences.

The initial stage of any evaluative intervention program is identification of objectives. In this case the aims are fairly straightforward: to improve children's understanding of others and to help children form positive attitudes about other people from different social groups. However, methodological issues need to be addressed. A major question is: What is the internal and external validity of the program?

The demands of internal validity require the researcher to seek out the answers to such questions as, Is the program having the intended result? Is the program indeed producing its defined objective? Are there other unintended effects of the program? One approach is to employ different types of outcome measures, such as task performance measures, rating measures, and observational measures, to assess goal-specific dependent variables as well as to measure other kinds of behavior. For example, sets of indexes for intergroup understanding and other types of abilities may be used to determine the extent to which the measures reveal evidence for convergent and discriminant validity (Campbell and Fiske 1959). Here the intent is to determine to what degree the various measures of intergroup understanding are interrelated and whether the measures are relatively independent from other abilities such as general intelligence. To the extent that they are independent, the program is having a specific effect. If, on the other hand, the different measures of intergroup understanding are not significantly correlated, the effects of the program may be equivocal or its measurement instrument-specific. A lack of significant correlation could also mean that the concept of intergroup understanding is not a unitary construct. In any case, this type of information would be very important in further defining the problem.

An additional methodological issue involves the problem of the "intended program versus the effective program." That is, given the interaction between the initial characteristics of the children randomly assigned to different program groups and the intended treatment itself, how are the children in the different programs perceiving the experience and what is the influence of this? The child's perception of the educational experience is far more important than the programmer's intentions. Any appraisal of the internal validity of an educational program must attempt to tackle this difficult but crucial problem.

Although the researcher may artificially manufacture inflated internal validity by selecting outcome measures that are similar to the kinds of activities that occur in the program itself, such recourse would defeat the demands for external validity. One external validity question is the generalizability of the intended effects. Are the abilities exhibited after program experience anything more than what was specifically learned while in the program? For example, if children are instructed to have greater sensitivity toward certain ethnic and/or religious or racial groups, would their sensitivities apply to different ethnic, religious, or racial groups? Furthermore, would they generalize to other kinds of social groups such as those defined by age, socioeconomic standing, or physical attractiveness? In other words, would a child who had been instructed to articulate similarities and differences with respect to racial groups, for example, and who understood the irrelevancies of many attributes, carry over the same disposition toward the disabled or other minority groups? A determination of the generalization of program effects is integral to the outcome evaluation process. Also, such a determination would provide the feedback necessary to modify programs for handling specific problems that might be detected.

The second external validity question concerns the durability of intended effects. Here longitudinal research is needed. Only by following up on the children enrolled in the special programs can it be known if the program effects are long lasting. Such longitudinal research may also uncover possible structural changes over time in program-specific dependent variables and should help to define more accurately the validating criterion of program success, which at this point remains informed conjecture.

The road between research and practice is two-way. What has been said has been directed primarily to the issue of translating research experience into practice. However, it is also true that the educator can teach the researcher a great deal about child development and behavior. Feedback from teachers concerning the feasibility and effectiveness of proposed methods in action can pinpoint other issues, about which data are needed for rationalizing or suggesting programmatic efforts.

REFERENCES

Aronfreed, J. 1968. Conduct and Conscience. New York: Academic Press.

_____. 1969. "The Concept of Internalization." In Handbook of Socialization Theory and Research, ed. D. A. Goslin. Chicago: Rand McNally.

Berkowitz, L. 1972. "Social Norms, Feelings, and Other Factors Affecting Helping and Altruism." In Advances in Social Psychology, ed. L. Berkowitz. New York: Academic Press.

Borke, H. 1971. "Interpersonal Perception of Young Children: Egocentrism or Empathy?" Developmental Psychology 5: 263-69.

_____. 1972. "Chandler and Greenspan's 'Ersatz egocentrism': A Rejoinder." Developmental Psychology 7: 107-09.

_____. 1973. "The Development of Empathy in Chinese and American Children between Three and Six Years of Age." Developmental Psychology 9: 102-08.

Burns, N., and L. Carey. 1957. "Age Differences in Empathic Ability among Children." Canadian Journal of Psychology 11: 227-30.

Campbell, D., and D. Fiske. 1959. "Convergent and Discriminant Validation by the Multitrait-Multimethod Matrix." Psychological Bulletin 56: 81-105.

Chandler, M. J. 1973. "Egocentrism and Antisocial Behavior: The Assessment and Training of Social Perspective-taking Skills." Developmental Psychology 3: 321-32.

_____, and S. Greenspan. 1972. "Ersatz Egocentrism: A Reply to H. Borke." Developmental Psychology 7: 104-06.

Cofer, C., and M. Appley. 1964. Motivation: Theory and Research. New York: John Wiley.

Coop, R., and Irving E. Sigel. 1971. "Cognitive Style: Implications for Learning and Instruction." Psychology in the Schools 8: 152-61.

Devries, R. 1970. "The Development of Role-taking as Reflected by the Behavior of Bright, Average, and Retarded Children in a Social Guessing Game." Child Development 41: 759-70.

Dymond, R. 1950. "Personality and Empathy." Journal of Consulting Psychology 14: 343-50.

Elkonin, D. B. 1960. "Some Results of the Psychic Development of Children of Pre-School Age." In Psychological Science in the USSR, ed. Y. A. Ponomarev (translation) Vol. 2. Moscow: Russian Soviet Federated Socialist Republic, Academy of Pedagogical Sciences.

Feffer, M. 1959. "The Cognitive Implications of Role-taking Behavior." Journal of Personality 27: 152-68.

_____. 1970. "Developmental Analyses of Interpersonal Behavior." Psychological Review 77: 197-214.

_____, and V. Gourevitch. 1960. "Cognitive Aspects of Role-taking in Children." Journal of Personality 28: 383-96.

Feshbach, N. D. 1973. "Empathy: An Interpersonal Process." Paper presented at the annual meeting of the American Psychological Association, Montreal, August 1973.

_____, and S. Feshbach. 1969. "The Relationship between Empathy and Agression in Two Age Groups." Developmental Psychology 1: 102-07.

_____, and K. Roe. 1968. "Empathy in Six- and Seven-Year-Olds." Child Development 39: 133-45.

Flavell, J. H. 1968. The Development of Role-taking and Communication Skills in Children. New York: John Wiley.

_____. 1971. "Stage-related Properties of Cognitive Development." Journal of Cognitive Psychology 2: 421-53.

Hebb, D. O. 1971. "Comment on Altruism: The Comparative Evidence." Psychological Bulletin 76: 409-10.

Hoffman, M. L. 1972. "Toward a Developmental Theory of Prosocial Motivation." Paper presented at the meeting of the National Institute of Child Health and Human Development, Eldridge, Maryland, May 1972.

_____. 1974. "Developmental Synthesis of Affect and Cognition and Its Implications for Altruistic Motivation." Ann Arbor: University of Michigan, Department of Psychology, Developmental Psychology Program.

Iannotti, R. J. 1975. "A Developmental Investigation of Role-taking, Empathy, Altruism, and Aggression." Ph.D. dissertation, State University of New York at Buffalo.

_____, and J. Meacham. 1974. "The Nature, Measurement, and Development of Empathy." Paper presented at the meeting of the Eastern Psychological Association, Philadelphia, Pennsylvania, April 1974.

Kohlberg, Lawrence. 1963. "Stages in Children's Conceptions of Physical and Social Objects, in the Years from Four to Eight: A Study of Developmental Theory." Unpublished manuscript, Harvard University.

Krebs, D. L. 1970. "Altruism: An Examination of the Concept and a Review of the Literature." Psychological Bulletin 73: 258-303.

Laurendeau, M., and A. Pinard. 1962. Causal Thinking in the Child. New York: International University Press.

Looft, W. R. 1972. "Egocentrism and Social Interaction across the Life-Span." Psychological Bulletin 78: 73-92.

Mead, G. H. 1934. Mind, Self, and Society. Chicago: University of Chicago Press.

Mehrabian, A., and N. A. Epstein. 1972. "A Measure of Emotional Empathy." Journal of Personality 60: 219-23.

Milgram, N. M. 1960. "Cognitive and Empathic Factors in Role-taking by Schizophrenic and Brain Damaged Patients." Journal of Abnormal and Social Psychology 60: 219-23.

Miller, P. H.; F. S. Kessel; and J. H. Flavell. 1970. "Thinking about People Thinking about People Thinking about . . .: A Study of Social Cognitive Development." Child Development 41: 613–23.

Mood, D.; J. Johnson; and C. Shantz. 1973. "Young Children's Understanding of the Affective State of Others: Empathy or Cognitive Awareness?" Detroit: Center for the Study of Cognitive Processes, Wayne State University.

Piaget, J. 1930. The Child's Conception of Causality. London: Kegan Paul.

_____. 1954. The Construction of Reality in the Child. New York: Basic Books.

_____. 1961. "The Genetic Approach to the Psychology of Thought." Journal of Educational Psychology 52: 275–81.

_____, and B. Inhelder. 1956. The Child's Concept of Space. London: Routledge and Kegan Paul.

Reese, H., and W. Overton. 1970. "Models of Development and Theories of Development." In Life-Span Developmental Psychology: Theory and Research, ed. L. R. Groulet and P. Baltes, pp. 115–45. New York: Academic Press.

Scott, N., and I. Sigel. 1965. "Effects of Inquiry Training in Physical Science on Creativity and Cognitive Styles of Elementary School Children." Washington, D.C.: Research report for U.S. Office of Education.

Selman, R. L. 1971. "Taking Another's Perspective: Role-taking Development in Early Childhood." Child Development 42: 1721–34.

_____. 1972. "Manual for Scoring Stages of Role-taking in Moral and Nonmoral Dilemmas." Unpublished manuscript, Harvard University.

_____. 1973. "A Structural Analysis of the Ability to Take Another's Social Perspective: Stages in the Development of Role-taking Ability." Paper presented at the meeting of the Society for Research in Child Development, Philadelphia, Pennsylvania, March 1973.

Shantz, C. Forthcoming. "The Development of Social Cognition."
    In Review of Child Development Research, ed. E. M. Hether-
    ington, vol. 5. Chicago: University of Chicago Press.

Sigel, Irving E.; T. Jarman; and H. Honesian. 1967. "Styles of
    Categorization and Their Perceptual, Intellectual, and Per-
    sonality Correlates in Young Children." Human Development
    10: 1-17.

Staub, E. 1971. "The Use of Role-playing and Induction in Chil-
    dren's Learning of Helping and Sharing Behavior." Child De-
    velopment 42: 805-16.

Stotland, E. 1969. "Exploratory Investigations of Empathy." In
    Advances in Experimental Social Psychology, ed. L. Berko-
    witz, vol. 4. New York: Academic Press.

Weinstein, E. A. 1969. "The Development of Interpersonal Com-
    petence." In Handbook of Socialization Theory and Research,
    ed. D. A. Goslin. Chicago: Rand McNally.

Welch, L. A. 1940. "A Preliminary Investigation of Some Aspects
    of the Hierarchical Development of Concepts." Journal of
    Genetic Psychology 22: 359-78.

7

CULTURAL PLURALISM:
IMPLICATIONS
FOR CURRICULUM
Mari-Luci Jaramillo

Most of us know the inherent dangers of trying to define in simplistic terms a concept as complex as cultural pluralism. Nevertheless, it is equally perilous to attempt to use the idea in multiple ways without agreeing beforehand on what it means, even if only in some general way. In order to start discussing my specific topic quickly, I will offer a simple definition that most educators probably can agree on: Cultural pluralism means that cultures can coexist with total cultural integrity, while at the same time having access on a proportional basis to the economic mainstream of the greater society.

If we are to operationalize this concept in the schools, we will have to change our thinking about the best way of dealing with equal educational opportunity. Perhaps looking at curriculum in more global terms will clarify our thinking. Figure 7.1 shows what we must believe in and what we must do before we can design a culturally pluralistic curriculum. Obviously, the compensatory education curriculum model that we derived from James Coleman's study (Coleman 1966) did not work too well, and we need to reassess our position. It is time we pursued a culturally pluralistic conceptual model. This model should be based on the famous Brown vs. Topeka court case (1954) if we want quality education for culturally diverse groups, such as exist in our present society. Arciniega has discussed this fully (Arciniega 1974).

Figure 7.2 shows how the model could work in our culturally diverse society. The selection of the four identifiable minorities and the placement of all others into one group is done not because all others are alike, but because the discrimination against these four is much greater. In order of priority, these four identifiable groups must most quickly be given educational opportunities and successes to enable them to enter the economic mainstream, or else they will never be full participants.

FIGURE 7.1

Two Interpretations of Equal Educational Opportunity

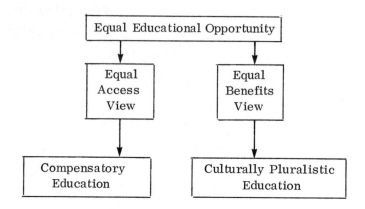

Source: Compiled by the author.

FIGURE 7.2

A Culturally Pluralistic Curriculum

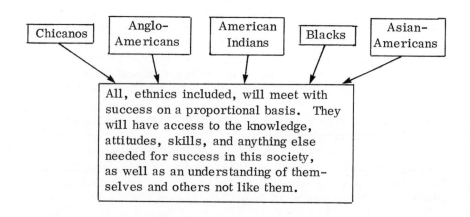

Source: Compiled by the author.

210

In order to even think about real curricular change, we must at least list some of the negative factors in existing curricula. As we are all aware, there has been almost total exclusion of minority studies in the schools. When minorities have been studied, a negative view has almost always been presented. There has also been a refusal to accept minority languages and/or dialects as bona fide media of instruction, except in a few isolated cases. In addition, there is almost total nonrepresentation of minorities in the decision-making levels in our schools, and as a consequence the minorities have had little input. The last big negative factor, of course, is the testing syndrome we adhere to in our schools, which has always hurt minority students more than it has helped them.

In order to correct the existing curricular weaknesses, the areas of theory, curriculum, and change strategies must be re-thought (Arciniega 1975). Figure 7.3 shows this graphically.

FIGURE 7.3

Areas of Interaction for Promoting a Culturally Pluralistic
Curriculum, by Levels of Education

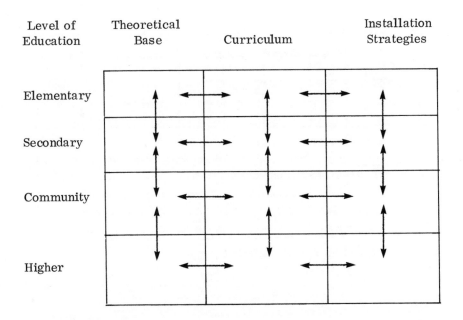

Source: Ideas from conversations with Tom Arciniega, College of Education, San Diego State College, 1975.

For curriculum revision as such, we must design programs and develop prototypes, and we must pilot, adapt and modify, produce, and disseminate these programs, based on the philosophy of cultural pluralism instead of that of the melting pot.

We must also analyze each school level by subject or by whichever other organizers we use, and we must see what has to be done to make them culturally pluralistic. We also must study the interdisciplinary aspects. A high school revision example may well resemble Figure 7.4.

FIGURE 7.4

A High School Example, Showing Interaction
within the Curriculum

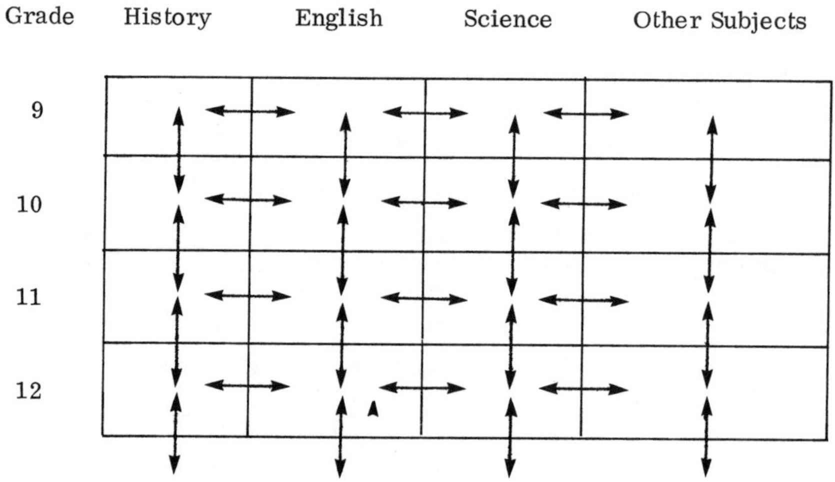

Source: Ideas from conversations with Tom Arciniega, College of Education, San Diego State, 1975.

Keeping these broader perspectives in mind will help us as we look at curriculum in more specific ways.

DEFINITIONS OF CURRICULUM

I now wish to address curriculum in more concrete terms, knowing full well that the ideal of massive curriculum change will be a long time in coming and that we must continue moving even if only in bits and pieces, as is being done.

An agreement on the definition of curriculum certainly appears to be in order. Among the hundreds of definitions in the literature, perhaps the simple working definitions that would be agreeable to most readers would include "the contrived environment . . . (in which) we attempt to influence persons" (Macdonald 1965, p. 2) and "planned aspects of schooling" (Berman 1968, p. 19). The rest of this chapter will be based on these two definitions.

CURRICULUM DEVELOPMENT

Curriculum as such does not have principles of its own, but merely activates and orchestrates principles from other areas. We accept principles from our knowledge about human growth and development, about society at large, and about "individuals."

We have always accepted the assumptions and implied principles that these areas have furnished us about learners. The fact that much of the research in and about these subjects is based on the white middle class has troubled many of us, but we have continued to use the information to help us develop the curriculum, soothing our consciences by telling ourselves we would only use it while developing our own and by allowing for variations from the norm for culturally different children. If we are to operationalize cultural pluralism in our schools, however, we must find better and more specific answers to the questions we asked before and to the new set of questions we must start asking now.

Let me share just a few of these new questions. Are the stages of intellectual development exactly alike across different cultures? For instance, will Jean Piaget's developmental stages (Piaget 1973, pp. 10-25), which he developed by observing his own children, hold constant for minority children in general? for children whose parents feel oppressed in numerous ways? for minority children who speak a foreign language in their own country? for minority children who live in traditional cultures that are surrounded by a "modern" dominant one? for minority children who live in urban settings? for minority children who live in rural settings?

A culturally pluralistic curriculum must answer these questions in the area of human growth and development. We do not have this research as yet, and it is desperately needed if we are to make sound changes in curriculum that would lead toward cultural pluralism.

We have another set of questions regarding our input from society at large. Do the social developmental stages (Havinghurst

1948, p. 15) apply to all children? Do child-rearing practices, cultural beliefs, taboos, and behaviors influence these stages? Is social independence dependent on culture? Does the social learning theory (Bandura and Walters 1963) that we are now using have relevance for the culturally different child? We do not really know. We have not yet explored these ideas in a very serious way, but we continue to hope that our assumptions are valid.

Much will also have to be reviewed in the different areas of learning. Do cultures influence learning and motivational styles? Some research is on the horizon (Ramirez 1970, pp. 45-46), but we need much more before we can make sound generalizations about curriculum development.

Even small group interaction, which is so much in vogue, should be questioned when applied to minorities. Does culture teach people to behave differently in groups? Can behavior that is "disruptive" in one culture not be disruptive in another? Do not some cultures teach that not everyone has to be overtly participating constantly--much to the dismay of teachers assigning group tasks? Many similar questions could be posited here.

Perhaps the area we should most question is that which we have identified as our cultural heritage. I do not believe that there is a need to explain here that we have limited ourselves to only one point of view in selecting content from this area; nor do I think we need more than a reminder that we have used the principle, or slogan, "to preserve our democratic way of life" as one of our main criteria. In reality what we have done has been to select much of the content and many of the skills that we hope will preserve our economic system, which may or may not be related to democracy as we know it and is certainly not the issue in this chapter. We have tried to give students the academic, technical, and social skills they need to prepare themselves for careers; and I might add that we have failed with many. We have paid only lip service to the multicultural, intercultural, interracial, and/or international relationships, which many of us think are equally important. In the area of cultural heritage, we have borrowed many principles, which we use to determine curriculum; but obviously all of these principles have come from a melting pot philosophy.

We must ask new questions in this area also. What does cultural heritage mean in a country of immigrants? Which groups have contributed? How? When? How much? Is their contribution worth preserving and studying, and if so, why? Is cultural survival as important as economic survival to certain groups? Is this true for all groups? Can one be a "good" American without identifying with a WASP orientation? Which are the best criteria of selection available to help determine curriculum in this area? With many of these questions unanswered, we move ahead in trying to meet the needs of a culturally diverse society.

The general questions we have asked ourselves in developing curriculum in the past have been questions such as the following: Should students be involved in planning curriculum, and if so, to what extent? How should the objectives of the curriculum be determined? On what basis is content selected? How will the learning experiences be selected? See Appendix A for additional sample questions related to the nature of man and the nature of society (Darling 1975). If we believe in cultural pluralism, we will continue to ask some of the same general questions, but a genuine commitment to cultural pluralism would certainly make it more difficult to accept blanket generalizations about students when answering these questions. We certainly must find out more about the ways in which minority groups view reality. We also must continue probing into the differences within cultures. However, we must be careful not to create a new set of stereotypes by again making blanket generalizations about all peoples. Top quality research is needed in these areas.

Since we have not emphasized human values in U.S. schools in the past, nor developed a social conscience to any large extent, nor systematically helped students understand themselves and others who are not like them, nor treated racism and prejudice openly, nor used the schools as institutions that could start combating racism; then it follows that a culturally pluralistic curriculum would attempt to do much that has seldom if ever been tried in our schools, since there is a genuine belief that the said curriculum would attempt to do all of this.

A culturally pluralistic curriculum would attempt to bring students closer to the coal of cross-cultural and/or cross-racial understanding, but I do not think it can ever hope to make everyone in this society totally multicultural. If a multicultural person internalizes the beliefs of several cultures and can totally operate in any of the given cultures, both cognitively and emotionally (Jaramillo 1972, pp. v-3), it is almost impossible to expect schools to accomplish this alone. In addition, completely internalizing the culture of another is not possible for everyone. Even those who are able to become completely bicultural, that is, who have the affective, as well as the cognitive, experience that is necessary for the complete internalization of two cultures, can sometimes experience anomie (Peal and Lambert 1962). It appears that since one learns at a very early age how to handle emotions in a given cultural setting, that is one area in which it is extremely difficult to operate in "another" way. I am discussing the reality and limitations of the classroom rather than the clinical case, in which over a period of concentrated treatment a change can occur in controlling or exhibiting emotions.

I repeat, a culturally pluralistic curriculum would bring students to a deeper understanding of ways that are different from their own and also a better understanding of their own ways, but it would be unrealistic to expect the majority of the students to become multicultural because of their experience of such a curriculum. Too many other forces are at play, and at best the new curriculum could only help them to understand others better. In the process of understanding others, they would perhaps become more aware of themselves.

One way of looking at the proposed changes is to divide the curriculum into planning and operational stages, for the purpose of discussion. Most of this chapter will be limited to the pre-activity or planning phase instead of the operational stage. A chapter devoted to the operational stage would deal with the actual instructional level.

If the concept of cultural pluralism is adopted, the implications for curriculum modification and change are many. It will require a major school change, including administration and organization. To illustrate this, I will use a fairly traditional framework for viewing some of the various components of the curriculum. These will be curriculum decisions, governance, goals, staffing, the role of the teacher along with her/his new attitudes and knowledge, the educational materials to be used, the learning environment, content, and the selection and organization of learning experiences and teaching strategies. I will discuss the various elements involved in the components just listed.

Decisions

Curriculum decisions will necessarily involve lay participation. Up to now we have not recognized ethnicity as an area of study. Previously, ethnic groups were not allowed to participate in school decisions or study their specific heritages. For example, Italians were not able to "Italianize" the curriculum because the Italian-American culture was not viewed as legitimate by those in control of the schools.

If cultural pluralism is to work, the members of ethnic groups will, along with "others," decide what the curriculum will be. They will demand that the ethnic cultures be studied as "regular" studies and that ethnic experiences be used to enrich all areas of the curriculum, whether these areas are subject matter as such or other organizers used in planning curriculum. This proposed guideline would legitimize ethnic cultures as areas of study.

Governance of Schools

We must admit that as of now the schools are merely responding to outside pressures to establish culturally pluralistic programs.
If these pressures were to stop, we have no way of knowing which of
the changes that have already been achieved would be stabilized
enough to continue developing. For this and other reasons we must
encourage those who believe in cultural pluralism to help govern
their schools. They, in turn, certainly need the support of committed professionals in order to achieve a true advancement toward
shared power.

In discussing school governance, we must also consider the
aims of a culturally pluralistic curriculum. Some believe that this
type of curriculum is primarily conceived to help minorities, while
others believe that the goal is to change racist attitudes in the majority. Some believe it is meant for all children, that is, meant to
broaden everyone's knowledge base. If this is so, then the governance of the schools must also be in the hands of all.

Of course, those who would come into control of the schools
would endorse the idea that "schools must accept and capitalize on
the strengths of cultural difference in a manner which leads to successful performance in school by minority children" (Arciniega 1974).
This would imply the reform of schools along culturally pluralistic
lines. In the governance of schools we need the "authentic involvement of the minority community in the decision-making structures of
the school system" (Arciniega 1974).

Goals

Without listing the goals of formal education, I think we can
agree that although they are very idealistic, in reality the student
who "knows" more subject matter is the one who usually meets the
criteria of a "good" student, never mind the goals.

The revised goals will certainly include the promotion of cultural differences. The goals will also "promote change efforts designed to effect attitudinal, normative, as well as cognitive changes
in the dominant culture" (Arciniega 1974). An obvious principle
arising from this is that cultural differences should be considered a
valuable human resource.

Differentiated Staffing

The staff should include a whole new subset of professionals who are experts in the distinct minority cultures and who can identify the potential areas of conflict in a culturally pluralistic curriculum. Not only can they identify potential conflict, but they can actually help people prepare for the built-in conflict when it cannot be avoided. They will work alongside the professionals.

These persons can also apply their knowledge about given cultures whether they have had formal or informal training. An example would be the people who know the oral history, traditions, and literature of a given group of people, yet do not have the system's credentials to teach. They would become the needed experts for this data collection. These people must be used as a legitimate resource. Under the present system, only after intensive literature searches fail to disclose information are these people used, and only until something written appears, however poor or inaccurate it may be.

There is a great possibility that ideal staffing patterns, which should reflect all cultural and/or racial groups, will never come to be in all places. Ideally, staffing should reflect the cultural diversity of society. Perhaps these subgroups of professionals will have to play the very important role of providing cultural models for the students. Of course, this will work only if they are given high status in the system.

Teachers

If our new curriculum is to work, many of our teachers will have to change their attitudes, learn some new concepts about minorities, undergo some new cultural experiences, and above all achieve some new self-understanding (Hunter 1974), p. 41).

Because of past teacher training practices, which were built on a melting-pot philosophy, most practicing teachers will have to be retrained in order to work in a school setting in which many diverse behaviors are not only accepted and valued, but actually sought and encouraged. The fact that much of the learning that will take place can not be prescribed beforehand will be very discouraging to those teachers who were led to believe that good lesson plans "control" the children's learning. The fact that content can not be totally decided upon before the actual instructional phase will also be alarming to the believers in the melting-pot theory, under which the same treatment was good enough for all students. They knew what content "good" Americans needed!

Discussing taboo topics such as discrimination and racism will also upset the many teachers who sincerely believe that everyone has equal access to opportunity and who cannot see the need for such study in public schools.

Of course the same applies to the teacher who has not previously taught and is undergoing professional training. Bringing the things we have been discussing into the colleges of education is just as crucial as bringing them into the public schools. Both levels of education need extensive curricular change.

The new and retrained teachers must be open, aware, and cognizant of minority needs if they are to be effective in the new curriculum. They will need to know the whys and hows of modifying the curriculum for children and youths of various ethnic groups (Dunfee 1970, p. 4).

As we move toward a culturally pluralistic curriculum, more and more teachers must learn, or at least study and understand, the languages of the minorities in order that these languages may be used as legitimate modes of instruction along with English.

Materials

In such fields as history, literature, social studies, and language arts, the contributions of neglected groups have been overlooked or ignored (Dunfee 1970, p. 2). Apparently omission has been a major factor, but what has been presented is also usually biased or in complete error.

These oversights must be corrected immediately if we are to have culturally pluralistic education. "Adequate treatment and presentation of the historical, cultural, and economic contributions made by minorities" (Arciniega 1974) is long overdue. Many of the materials should also reflect the minority languages, to give them status as a medium of instruction. The materials must emphasize minority contributions and be true to minority life styles. If at all possible they should be multilinguial and reflect the variety of cultures found in this nation. The present materials must be modified and adapted to the highest degree possible.

Learning Environment

Although a subtopic such as this is usually presented in the "learning" section, I shall briefly mention here the curricular implications the environment will have.

If teaching is to become highly individualized, reflecting the learning styles, rates of learning, and cultural experiences of the students in order to enable minority members to meet with school success, then the learning environment will become crucial. The learning environment must also help majority children change their attitudes and norms, as well as any erroneous concepts that they may have about minorities. Only a well-thought-out environment in which interpersonal relationships are valued will enable the type of learning that has been described to take place.

Content

We all know the kinds of myths schools use to teach about given ways of life. These become legitimate content, even though the selection of the said content is very arbitrary. Portions of the culture are transmitted from this myth collection. As an example of an Anglo-American myth, I offer the following: "Everybody reads Shakespeare." That belief (myth) is certainly evident in our curriculum, regardless of the criteria we use to defend the selection. Anglo-Americans have conquered this myth world quite well. Generalizations can be made about them that "everyone that's anyone" can substantiate almost as truth. Ethnics must also legitimize their myth worlds in order that certain givens may be included in the curriculum. Admittedly this is a long process, but we must try to help it move forward.

Also related to content selection is the question of priorities. The study of contemporary models and problems is as important as history as it is presently taught. A dynamic culturally pluralistic curriculum must prove to its students that ethnics are achieving, in order to reinforce what the students are studying. What the students perceive can be devastating. Perhaps a real-life incident will demonstrate this point well. When a friend of mine from another state was getting ready to move to New Mexico, his third-grade daughter commented that she would now have to be with lots of dumb Mexicans. After a long conversation, the father concluded that from his daughter's perspective, based on the limited experiences she had had, Mexicans could indeed be classified as dumb-- always in the low groups, in trouble with school authorities, and so on. We must offer curricular experiences that will enable minority group members to meet with success, so that they in turn will become the cultural models for nonminority students to observe.

All segments of the curriculum must be analyzed in order to locate those areas to which contributions by the minorities can be added as entirely new content or as reinforcing what has been presented before.

Any discussion about content, regardless of its brevity, should include a sentence or two about the newer emphasis on process instead of on content alone. The learner himself is the subject, and the process actually becomes the content (Fersh 1975). For this reason the way in which it is taught is as important as what is taught.

Selection and Organization of Learning Experiences and Teaching Strategies

After we have acquired the basic data that this chapter has suggested we need, the selection of experiences must be based on the learning principles that evolve. Surely we will continue to use a framework using multiple objectives (Taba 1962), which requires integrated teaching strategies and learning experiences to avoid the fragmenting of knowledge, attitudes, skills, and critical thinking. These integrated experiences, even by themselves, will help us understand ourselves and others better. They will place all of us in proper perspective. The assumptions we use in selecting affective experiences need even stronger support, since many people do not even agree that these experiences are necessary in the teaching-learning situation.

The actual selection and organization will remain much the same as we know it today. It will still be spiral, adding new dimensions as the student progresses through the educational system.

CONCLUSION

The foregoing discussion is an attempt to provide a framework for the types of questions to be asked in planning and developing a culturally pluralistic curriculum. For a variety of reasons, most of the discussion has led us toward modifying or changing existing elements in the curriculum rather than toward the total change needed. Changes such as those proposed occur slowly, never radically. Even though the changes are needed desperately, we will not see them take place over night. We will have to work diligently to get even the minute changes that have been suggested.

A totally new concept in curriculum would be acceptance of the idea that schools should become instrumental in giving skills to students to help them change society. A new set of questions that would have to be posited would be as follows:

What are these skills? Are they political? Social? Do they involve other academic skills not now taught? Are these skills needed in isolation or do they work better in patterns or in other combinations?

Once the skills are identified, will they be different or the same for minority members and nonminority members? Will students alone be able to create societal change to any effective degree? Who else should be studying changes? Who else should be educated by the schools? Should school efforts be limited to making the schools better in a humanistic way, with no illusions that schools can directly influence society?

We have tried so many times without success, but could we get away from subject matter organizers and look at new kinds of organizers? Might some new ones include conceptualizing? inquiring? experimenting? reading? playing?

Yes, schools can become better and more effective in helping this society see and use a great human resource, its cultural diversity. We still can become a real democracy.

APPENDIX A: RANDOM QUESTIONS ABOUT HUMAN NATURE

What is the function of humanity on earth? Is it self-preservation and self-fulfillment? Is it societal preservation and societal fulfillment? Are human beings a transient biological phenomenon on earth? Is a human being a unique animal? If so, in what ways?

Do human values transcend societies? If so, what are the important ones? Should schools teach these values to children? Can they avoid teaching values? If values should be taught, then what values should be taught?

Is every person predestined from conception to possess certain mental and physical abilities that may be realized but not improved upon?

Do people possess certain instincts? If so, what are they? Are people social beings? Are they inherently creative?

Is a person inherently a changing or a static being? What is the basic orientation of the human race, and how is this changing?

Is everyone a "clean slate" when born, and does each person become whatever is stamped on the slate, or is the individual a product of evolution, with some innate cultural tendencies passed through the genes?

Do people have a hierarchy of needs, as suggested by Abraham Maslow (1968)? Do they go through stages of intellectual development, as indicated by Jean Piaget (1973)?

APPENDIX B: RANDOM QUESTIONS ABOUT THE
NATURE OF SOCIETY

What are the dominant social forces at work today? What are
the groups associated with those forces?

What are the major social problems today? What are their
roots? What are their manifestations?

What are the fruits and benefits of society in the United States
today? What kind of society should emerge to meet legitimate expressed societal needs? What traditions need to be maintained and/or
preserved? What traditions need to be changed?

What kind of society should exist in elementary schools? What
kinds of groups should exist? What kind of social structure should
the children learn to function within the elementary school?

How would you consider such relationships as child to adult,
child to peer, child to sibling surrogate, child to parent, and child
to neighborhood?

Should the social systems functioning in the elementary school
be a reflection of the traditional or the emerging societal structures?

Assuming that societies change, what forces bring about that
change? Are they evolutionary or revolutionary?

Is war a natural product of society?

What is the role of the creative person in society?

Are hierarchical relationships inherent in societies?

REFERENCES

Arciniega, Tom. 1974. Paper presented at the Conference on
    Quality Education: Practical Alternatives. Los Angeles,
    California, December.

_____. 1975. Conversations with author (February).

Bandura, A., and R. H. Walters. 1963. Social Learning and Per-
    sonality Development. New York: Holt, Rinehart and Winston.

Berman, Louise M. 1968. New Priorities in the Curriculum.
    Columbus, Ohio: Charles E. Merrill Publishing Company.

Brown v. Topeka. 1954. 347 U.S. 483.

Coleman, James., et al. 1966. Equality of Educational Opportunity. U.S. Department of Health, Education and Welfare, Office of Education, National Center for Educational Statistics. Washington, D.C.: Government Printing Office.

Darling, David. 1975. Conversation with author, February. Sample questions are from his Graduate Curriculum Class at the University of New Mexico.

Dunfee, Maxine. 1970. Ethnic Modification of the Curriculum. Washington, D.C.: Association for Supervision and Curriculum Development.

Fersh, Seymour. 1975. "Intercultural Education: The Value of Our Directions and the Direction of our Values." Lecture presented at the annual meeting of the American Association of Colleges of Teacher Education, Chicago, February.

Hunter, William A. 1974. Multicultural Education Through Competency Based Teacher Education. Washington, D.C.: American Association of Colleges for Teacher Education.

Havinghurst, Robert J. 1948. Developmental Tasks and Education. New York: Longmans, Green and Co.

Jaramillo, Mari-Luci. 1972. "Toward a Philosophy of Education for the Chicano: Bilingualism and Intellectual Development." Adelante: An Emerging Design for Mexican American Education. Austin: School of Communication, University of Texas.

Macdonald, James B. 1965. "The Person in the Curriculum." Speech delivered at the 1965 Teachers College Curriculum Conference, Columbia University, November 9.

Maslow, Abraham H. 1968. Toward a Psychology of Being. (Second edition) New York: Van Nostrand.

Peal, Elizabeth, and Wallace E. Lambert. 1962. "The Relation of Bilingualism to Intelligence." Psychological Monographs: General and Applied 76, no. 27.

Piaget, Jean. 1973. The Child and Reality: Problems of Genetic Psychology. New York: Grossman Publishers.

Ramirez, Manuel. 1970. "Cultural Democracy: A New Philosophy for Educating the Mexican American Child." The National Elementary Principal (National Education Association of the United States) 50, no. 2.

Taba, Hilda. 1962. Curriculum Development, Theory and Practice. New York: Harcourt, Brace and World.

CHAPTER

8

CULTURAL PLURALISM:
IMPLICATIONS FOR
CURRICULUM REFORM
James A. Banks

Several crucial questions concerning the relationship between
the school and ethnicity arose during the Pluralism in a Democratic
Society conference that must be discussed and clarified before we
can design sound curricular programs that relate to pluralism in the
United States. One of these key questions relates to what should be
the role of public institutions like the common school in the area of
ethnicity. Should the common schools promote, remain neutral to,
or ignore the ethnic characteristics of their students and the ethnic
diversity within American life?

There was considerable agreement among the conference participants that the school should not ignore ethnicity and should play
some kind of deliberate role in teaching students about issues related
to ethnicity within American society. However, there was little
agreement about the proper role of the school, although many fruitful and provocative ideas were advanced about what the school should
and should not do about issues related to ethnicity.

These views ranged from those of Michael Novak (Chapter 2 of
this book), who argued that ethnicity should be an integral part of the
school curriculum, to those of Nathan Glazer (Chapter 1), who cau-
tioned that too much emphasis on ethnicity in the schools might be
inimical to the common culture and promote the Balkanization of
American society. Mari-Luci Jaramillo (Chapter 7) argued that the
school should promote ethnic identity and attachments but should be
primarily concerned with the "visible minorities" because of their
urgent needs and unique problems. It is a question of priorities,
argued Jaramillo. In his insightful chapter, David E. Apter (Chapter 3) pointed out that primordial and ethnic attachments persist in
a modernized democratic state and that primordialism and assimilation are competing forces. Apter's analysis suggests that the

common schools cannot ignore ethnic attachments because they are integral parts of democratic societies.

I will identify two major ideological positions related to ethnicity and cultural pluralism that surfaced at the conference in varying forms and are evident in most theoretical discussions on ethnicity and pluralism in the United States. The major assumptions and arguments of these positions will be discussed, and their limitations as guides to curriculum reform will be identified. I will then describe an eclectic ideological position that reflects both major ideologies and present my recommendations for curriculum reform within that context.

It is very important for the reader to realize that the ideological positions I will identify and describe are ideal types in the Weberian sense. The views of no particular writer or theorist can be accurately described by either of the two major positions in their ideal forms. However, various views on ethnicity and pluralism can be roughly classified, using a continuum that has the two ideologies, in their ideal forms, at the extreme ends.

The two major positions are the cultural pluralist ideology and the assimilationist ideology. I am not the first observer to structure a typology related to the ideologies and theories of pluralism in the United States. Milton M. Gordon (1964, p. 84) classified theories of assimilation into three major categories: Anglo-conformity, the melting pot, and cultural pluralism. John Higham (1974) also identifies three ideologies: the integrationist, the pluralist, and the pluralistic integrationist. These two typologies, as well as the one that I am presenting, are in some ways similar but are different conceptualizations.

THE CULTURAL PLURALIST IDEOLOGY

The cultural pluralist ideology, in varying forms, is being widely articulated by writers today. Some writers, such as Stokely Carmichael and Charles V. Hamilton (1967), endorse a strong version of pluralism, while writers such as Michael Novak (1975) and Robert L. Williams (1975) endorse a much weaker form of cultural pluralism. The pluralist makes various assumptions about the nature of American society, the function of the ethnic group in socializing the individual, and the responsibility that the individual member of a presumed oppressed ethnic group has to the "liberation struggle" of that group. The pluralist also makes certain assumptions about research, learning, teacher training, and the proper goals of the school curriculum.

The pluralist argues that ethnicity and ethnic identities are very important in American society. The United States, according to the pluralist, is made up of competing ethnic groups, each of which champions its own economic and political interests. It is extremely important, argues the pluralist, for the individual to develop a commitment to his or her ethnic group, especially if that ethnic group is oppressed by more powerful ethnic groups. The energies and skills of each member of an ethnic group are needed to help in the liberation struggle of that group. Each individual member of an ethnic group has a moral obligation to join the liberation struggle. Thus the pluralist stresses the rights of the ethnic group over the rights of the individual. The pluralist also assumes that an ethnic group can attain inclusion and full participation within a society only when it can bargain from a powerful position and when it has closed ranks within (Carmichael and Hamilton 1967; Sizemore 1969).

The pluralist views the ethnic group as extremely important in the socialization of the individual within a highly modernized society. It is within their own particular ethnic groups that individuals develop their languages, life styles, and values and experience important primary group relationships and attachments. The ethnic community also serves as a supportive environment for the individual and helps to protect the individual from the harshness and discrimination he or she might experience in the wider society. The ethnic group thus provides a sense of identity and psychological support, both of which are extremely important within a highly modernized and technological society that is controlled primarily by one dominant ethnic group. The pluralist views the ethnic group as exceedingly important and believes that public schools should actively promote the interests of the various ethnic groups in their policies and in the curriculum.

The pluralist makes assumptions about research that differ from those made by the assimilationist. The pluralist assumes that ethnic minority cultures in the United States are not disadvantaged, deviant, or deficient but that they are well ordered and highly structured but different from each other and from the dominant Anglo-American culture. Thus the pluralist uses a culture difference model when researching ethnic groups, while the assimilationist researcher uses a deficit model or a genetic model (Baratz and Baratz 1970; Simpkins, Williams, and Gunnings 1971). Because of their different research assumptions, the cultural pluralist researcher and the assimilationist researcher frequently derive different and often conflicting research conclusions. Researchers such as Stephen and Joan Baratz (1970), Jane R. Mercer (1974), and Robert L. Williams (1975) have used the cultural difference model extensively in their research studies on ethnic groups and have done a great deal to legitimize it within the social science and educational communities.

The cultural pluralist also assumes that ethnic minorities have unique learning styles and that the school curriculum and teaching strategies should be revised to make them more consistent with the cognitive and life styles of ethnic-group students. Manuel Ramirez III and Alfredo Castaneda (1974) have written insightfully about the unique learning styles of Mexican-American youths. A recent study by Susan S. Stodolsky and Gerald Lesser (1967) also supports the notion that the cognitive styles among ethnic groups sometimes differ.

Pluralists, because of their assumptions about the importance of the ethnic group in the lives of children, believe that the curriculum should be drastically revised to make it reflect the cognitive styles, cultural history, and present experiences and aspirations of ethnic groups, especially the visible minorities. The cultural pluralist believes that if the school curriculum were more consistent with the experiences of ethnic groups, the learning and adjustment problems that minority students experience in school would be greatly reduced. Thus the cultural pluralist argues that learning materials should be culture-specific and that the major goal of the curriculum should be to help the child to function more successfully within his or her own ethnic culture. The curriculum should be structured in such a way that it stresses events from the points of view of the specific ethnic groups. The curriculum should promote ethnic attachments and allegiances and help students gain the skills and commitments that will enable them to help their ethnic groups gain power and exercise it within the larger civic culture.

THE ASSIMILATIONIST IDEOLOGY

The assimilationist believes that the pluralist greatly exaggerates the extent of cultural differences within American society. The assimilationist does not deny that ethnic differences exist within American society or that ethnicity is very important to some groups. However, the assimilationist and the pluralist interpret ethnicity in the United States quite differently. The assimilationist tends to see ethnicity and ethnic attachments as fleeting and temporary within an increasingly modernized world. Ethnicity, argues the assimilationist, wanes or disappears under the impact of modernization and industrialization. The assimilationist believes that ethnicity is more important in the developing societies than in the highly modernized societies and that it crumbles under the forces of modernization and democratization. The assimilationist sees the modernized state as being universalistic rather than as characterized by strong ethnic allegiances and attachments. (See Chapter 3.)

Not only do the assimilationists view ethnicity as somewhat noncharacteristic of modernized societies, but they also believe

that strong ethnic attachments are dysfunctional within a modernized
state. Assimilationists believe that the ethnic group promotes group
rights over the rights of the individual and that the individual must
be freed of ethnic attachments in order to have choices within society.
The assimilationist also views ethnicity as a force that is inimical to
the goals of a democratic society. Ethnicity, argues the assimilationist, promotes divisions, revives ethnic conflicts, and leads to the
Balkanization of society. The assimilationist sees integration as a
societal goal in a modernized state, as opposed to ethnic segregation
and separatism.

The assimilationist believes that the best way to promote the
goals of American society and to develop commitments to the ideals
of American democracy is to promote the full socialization of all individuals and groups into the common culture. Every society, argues the assimilationist, has values, ideologies, and norms to which
each member of that society must develop commitments if it is to
function successfully and smoothly. In the United States these values
are embodied in the American Creed and in such documents as the
United States Constitution and the Declaration of Independence. In
each society there is also a set of common skills and abilities that
every successful member of that society must master. In our nation
these include the speaking and writing of the English language.

The primary goal of the common school, like the goals of other
publicly supported institutions, should be to socialize individuals into
the common culture and enable them to function more successfully
within it. At best the school should take a position of "benign neutrality" in matters related to the ethnic attachments of its students.
(See Chapter 1.) If ethnicity and ethnic attachments are to be promoted, this should be done by private institutions like the church,
the community club, and the private school.

Like the cultural pluralist, the assimilationists make assumptions about research that is related to minorities, and their conclusions reflect their assumptions. Assimilationists usually assume
that subcultural groups that have characteristics that cause their
members to function unsuccessfully in the common culture are deficient, deprived, and pathological and that they lack needed functional
characteristics. Researchers who embrace an assimilationist ideology usually use the genetic or the social pathology research model
when studying ethnic minorities (Jensen 1969; Shockley 1972).

The assimilationist learning-theorist assumes that learning
styles, such as the stages of cognitive development identified by
Piaget, are universal across cultures and that certain early socialization practices, such as those exemplified among middle-class
Anglo-Americans, enhance learning, while other early socialization
practices, such as those found within most lower-class ethnic groups,

retard the child's ability to conceptualize and to develop his or her verbal and cognitive abilities. Consequently, assimilationist learning theorists often recommend that ethnic minority youths from lower-class homes enter compensatory educational programs at increasingly early ages. Some have suggested that these youths should be placed in a middle-class educational environment shortly after birth (Caldwell 1967).

The assimilationist believes that curriculum materials and teaching styles should be primarily related to the common culture. Emphasis should be on our common civilization, since all American citizens must learn to participate in a common culture that requires universal skills and competencies. Emphasis on cultural and ethnic differences might promote the disunification of our society and fail to promote socialization into the common civic culture. The primary mission of the schools should be to socialize youths into the civic culture of the United States.

The curriculum should stress the commonality of the heritage all people share in the United States. This includes the great documents in American history such as the Declaration of Independence, and it also includes events such as the American Revolution and the two great world wars. The curriculum should also help the child develop a commitment to the common culture and the skills to participate in social action designed to make the practices in this nation more consistent with our professed ideologies. The school should develop within youths a critical acceptance of the goals, assumptions, and possibilities of this nation.

Attacks on the Assimilationist Ideology

Historically the assimilationist ideology has dominated American intellectual and social thought, as Nathan Glazer (Chapter 1) perceptively observes. Social and public policy in U.S. society has also been most heavily influenced by the assimilationist ideology. Historically the schools and other U.S. institutions have viewed the acculturation of the immigrants and their descendants as one of their major goals. The nativists and the Americanizers wanted to make the immigrants "good, law-abiding Americans" (Higham 1972). Occasionally in U.S. history a few voices in the wilderness have championed cultural pluralism; but their cries have usually fallen on deaf ears.

Around the turn of the century, when masses of Southern, Eastern, and Central Europeans were immigrating to the United States and were being attacked by the American nativists, the liberal philosophers and writers, usually of immigrant descent, strongly defended the immigrants and argued that their cultures could greatly enrich American civilization and that the immigrants had a right to maintain their ethnic cultures in a democratic nation like the United States. These writers, who included Horace M. Kallen (1924), Randolph S. Bourne (1916), and Julius Drachsler (1920), set forth the concept of cultural pluralism and used it to defend these immigrants and their right to have cultural democracy in the United States. Kallen argued cogently that the cultures of the various immigrant groups would greatly strengthen American civilization. He viewed a society made up of diverse ethnic cultures as "an orchestration of mankind." Despite the passionate arguments and eloquence of philosophers like Kallen and Drachsler, the assimilationists triumphed in the United States and were symbolized by the passage of the highly restrictive immigration act of 1924.

The Third World Rejects the Assimilationist Ideology

In the 1960s the Afro-Americans began a fight for their rights that was unprecedented in their history. Other nonwhite ethnic groups, who were made acutely aware of their ethnic status by the black revolt and encouraged by what they perceived as the benefits gained by Afro-Americans, also began to make unprecedented demands upon U.S. civic and public institutions. These groups demanded more control of their communities, more ethnic teachers for their youths, and new interpretations of U.S. history and culture that more accurately and sensitively described their experiences. Ethnic minority groups began to seriously question both the societal goals and the dominant ideology within American society.

The assimilationist ideology and the practices associated with it were strongly attacked by third-world intellectuals, researchers, and social activists. The rejection of the assimilationist ideology by nonwhite intellectuals and leaders is historically very significant. This rejection represents a major break from tradition within ethnic groups, as Glazer observes. (See Chapter 1.) Traditionally, most intellectuals and social activists among U.S. minorities have supported assimilationist policies and regarded acculturation as a requisite for full societal participation. There have been a few staunch separatists among Afro-Americans and other ethnic groups throughout American history, but these leaders have represented a cry in the wilderness. Significant, too, is the fact that in the 1960s many white liberal writers and researchers also began to attack the assimilationist ideology and the practices associated with it. This represented a major break from white liberal tradition. Some white liberal writers and researchers attacked the assimilationist ideology

much more vigorously than did many black intellectuals and writers.
Some of the most passionate and perceptive advocates of the teaching
and acceptance of black English in the schools, for example, are
liberal white researchers such as Joan C. Baratz and Roger Shuy
(1969) and William Labov (1970).

Third-world writers and researchers attacked the assimilationist ideology for many reasons. They saw it as a weapon of the
oppressor that was designed to destroy the cultures of ethnic groups
and to make their members personally ineffective and politically
powerless. These writers also saw assimilationism as a racist
ideology that justified damaging school and societal practices that
victimized minority group children. Many minorities also lost faith
in the assimilationist ideology because they had become disillusioned
with what they perceived as its unfulfilled promises. The rise of
ethnic awareness and ethnic pride also contributed to the rejection
of the assimilationist ideology by many ethnic minorities in the 1960s.
Many minority leaders and writers searched for an alternative ideology and endorsed some version of cultural pluralism. They viewed
the pluralist ideology as much more consistent with the liberation of
oppressed and stigmatized ethnic groups than the assimilationist
ideology.

In the mid-1970s cultural pluralism has come into vogue
among curriculum specialists and has been widely discussed and
written about by educators. The pluralist ideology is verbally endorsed by many curriculum specialists in the schools, although many
of the school people who verbally endorse cultural pluralism have not
seriously examined all of the ramifications of the pluralist ideology
and its full policy and curricular implications. The December 1975
issue of Educational Leadership, a leading curriculum journal, was
devoted to the implications of cultural pluralism for the curriculum.
This special issue of the journal suggests the wide popularity of the
concept among school people and curriculum specialists.

A CRITIQUE OF THE PLURALIST AND
ASSIMILATIONIST IDEOLOGIES

Although both the pluralist and the assimilationist positions
make some useful assumptions and set forth arguments that curriculum specialists need to seriously consider as they attempt to revise
the school curriculum, neither ideology, in its ideal form, is sufficient to guide the revision of the curriculum in the common schools.
The pluralist ideology is useful because it informs us about the importance of ethnicity within our nation and the extent to which an individual's ethnic group determines his or her life chances in American

society. The assumptions that the pluralist makes about the nature of minority cultures, the learning styles of minority youths, and the importance of ethnic identity to many American children are also useful to the curriculum builder.

However, the pluralist exaggerates the extent of cultural pluralism within American society and fails to give adequate attention to the fact that gross cultural, if not structural, assimilation has taken place in American society. Gordon, who seriously questions the extent of cultural pluralism in American society (1964, p. 159), writes, "Structural pluralism . . . is the major key to the understanding of the ethnic makeup of American society, while cultural pluralism is the minor one." Exaggerating the extent of cultural differences between and among ethnic groups might be as detrimental for school policy as ignoring the differences.

The pluralist also fails to give adequate attention to the fact that most members of ethnic groups participate in a culture that is wider and more universalistic than the cultures in which they have their primary group attachments. Thus the pluralist appears unwilling to prepare youths to cope adequately with the "real world" beyond the ethnic community. The cultural pluralist has also not clarified, in any meaningful way, the kind of relationship that should exist between antagonistic and competing ethnic groups that have different allegiances and conflicting goals and commitments. In other words, the pluralist does not have an adequate concept of the way a strongly pluralistic nation will maintain an essential degree of societal cohesion.

The assimilationist argues that the school within a common culture should socialize youths to enable them to become effective participants within that culture and to encourage them to develop commitments to its basic values, goals, and ideologies. The assimilationist also argues that the schools should help youths to attain the skills that will enable them to become effective and contributing members of the nation-state in which they live. It is important for curriculum developers to realize that most societies expect the common schools to help socialize youths in such a way that they will become productive members of the nation-state and develop strong commitments to the idealized societal values. Curriculum developers should keep the broad societal goals in mind when they reform the curriculum for the common schools.

However, the assimilationists make a number of highly questionable assumptions and promote educational practices that often hinder the success of youths who are socialized within ethnic communities that have cultural characteristics quite different from those of the school. The assimilationsts' assumption that learning styles are universalistic rather than to some extent culture-specific is

questionable. The assumption that all children can learn equally
well from teaching materials that only reflect the cultural experiences of the majority group is also questionable and possibly detrimental to those minority group children who have strong ethnic
identities and attachments.

When assimilationists talk about the "common culture," most
often they mean the Anglo-American culture and are ignoring the
reality that the United States is made up of many different ethnic
groups, each of which has some unique cultural characteristics that
are a part of America. The curriculum builder should seriously examine the "common culture" concept and make sure that the view of
the common American culture that is promoted in the school is not
racist, ethnocentric, or exclusive, but is multiethnic and reflects
the ethnic and cultural diversity within American society. We need
to redefine what the common culture actually is and make sure that
our new conceptualization reflects the social realities within this nation, that it is not a mythical and idealized view of American life
and culture.

THE PLURALIST-ASSIMILATIONIST IDEOLOGY

Since neither the cultural pluralist nor the assimilationist ideology can adequately guide curriculum reform within the common
schools, we need a different ideology that reflects both of these positions and yet avoids their extremes. We also need an ideology that
is more consistent with the realities in American society. We might
call this position the pluralist-assimilationist ideology and imagine
that it is found near the center of our continuum, which has the cultural pluralist and assimilationist ideologies at the extreme ends.
(See Table 8.1.)

Historically, the pluralist-assimilationist ideology has not
been a dominant ideology in American society. However, the experiences of some ethnic groups in America, the Orthodox Jews being the most salient example, are highly consistent with the pluralist-
assimilationist's vision of society. Although the pluralist-assimilationist's ideology is less theoretically developed than the other two
positions, the pluralist-assimilationist, like the other ideologists,
makes a number of assumptions about the nature of American society; about what the goals of the nation should be; and about research, learning, teacher training, and the school curriculum.

The pluralist-assimilationist believes that the cultural pluralist exaggerates the importance of the ethnic group in the socialization of the individual and that the assimilationist greatly understates
the role of ethnic groups in American life and in the lives of individuals.

TABLE 8.1
Ideologies Related to Ethnicity and Pluralism in the United States

Cultural Pluralist Ideology	Pluralist-Assimilationist Ideology	Assimilationist Ideology
Separatism	Open society biculturalism	Total integration
Primordial particularism	Universalized primordialism	Universalistic
Minority emphasis	Minorities and majorities have rights	Majoritarian emphasis
Primacy of group rights	Limited rights for the group and the individual	Individual rights are primary
Unification through common ancestry and heritage	Ethnic attachments and ideology of common civic culture compete for allegiances of individuals.	Ideology of the common culture unifies
Research Assumption Ethnic minority cultures in the United States are well ordered, highly structured, but different in such aspects as language, values, and behavior.	Research Assumption Ethnic minority cultures in the United States have some unique cultural characteristics. However, minority and majority groups share many cultural traits, values, and behavior styles.	Research Assumption Subcultural groups that have characteristics that make its members function unsuccessfully in the common culture are deprived, pathological, and lack needed functional characteristics.
Cultural difference research model	Bicultural research model	Social pathology research model and/or genetic research model
Minorities have unique learning styles.	Minorities have some unique learning styles, but share many learning characteristics with other groups.	Human learning styles and characteristics are universal.
Curriculum Materials and teaching styles that are culture-specific should be used. The goal of the curriculum should be to help the child function more successfully within his or her own ethnic culture and help to liberate his or her ethnic group from oppression.	Curriculum The curriculum should respect the ethnicity of the child and make use of it in positive ways. The goal of the curriculum should be to help the child learn how to function effectively within the common culture, his or her ethnic culture, and other ethnic cultures.	Curriculum Materials and teaching styles that are related to the common culture should be used. The curriculum should help the child develop a commitment to the common civic culture and its formulated ideologies, such as the American Creed.
Teachers Minority students need skilled teachers of their same race and ethnicity for role models, to help them learn more effectively and develop more positive self-concepts and identities.	Teachers Students need skilled teachers who are very knowledgeable about and sensitive to their ethnic cultures and cognitive styles.	Teachers A skilled teacher who is familiar with learning theories and is able to implement those theories effectively is a good teacher for any group of students, regardless of their ethnicity, race, or social class. The goal should be to train good teachers of children.

Thus the pluralist-assimilationist believes that both the pluralist and the assimilationist have distorted views of the realities in American society. The pluralist-assimilationist assumes that although the ethnic group and the ethnic community are very important in the socialization of individuals, these same individuals are also strongly influenced by the common culture during their early socialization, even if they never leave the ethnic community or enclave. The common culture influences every member of American society through such institutions as the schools, the mass media, the courts, and the technology that most Americans share. Thus, concludes the pluralist-assimilationist, although ethnic groups have some unique cultural characteristics, all groups in America share many cultural traits. As more and more members of ethnic groups become upwardly mobile, ethnic group characteristics become less important but do not disappear. Many ethnic group members who are culturally quite assimilated still maintain separate ethnic institutions and symbols (Gordon 1964).

The pluralist-assimilationist regards neither the separatism of the pluralist nor the total integration of the assimilationist as ideal societal goals, but rather envisions an "open society," in which individuals from diverse ethnic, cultural, and social-class groups have equal opportunities to function and participate. In an open society, individuals can take full advantage of the opportunities and rewards within all social, economic, and political institutions without regard to their ancestry or ethnic identity (Banks 1974). They can also participate fully in the society while preserving their distinct ethnic and cultural traits, and they are able to "make the maximum number of voluntary contacts with others without regard to qualifications of ancestry, sex, or class" (Sizemore 1972, p. 281).

In the multiethnic, open society envisioned by the pluralist-assimilationist, individuals would be free to maintain their ethnic identities. They would also be able and willing to function effectively within the common culture and within other ethnic cultures. Individuals would be free to act in ways consistent with the norms and values of their ethnic groups as long as they did not conflict with the dominant American idealized values such as justice, equality of opportunity, and respect for human life. All members of society would be required to conform to the American Creed values. These values would be the unifying elements of the culture that would maintain and promote societal cohesion.

Because of their perceptions of the nature of American society and their vision of the ideal society, pluralist-assimilationists believe that the primary goal of the curriculum should be to help children learn how to function more effectively within their own ethnic cultures, within the wider common culture, and within other ethnic communities. However, pluralist-assimilationists feel strongly that during the process of education the school should not alienate children from their ethnic attachments but help them to clarify their ethnic identities and make them aware of other ethnic and cultural alternatives.

The pluralist-assimilationist believes that the curriculum should reflect the cultures of various ethnic groups and the common culture. Students need to study all of these cultures in order to become effective participants and decision makers in a democratic society. The school curriculum should respect the ethnicity of the child and make use of it in positive ways. However, the students should be given options regarding their political choices and the actions that they take with regard to their ethnic attachments. The school should not "force" students to be and feel ethnic if they choose to free themselves of ethnic attachments and allegiances.

The pluralist-assimilationist also assumes that the children of ethnic minorities do have some unique learning styles, although they share many learning characteristics with other children. Educators should be knowledgeable about the aspects of their learning styles that are unique, in order to help these children attain more success within the school and in the larger society.

Although the pluralist-assimilationist ideology can best guide curriculum reform and school policy, difficult questions regarding the relationship of the school and the child's ethnic culture are inherent within this position. The pluralist-assimilationist argues, for example, that the school should reflect both the child's ethnic culture and the common societal culture. The following questions emerge. How does the individual function within two cultures that sometimes have contradictory and conflicting norms, values, and expectations? What happens when the ethnic cultures of the students seriously conflict with the goals and norms of public institutions such as the school? Do the institutions change their goals? If so, what goals do they embrace? The assimilationist solves this problem by arguing that the child should change to conform to the expectations and norms of public institutions.

Although I support the pluralist-assimilationist position and will present my proposals for curriculum reform within that ideological framework, it is very difficult to satisfactorily resolve all of the difficult questions inherent within this ideology. However, public institutions like the school can and should "allow" ethnic group members to practice their culture-specific behaviors as long as they do not conflict with the major goals of the school. One of the school's major goals is to teach children how to read, to write, to compute, and to think. The school obviously cannot encourage "ethnic" behavior if it prohibits children from reading. On the other hand,

some children might be able to learn to read more easily from
<u>Graciela</u> than from <u>Dick and Jane.</u>

THE GOALS OF CURRICULUM REFORM

To help students learn how to function effectively within and
across various cultures, curriculum reform must have several
major goals. One of these goals should be to help individuals clarify
their ethnic identities and function effectively within their own ethnic
communities. An individual must clarify his or her own sense of
ethnic and personal identity before he or she can positively relate to
individuals who belong to other ethnic and racial groups. We need
to foster the development of self-acceptance but discourage ethnic
ethnocentrism. Although individuals within a pluralistic society
must learn to accept their own ethnic identity and to become comfortable with it, they must also learn to function effectively within
other ethnic cultures and to respond positively to individuals who belong to other ethnic groups. (See Figure 8.1.) They also need to
learn how to interact with members of outside groups and how to resolve conflicts with them.

Both of the above goals are equally significant within a pluralistic nation. The attainment of one is not likely to occur unless both
are realized and fostered. It is extremely difficult for a Mexican-
American child to accept his or her cultural heritage if it is demeaned by "significant others" in institutions such as the school.
It is also very difficult for Anglo-Americans to learn to respond to
nonwhites positively and sensitively if they are unaware of the perceptions of their culture that are held by other ethnic groups and of
the ways in which the dominant culture evolved and attained the power
to shape the United States in its image.

We have never fully realized the positive effects that can occur
from the diverse nature of our society because historically the major
goal of most social institutions has been to Anglicize ethnic groups,
to disregard their ethnic cultures, and to foster a monocultural societal ideal. The result has been that almost every ethnic group has
struggled to become culturally like Anglo-Americans. Those groups
that have been the most successful have attained the highest levels
of social and economic mobility. The ethnic groups in our society
that are the most "ethnic" tend to be heavily concentrated in the
lower and working classes. Because most of the institutions within
our society tend to foster and to idealize Anglo-Saxon cultural characteristics and do not encourage Anglo-Americans to function in
other ethnic cultures, Anglo-Americans are rarely required to function within other ethnic communities. Members of other ethnic

groups tend to reject their ethnic cultures and to strive to attain Anglo-American cultural traits. However, this is less true today than in the past. Ethnic diversity and biculturalism will not become ideals in our society until members of the dominant ethnic group and of other ethnic groups better understand their own cultures and learn to function within and across cultures.

FIGURE 8.1

The Sociocultural Environment of Ethnic Youths

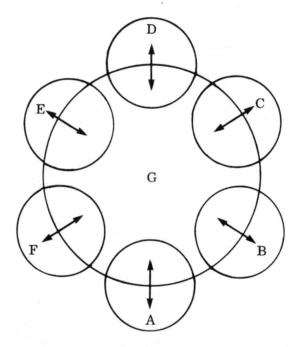

Note: The ethnic minority youth functions within two socioethnic environments, that of his or her ethnic subsociety and that of the dominant ethnic group, Anglo-Americans. The circles labeled A through F represent ethnic minority subsocieties. The circle labeled G represents the dominant ethnic society. The school should help ethnic minority children to learn to function successfully within their own ethnic subsociety, other ethnic subsocieties, and the dominant ethnic society. It should help Anglo-Americans to learn to function in all of these ethnic subsocieties and present them with cultural and ethnic alternatives.

Source: Compiled by the author.

A reformed curriculum should also help students to develop
the ability to make reflective decisions to enable them to resolve
personal problems and, through social action, influence public policy and develop a sense of political efficacy (Banks 1975). In many
ethnic-studies units and lessons, emphasis is on the memorization
and testing of isolated historical facts about shadowy ethnic heroes
and about events of questionable historical significance. In these
types of programs, ethnic studies is merely an extension of the regular history or social studies program.

Curriculum reform should have goals that are more consistent
with the needs of a global society. Events within the last decade have
dramatically indicated that we live in a world society that is beset
with momentous social and human problems, many of which are related to ethnic hostility and conflict. Effective solutions to these
tremendous problems can be found only by an active, compassionate,
and informed citizenry capable of making sound public decisions that
will benefit the world community. It is imperative that the school,
and social studies in particular, play a decisive role in educating
citizens who have both the vision and the courage to make our world
more humane.

ETHNIC STUDIES: A PROCESS OF
CURRICULUM REFORM

To help students learn how to function more effectively within
various ethnic cultures and within the common culture, ethnic studies
should be viewed as a process of curriculum reform that will result
in the creation of a new curriculum that is based on new assumptions
and new perspectives and that will help students gain novel views of
the American experiences and a new conception of what it means to
be American. Since the English immigrants gained control over
most economic, social, and political institutions early in our national history, to Americanize has been interpreted to mean to Anglicize. Especially during the height of nativism in the late 1800s and
the early 1900s, the English-Americans defined Americanization as
Anglicization (Higham 1972). This notion of Americanization is still
widespread within our society and schools today. Thus when we think
of American history and American literature we tend to think of
Anglo-American history and literature as written by Anglo-American
authors.

Reconceptualizing American Society

Since the assumption that only that which is Anglo-American is
American is so deeply ingrained in curriculum materials and in the

hearts and minds of many students and teachers, we cannot significantly change the curriculum by merely adding a unit or a lesson
here and there about Afro-American, Jewish-American, or Italian-
American history. Rather, we need to seriously examine the conception of American that is perpetuated in the curriculum and the
basic purposes and assumptions of the curriculum.

It is imperative that we totally reconceptualize the ways in
which we view American society and history in the school curriculum.
We should teach American history from diverse ethnic perspectives
rather than primarily or exclusively from the points of view of Anglo-
American historians and writers. Most American history courses
are currently taught primarily from an Anglo-American perspective.
These types of courses and experiences are based on what I call the
Anglo-American Centric Model or Model A. (See Figure 8.2.) Ethnic studies, as a process of curriculum reform, can and often do
proceed from Model A to Model B, the Ethnic Additive Model. In
courses and experiences based on Model B, ethnic content is an additive to the major curriculum thrust, which remains Anglo-American
dominated. Many school districts that have attempted ethnic modification of the curriculum have implemented Model B types of curriculum changes. Black studies courses, Chicano studies courses, and
special units on ethnic groups in the elementary grades are examples
of Model B types of curricular experiences.

However, I am suggesting that curriculum reform proceed
directly from Model A to Model C, the Multiethnic Model. In courses
and experiences based on Model C, the students study historical and
social events from several ethnic points of view. Anglo-American
perspectives are only one group of several and are in no way superior or inferior to other ethnic perspectives. I view Model D, or
the Multinational Model, types of courses and programs as the ultimate goal of curriculum reform. In this curriculum model the students study historical and social events from multinational perspectives and points of view. Since we live in a global society, students
need to learn how to become effective citizens of the world community. This is unlikely to happen if they study historical and contemporary social events only from the perspectives of ethnic cultures
within this nation.

Teaching Multiethnic Perspectives

When studying a historical period, such as the Colonial period,
in a course organized on the Multiethnic Model (Model C), the inquiry
would not end when the students viewed the period from the perspectives of Anglo-American historians and writers; rather, they would

FIGURE 8.2 Ethnic Studies as a Process of Curriculum Change

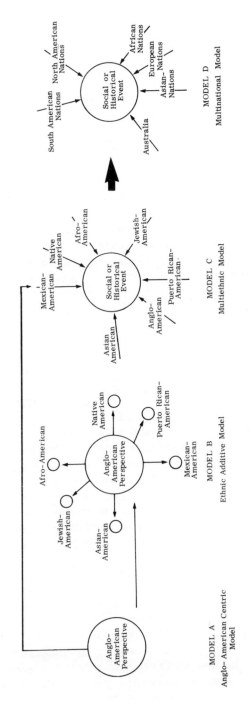

MODEL A
Anglo-American Centric Model

MODEL B
Ethnic Additive Model

MODEL C
Multiethnic Model

MODEL D
Multinational Model

Note: Ethnic studies is conceptualized as a process of curriculum reform that can lead from a total Anglo-American perspective on our history and culture (Model A), to multiethnic perspectives as additives to the major curriculum thrust (Model B), to a completely multiethnic curriculum in which every historical and social event is viewed from the perspectives of different ethnic groups (Model C). In Model C the Anglo-American perspective is only one of several and is in no way superior or inferior to other ethnic perspectives. Model D, which is multinational, is the ultimate curriculum goal. In this curriculum model, students study historical and social events from multinational perspectives and points of view. Many schools that have attempted ethnic modification of the curriculum have implemented Model B types of programs. It is suggested here that curriculum reform move directly from Model A to Model C and ultimately to Model D. However, in those districts that have implemented Model B types of programs, it is suggested that they move from Model B to Model C and eventually to Model D types of curricular organizations.

Source: Compiled by the author. Copyright (c) 1975 by James A. Banks. Reproduction without the author's permission is strictly prohibited.

243

be confronted with these kinds of questions: Why did Anglo-American historians name the English immigrants colonists and the other nationality groups immigrants? How do Native American historians view the Colonial period? Do their views of the period differ in any substantial ways from the views of Anglo-American historians? Why or why not? What was life like for the Jews, blacks, and other ethnic groups in America during the seventeenth and eighteenth centuries? How do we know? In other words, in courses and programs organized on Model C, students would view historical and contemporary events from the perspectives of different ethnic and racial groups.

I am not suggesting that we eliminate or denigrate Anglo-American history or Anglo-American perspectives on historical events; I am merely suggesting that Anglo-American perspectives should be among many different ethnic perspectives taught in social studies and in American history. Only by approaching the study of American history in this way will students gain a global rather than an ethnocentric view of our nation's history and culture.

A historian's experience and culture, including his or her ethnic culture, cogently influences his or her views of the past and present (Commager 1966). However, it would be simplistic to argue that there is one Anglo-American view of history and contemporary events or one black view. Wide differences in experiences and perceptions exist both within the across ethnic groups. However, those who have experienced a historical event or a social phenomenon such as racial bigotry or internment often view the event differently from those who have watched from a distance. There is no single Anglo-American perspective on the internment, as there is no one Japanese-American view of it. However, accounts written by those who were interned, such as Shizuye Takashima's powerful A Child in Prison Camp (1971) often provides insights and perspectives on the internment that cannot be provided by people who were not interned. Individuals who viewed the internment from the outside can also provide us with unique and important perspectives and points of view. In a sound social studies curriculum, both perspectives would be studied.

Only by looking at events such as the internment from many different perspectives can we fully understand the complex dimensions of American history and culture. Various ethnic groups within our society are often differently influenced by events and respond to and perceive them differently. One of the goals of ethnic studies should be to change the basic assumptions about what it means to be American and to present students with new ways of viewing and interpreting American history and culture. Any goals that are less ambitious, while important, will not result in the substantial and radical curricular reform that I consider imperative.

Ethnic Studies and Ethnic Conflict

Those of us in ethnic studies write and talk most frequently about the positive effects that cultural diversity can have on American society. However, we rarely speak candidly about the conflict inherent within a society that is made up of diverse ethnic groups with conflicting goals, ideologies, and strong feelings of ethnocentrism. Some educators are deeply concerned that ethnic studies, by fostering ethnic pride, might lead to extreme ethnic conflict and the disunity of American society. In designing ethnic studies programs and experiences, we must give serious and thoughtful consideration to this complex question. Otherwise, this legitimate concern may become a rationalization for inaction and a justification for the status quo.

Whether the content and programs of ethnic studies contribute to the development of dysfunctional ethnic polarization and social conflict or help to bring about democratic social change depends to some extent on the ways in which ethnic studies programs are conceptualized and taught. Ethnic studies programs that focus exclusively on the sins of Anglo-Americans and the virtues of oppressed minorities are not likely to help students to develop the kinds of skills and attitudes that they need to function successfully within our pluralistic society. Ethnic studies should focus on helping students to develop humanistic attitudes and the skills to engage in reflective social action that will influence public policy. An ethnic studies program that fosters humanism and reflective social action will enable students to participate more effectively in the reformation of our society and in the elimination of ethnic conflict and polarization.

Ethnic Studies: For All Students

The broad view of ethnic studies that I have described in this chapter suggests that all students, regardless of their ethnicity, race, or social class, should take part in ethnic studies, which I define in part as the study of American history and culture from diverse ethnic perspectives. Studying American history and culture from different ethnic perspectives can help students broaden their views of American society and become more aware of cultural and ethnic alternatives. Most Americans are socialized within tight ethnic enclaves, in which they primarily learn one cultural life style and one way to be human. Consequently, most of our students are ethnically illiterate. The curriculum in most schools is mainly an extension of the home and community culture of Anglo-American students.

The school should present all students with cultural and ethnic alternatives and help them to become more ethnically literate (Banks 1973). Minority students should be helped to attain the skills and perceptions needed to function effectively both within their ethnic cultures and within the common culture. Anglo-American students must also be helped to function across ethnic cultures and to learn that they have cultural options. We severely limit the potentiality of students when we merely teach them aspects of their own ethnic cultures and reinforce their ethnic group ethnocentrism. Anglo-American students should realize that using black English is one effective way to communicate, that Native Americans have values, beliefs, and life styles that may be functional for them, and that alternative ways of behaving and of viewing the universe that they may wish to embrace are practiced within the United States. By helping all students to view the world beyond their cultural and ethnic perspectives and to function effectively across cultures, we will enrich them as human beings and enable them to live more productive and fulfilling lives.

REFERENCES

Banks, James A. 1973. "Teaching for Ethnic Literacy." Social Education 37: 738-50.

_____. 1974. "Curricular Models for an Open Society." In Education for an Open Society, ed. Delmo Della-Dora and James E. House, pp. 43-63. Washington, D.C.: Association for Supervision and Curriculum Development.

_____. 1975. Teaching Strategies for Ethnic Studies. Boston: Allyn and Bacon.

Baratz, Joan C., and Roger Shuy, eds. 1969. Teaching Black Children to Read. Washington, D.C.: Center for Applied Linguistics.

Baratz, Stephen S., and Joan C. Baratz. 1970. "Early Childhood Intervention: The Social Science Base of Institutional Racism." Harvard Educational Review 40: 29-50.

Bourne, Randolph S. 1916. "Trans-National America." The Atlantic Monthly 118: 95.

Caldwell, Betty. 1967. "What Is the Optimal Learning Environment for the Young Child?" _American Journal of Orthopsychiatry_ 37: 9-21.

Carmichael, Stokeley, and Charles V. Hamilton. 1967. _Black Power: The Politics of Liberation in America_. New York: Vintage Books.

Commager, Henry S. 1966. _The Nature and the Study of History_. Columbus, Ohio: Charles E. Merrill.

Drachsler, Julius. 1920. _Democracy and Assimilation_. New York: Macmillan.

Gordon, Milton M. 1964. _Assimilation in American Life: The Role of Race, Religion, and National Origins_. New York: Oxford University Press.

Higham, John. 1972. _Strangers in the Land: Patterns of American Nativism, 1860-1925_. New York: Atheneum.

_____. 1974. "Integration vs. Pluralism: Another American Dilemma." _The Center Magazine_ 7: 67-73.

Jensen, Arthur R. 1969. "How Much Can We Boost IQ and Scholastic Achievement?" _Harvard Educational Review_ 39: 1-123.

Kallen, Horace M. 1924. _Culture and Democracy in the United States_. New York: Boni and Liveright.

Labov, William. 1970. "The Logic of Nonstandard English." In _Language and Poverty: Perspectives on a Theme_, ed. Frederic Williams, pp. 153-89. Chicago: Markham.

Mercer, Jane R. 1974. "Latent Functions of Intelligence Testing in the Public Schools." In _The Testing of Black Students_, ed. Lamar P. Miller, pp. 77-94. Englewood Cliffs, N.J.: Prentice-Hall.

Ramirez, Manuel, III, and Alfredo Castaneda. 1974. _Cultural Democracy, Bicognitive Development and Education_. New York: Academic Press.

Shockley, William. 1972. "Dysgenics, Geneticity, Raceology: Challenges to the Intellectual Responsibility of Educators." Phi Delta Kappan 53: 297-307.

Simpkins, Gary; Robert L. Williams; and Thomas S. Gunnings. 1971. "What a Culture a Difference Makes: A Rejoinder to Valentine." Harvard Educational Review 41: 535-41.

Sizemore, Barbara A. 1969. "Separatism: A Reality Approach to Inclusion?" In Racial Crisis in American Education, ed. Robert L. Green, pp. 249-79. Chicago: Follett Educational Corporation.

_____. 1972. "Is There a Case for Separate Schools?" Phi Delta Kappan 53: 281.

Stodolsky, Susan S., and Gerald Lesser. 1967. "Learning Patterns in the Disadvantaged." Harvard Educational Review 37: 546-93.

Takashima, Shizuye. 1971. A Child in Prison Camp. Montreal: Tundra Books.

Williams, Robert L. 1975. "Moderator Variables as Bias in Testing Black Children." The Journal of Afro-American Issues 3: 77-90.

MELVIN M. TUMIN studied at the University of Newark, the University of Wisconsin, and Northwestern University. He is the author of <u>Social Inequality</u>; <u>Segregation and Desegregation</u>; <u>Quality and Equality in Education</u>; and <u>Patterns of Society</u>, among other books, and is an editor of <u>Race and Intelligence.</u> He is presently working on a book entitled <u>Theories of Human Nature.</u> He currently serves as Professor of Sociology and Anthropology at Princeton University.

WALTER PLOTCH studied at Queens College of the City University of New York, and Harvard University. He is general editor of the <u>Job Corps Intergroup Relations Series</u> and a contributor to various educational journals. He has directed programs on racial and ethnic problems, urban affairs, and crisis intervention throughout the United States for federal, state and local governments, major school systems, colleges, and voluntary associations. Formerly National Education Director of the Anti-Defamation League of B'nai B'rith, he presently heads his own public affairs consulting firm.

David E. Apter is Henry Heinz II Professor of Comparative Political and Social Development at Yale University.

James A. Banks is Professor of Education at the University of Washington.

Florence B. H. Davidson is the Executive Director of the Massachusetts Psychological Center.

Nathan Glazer is Professor of Psychology at Harvard University.

Mari-Luci Jaramillo is Associate Professor, Department of Education at the University of New Mexico.

James E. Johnson is a post-Doctoral Fellow at the Institute for Research in Human Development, Educational Testing Service, Princeton, N.J.

Michael Novak is Executive Director of the Ethnic Millions Political Action Committee.

Irving E. Sigel is a Senior Research Psychologist at the Institute for Research in Human Development, Educational Testing Service, Princeton, N.J.

Charles A. Tesconi, Jr. is Associate Professor of Education at the University of Illinois at Chicago Circle.

Judith V. Torney is Associate Professor of Psychology at the University of Illinois at Chicago Circle.

CARRASCOLENDAS: Bilingual Education through Television
Frederick Williams
Geraldine Van Wart

ETHNICITY AND SUBURBAN LOCAL POLITICS
David J. Schnall

IMMIGRANT PROFESSIONALS IN THE UNITED STATES:
Discrimination in the Scientific Labor Market
Bradley W. Parlin

SOUTHERN NEWCOMERS TO NORTHERN CITIES:
Work and Social Adjustment in Cleveland
Gene B. Petersen
Laure M. Sharp
Thomas F. Drury

A SURVEY OF PUERTO RICANS ON THE U.S.
MAINLAND IN THE 1970s
Kal Wagenheim